THE BOWLER'S ART

Leg spin attack: Shane Warne in action at the Sydney Cricket Ground, Australia vs West Indies, 1 December 1996.
(Stephen Laffer)

CRICKET:
THE
BOWLER'S ART

BRIAN WILKINS

Kangaroo Press

DEDICATION

To my wife and children who have put up with my passion for cricket for so long.

ACKNOWLEDGMENTS

The author wishes to thank all those friends who have helped to make this a better book than it otherwise would have been. In particular the author acknowledges the assistance of the following:

Dick Hince, Central Institute of Technology

Dr Colin Cook, Victoria University of Wellington

Bert Christensen, Central Institute of Technology

Roger Stanton, Central Institute of Technology

Dr David Wratt, New Zealand Meterological Service

Stephen Green, Curator of the Lord's Museum

'Wo' Wilson, Basin Reserve Cricket Museum

Richie Benaud

Associate Professor Richard Flay of the Dept of Mechanical Engineering, University of Auckland, for allowing the author to use the wind tunnel for new work included in the second edition.

A.G. Thompson Ltd, Victoria, Australia, for supplying the Kookaburra cricket balls.

Dr Jim Pearce of Victoria University of Wellington for help in the preparation of this book.

The publishers are grateful to the following for permission to use copyright material:

Methuen and Eyre and Spottiswoode for extracts from *The Complete Leg-Break Bowler* by C. S. Marriott

The University of Newcastle, Australia for figures from a project report by A. Imbrosciano on 'The swing of a cricket ball'.

Thomas Nelson for the illustration from *Grimmett on Cricket*

Lord's Museum for the photograph of Simpson-Hayward

The University of Notre Dame for the photograph by F.N.M. Brown

The University of Pennsylvania Press for the extracts from *A Century of Philadelphia Cricket*

George Beldam for his father's photographs.

It has not been possible to trace the owners of certain photographs, but proper acknowledgment has been made to these and to extracts from various publications.

This edition published in 1997 by Kangaroo Press
an imprint of Simon & Schuster Australia
20 Barcoo Street (P.O. Box 507)
East Roseville NSW 2069 Australia
Printed in Singapore by Color Symphony Pte Ltd

ISBN 0 86417 899 9

CONTENTS

NOTES ON THE PHOTOGRAPHS

The ball photographs were devised and taken by the author.

The grip photographs were devised by the author and taken by Brett Robertson, photographer at Victoria University of Wellington, who also carried out the photographic processing.

Front cover illustration by Sarah Wilkins

PREFACE

When the Hambledon player Lamborn bowled the first off-spin, cricketers received a shock. Such development has continued to enrich the game for two hundred years.

My aim, in this book, is to make modern knowledge about cricket simple and easily understood.

No book on cricket has all the answers but I would hope that cricketers can use my work to help them avoid unnecessary time-wasting and confusion.

What happens to a cricket ball in the bowler's hand and on its journey towards the bat, has never ceased to interest cricketers. The more we understand, not only does the game become more interesting, but the more chance we have of putting this knowledge to use.

Cricket writers, in their enthusiasm to explain bowling, have often been rather too careless about distinguishing fact from speculation. As a result, much of the more technical comment on cricket is either misleading or just plain wrong and unlikely to be of use to anyone.

Misunderstanding is not always the fault of cricketers: some writers and investigators have given the impression that they have taken a catch when, in reality, they were still fumbling; a trap which I myself cannot guarantee to avoid!

Does it matter if we get it wrong? Haven't we enjoyed playing and watching the game for two hundred years without needing to worry too much about knowing more? One answer is that the citizens of the modern world have shown an insatiable curiosity to find out more about everything: we can't exclude cricket.

For a cricketer, the important question is, will more knowledge help me to play better? I hope so: that is one of the two main purposes of this book; the other is to tell a fascinating story. If the opposing team have done their homework, and we haven't, are they not more likely to beat us?

And who will deny that we will make better Laws for the game if we have a truer understanding of cause and effect? For example unless we understand the truth about tampering with the ball and how it brings about 'reverse swing' how can we apply existing Laws, or make new Laws, to deal with it? Wrong understanding is almost certain to lead to wrong Laws, or the wrong application of existing Laws.

Looking back at the talents of bowlers from the years 1890–1940 one is struck by their ability to spin the ball, not only as slower bowlers, but at all speeds, fast and slow. It is generally agreed that cricket will be a better game, both for players and spectators, when spin returns to its essential place. One of the aims of this book is to make it easier for bowlers to use the full range of bowling skills and this includes knowing how to spin at any pace. If we provide pitches that give bowlers a fair reward for these skills cricket will be a better game.

Women cricketers are probably hardened by now to the constant assumption on the part of authors that cricketers are males, and, simply for the convenience of not having to use extra words, this book is no better. Bowler, fortunately, is a universal term. One of the earliest known illustrations of cricket, or a game similar to it (c.1340), shows the bowler to be a woman.

Unless stated otherwise, the bowlers and batsmen referred to in this book are right-handed.

It would probably help the reader to have a cricket ball at hand: grasp the ball, grasp the meaning.

The first edition of this book was very favourably received by the cricket community. In this, the second edition, I have made changes to most chapters by introducing new topics and new ways of looking at bowling generally.

I report new information I have obtained on which to base a solid understanding of ball tampering, and also new information on the way pitches influence the game. Both are important issues for cricket entering the new millennium. I have obtained some of this new information by firing balls from a 'ball gun' which allows the ball to be fired with the seam in any chosen position. Watching the ball swing one way or the other as it flies across a large laboratory room at speed has been an interesting and informative experience.

I was a cricketer long before I became interested in doing the work needed to write this book. I hope that cricketers and cricket lovers will enjoy, and learn from, looking at the deeds of great bowlers, and the vast storehouse of cricket experience, in a thoroughly modern way.

Brian Wilkins

NOTE ON THE GRIP PHOTOGRAPHS

The grips, photographed in the author's hand, are shown in order to illustrate important principles. Hands of a different size and shape, and perhaps with different peculiarities of bone structure, will require modifications to the illustrated grips. Maximum comfort and efficiency should be the aim.

THE BALL IN THE AIR

This is both a why and a how book, as well as being a book which links the present with the past; why a ball moves in the air and off the pitch, and how a bowler can get the best results from his hard work and skill.

A cricket ball deviates in the air when the air flow around it is distorted. This occurs because the stitching, or some other roughness, or the spin on the ball, makes the air flow different on one side compared to the flow on the opposite side.

To understand good (and bad!) bowling, and the fascination of cricket, we need a clear and simple language to describe what a cricket ball is doing, or may do. There will be plenty of uncertainties for the ball on its way towards the bat, such as the quality and the quantity of the air it must pass through, and the response of the pitch. But, at least, we can be perfectly clear about its direction, the spin it carries, the axis about which it spins, the angle of the seam, whether the seam appears to wobble from side to side, and the expected direction of deviation, whether it comes from swing, or spin-swerve, or turn off the pitch, or any combination of these.

Fig. 1 is a sample of how these basic facts, direction, spin, and seam angle, are shown throughout the book, and unless stated otherwise, the spin photographs always show the view seen from behind the ball: the view seen by the bowler as it leaves his hand.

Cricketers use the seam for swing, for grip in spinning, and for bite on the pitch. Many different types of spin will be illustrated in this book: the photos are designed to cope with every possible type.

Cricket is a three dimensional game: it has length, breadth, and height. Games such as snooker and chess are two dimensional. I will leave the reader to think of a one dimensional sport: bungy-jumping perhaps. Cricketers added a generous

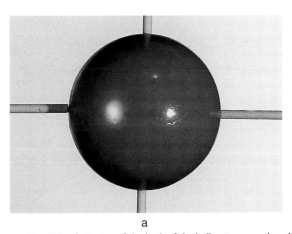

a   b

Fig. 1 Bowler's view of the back of the ball as it moves directly away from the eye in line with the point where the four rods meet. Unless otherwise stated, all of the ball photographs in this book have the ball moving away in that direction. Figure **1b** also shows the axis of spin, direction of spin, and seam angle. Here the seam angle is at 45° to the direction of flight.

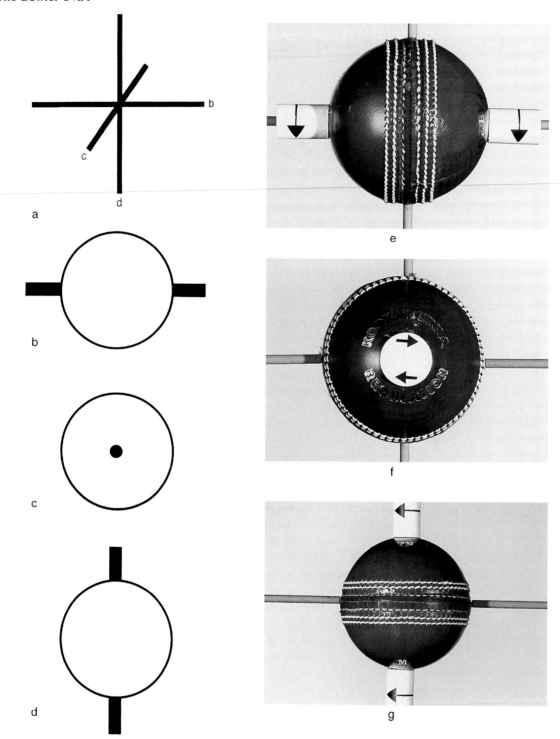

Fig. 2 'Pure' spin about the three axes (**a**). The two horizontal axes show (**b**) across the line of flight, and (**c**) in line with the flight; while (**d**) is vertical. Two directions of spin are possible about each axis; one of each of these is seen in the three ball photos, (**e**), (**f**), and (**g**).

measure of a fourth dimension, time, to their activities, long before Einstein gave it to modern physics.

The axis of the spinning ball in Figure 1b is horizontal and the seam spins like a tyre on a wheel. In all bowling the 'tyre on the wheel' is the most common way of spinning the ball. Everything is possible, including the delivery where the axis goes in through the seam on one side of the ball and comes out through the seam on the other side.

At the beginning we need to get the big picture clear, and that means looking at spin about the three main axes (Fig. 2a); the side-to side (or crossways) axis (Fig. 2b); the axis pointing down the pitch (Fig. 2c), and the vertical axis (Fig. 2d).

We can call these spins 'pure', but most bowling, except medium and fast, where the bowler's hand frequently comes straight down off the back of the ball to give pure back-spin around a side-to-side axis as in Figure 2b, or a spin bowler bowling top-spin about the same axis, is likely to be 'mixed'; i.e. around an axis pointing somewhere between the three main axes, as in many of the photographs in this book.

1

UNDER-ARM TO OVER-ARM

Pick up a cricket ball, or any ball of similar size, and note the important role played by the thumb in this action. It is likely that any one of the fingers involved could be lifted from the ball without an appreciable loosening of the grip. But not so the thumb, which comprises almost half of the natural grasp.

Cricketers of earlier centuries would not have picked it up differently. Nyren (1764–1837), writing in 1833, advises: 'The best method of holding the ball to bowl is between the thumb and fingers, firmly enough to steady it yet that it may leave the hand with ease'.[1] G. H. Simpson-Hayward (1875–1936), one of the last of the under-arm or lob bowlers, is shown in a photograph (Fig. 3c) taken just prior to the release of the ball, leaning forward with the bowling hand swinging through just above knee level, the ball held with the thumb on one side and the fingers on the other, ready to impart sharp off-spin.

An unusual type of off-break, combined with back-spin to give a flattish trajectory, was bowled by Walter Mead (1868–1954). This delivery, revived by Grimmett half a century later and named 'the flipper' by the Australians, employs the thumb in a key role. We look more closely at spinning techniques which depend on the thumb in Chapter 20.

One of Australia's best all-rounders — medium-pacer Monty Noble (1873–1940) — embarked, in 1898, on a notable career based on a devastating spin-swerve, spinning the ball from between thumb and forefinger. He learned his grip from American baseballers who toured Australia to promote their sport.

Half a century later, in 1948, Clarrie Grimmett (1891–1980) revealed his 'mystery ball' in his book *Grimmett on Cricket,*[2] the driving force for that enigmatic delivery being the thumb.

Continuing our exploration of the capabilities of the human hand grasping the ball between thumb and fingers, we may bring the ball through somewhere under the armpit and propel it along the ground. Such was bowling until about the middle of the eighteenth century. Until then bowling was nothing more than the strict meaning of the word, i.e. rolling the ball along the ground. Under-arm bowlers then had no incentive to use anything other than speed, with perhaps a cunning eye for a lump or a hollow on the way.

Once the ball came to be delivered through the air, 'pitched' to bounce somewhere near the batsman, the early records show that run-making became easier. To counter this, bowlers soon discovered the possibilities arising from 'twist' (spin) to accompany their under-arm push, swing or jerk.

The transition from 'bowling' to 'pitching' is thought to have taken the best part of twenty-five years,[3] a long period during which the importance of 'length' was appreciated, and during which it was slowly realised that speed was no longer essential.

Noah Mann Snr., of the Hambledon Club, is the first recorded 'under-curver', the pioneer of the ball which curves in the air, not because of shine or seam, but through spin. Mann's descendants in skill therefore include not only G. H. Hirst (1871–1954) and S. F. Barnes (1873–1967), but every single cricketer, baseball or softball pitcher who has ever spun a ball.

The hand coming from below the armpit can easily twist one way or the other. Nyren,[4] writing not long after this period, describes most of the

Fig. 3a Alfred Mynn, the greatest leg-break bowler of his day–from *The Cricket Field* by J. Pycroft (St James Press, 1922)

THE BOWLER.

b

c

b

Fig. 3 b is an unnamed round-arm bowler (from *Cricket* by John Wisden, 1873); **c** is G. H. Simpson-Hayward (MCC Collection); **d** is M. A. Noble.

bowlers who gave the ball spin as twisting in from the leg to off after pitching. In other words, the original and natural method of spinning the ball was leg-spin, the hand and ball coming out from under the armpit while turning anti-clockwise. There is no apparent reason why leg-spin should be more natural than off-spin, but the early writers are in no doubt that leg-spin was adopted first. The basic action in under-arm leg-spin is no different from that of over-arm leg-spin, the hand turning anti-clockwise in both cases.

An early 19th-century memory of spin:

The grandstand was immediately behind the wicket. Farmer Miles, a fine-set-up man, was the best bowler, and he bowled under-arm, rather a quick medium pace, and pitched a good length and bowled very straight, his balls curling in from leg; for be it remembered that but two years had elapsed since it was allowed to turn the hand uppermost, in delivery. I was seven years old at the time, and was perfectly fascinated at the sight; and the gardener, an old cricketer, stood by me all day and explained the game. Before the sun had set I had mastered most of the main points of it. One thing I am certain of, which is that there was an on-break from Farmer Miles' bowling; for I watched the balls pitch and curl.[5]

Meanwhile, another pioneer, Lamborn ('the Little Farmer') was practising a different type of delivery against gates while tending his sheep. Lamborn may well have been a good deal brighter than the somewhat slow-witted shepherd portrayed by Nyren who described him as:

Right-handed, and he had the most extraordinary delivery I ever saw. The ball was delivered quite low, and with a twist; not like that of the generality of right-handed bowlers, but just the reverse way that is, if bowling to a right-handed hitter, his ball would twist from the off stump into the leg. He was the first I remember who introduced

this deceitful and teasing style of delivering the ball. When All England played the Hambledon Club, the Little Farmer was appointed one of our bowlers; and, egad! this new trick of his so bothered the Kent and Surrey men, that they tumbled out one after another, as if they had been picked off by a rifle corps. For a long time they could not tell what to make of that cursed twist of his.[6]

Lamborn's under-arm twist of the hand was therefore clockwise and Nyren adds that, because of a general lack of intelligence ('deficiency'), and with 'a comprehension not equal to the speed of lightning', Lamborn needed to be told to pitch the ball a little outside the off stump 'when it would twist full in upon the stumps'. Sensitive off-spinners may be glad that Nyren is not around today!

Although we will never again see the classic under-arm bowlers, Nyren's lyrical description of Harris takes us as close as we will ever get to seeing in our mind's eye the late eighteenth-century equivalent of the athletic bowlers of the modern era:

His attitude when preparing for his run previously to delivering the ball would have made a beautiful study for the sculptor. First of all, he stood erect like a soldier at drill; then, with a graceful curve of the arm, he raised the ball to his forehead, and drawing back his right foot, started off with his left. His mode of delivering the ball was very singular. He would bring it from under the arm with a twist and nearly as high as his armpit, and with this action push it, as it were, from him. How it was that the balls acquired the velocity they did by this mode of delivery I never could comprehend. In bowling, he never stooped in the least in his delivery, but kept himself upright all the time. His balls were very little beholden to the ground when pitched; it was but a touch, and up again; and woe to the man who did not get into block them, for they had such a peculiar curl, that they would grind his fingers against the bat: many a time have I seen blood drawn in this way from a batter who was not up to the trick.[7]

The first bowler recorded as having stretched out his arm horizontally, at least to some extent, to bowl round-arm, was warned against persisting with it. This was Tom Walker in the 1780s. Having once experienced the satisfying full swing of the extended arm, cricketers were not to be denied.

The reaction of bowlers to changing batting methods was an important factor. One of the Hambledon men, Tom Seuter, is the first batsman recorded as leaving his crease, a technique which came to be used more frequently early in the century, particularly against the high-tossing slow lob bowlers.

An attempt to ban round-arm bowling (bowling from shoulder level) by a law change in 1816 failed. After a period in which it was widely tolerated unofficially, a new Code of Laws legalised round-arm bowling in 1835. But the tide was unstoppable and by this time over-arm was already employed — when umpires allowed it.

Old methods were not forgotten however, and the first of many fine exponents who revived under-arm was William Clarke, a star of the mid-nineteenth century, who achieved 'a consistent spin from leg'.

The new breed of round-arm bowlers maintained the skills discovered by their under-arm predecessors. However, the round-arm technique involved a significant change in the position of the hand at the moment of delivery.

Whereas the under-armers generally delivered the ball with the palm facing upwards, round-arm delivery used a downward-facing palm at least for a good part of the action, hence the alternative name 'over-hand' which was used at the time.

Hillyer, in the 1840s, had a tremendous 'curl' (assumed to be a curve), as well as a 'quick sharp break' from the leg to off, 'often uprooting the middle or off stump'.[8] Willsher, a crack left-hand bowler of the 1860s, was described as:

... fast and ripping with a twist from the leg to the off... (he) came up to the wicket with a quick-march kind of step, raised his hand high above his head, bringing it down to shoulder level at the last moment with a quick jerky movement which seemed to put spin and impetus on the ball that caused it to rise like lightning from the pitch.[9]

Another famous, pacey lefthander from Kent, Derek Underwood, is surely a worthy descendant from the Willsher lineage.

The revolutionary bowler of the round-arm period was Alfred Mynn (1807–1861) (Fig. 3a), tall and powerful, who bowled a ball which generally broke in from the leg to off and rose rapidly at a speed described as greater than anything previously seen on the cricket field. One of the only batsmen to master him was Nicholas Wanostrocht, alias 'Felix', who needed the help of practice against a bowling machine, the 'Catapulta', to become accustomed to such speed.

Although it is more difficult to bowl straight using round-arm than with under- or over-arm, Alfred Shaw (1842–1907) had no problem. With an easy, slow-medium round-arm action he could turn the ball both ways, particularly from the off, bowling 24 700 overs in first class cricket, conceding 24 107 runs and taking 2051 wickets (average 11.75).

When the Marylebone Club eventually legalised over-arm bowling in 1864, the roughly semicircular eighty year journey of the hand from near the armpit, to the sideways extended arm, to high above the head, was complete. The maximum height at delivery, which under-arm bowlers had sought by bowling as high up under the armpit as possible, was now achieved in a more natural and spectacular way, but pace, flight, spin both from leg and from off, and spin-swerve were all well established before over-arm came on the scene.

A century of over-arm was bound to bring new developments. Some are not as new as we might think, the flipper, for example; others were made possible by the use of shiny balls and prominent seams.

Early in the century, Nyren had written a dire warning to young cricketers:

> *I cannot approve of his (Lambert's) recommending a young player to give a twist to his balls: for in the first place, there are a hundred chances against his accomplishing the art and ten hundred favour of the practice spoiling his bowling altogether.*[10]

In spite of Nyren, the great bowlers of the mainly round-arm era were those who did indeed impart a goodly twist.

2
SPIN TO SWERVE

Noah Mann's 'under-curver' was not the first spinning ball recorded as curving through English air. Benjamin Robins (1707–1751) was a British mathematician and military engineer who laid the foundation for modern field artillery theory and practice. In 1742, thirty-five years before Mann joined the Hambledon Club, Robins published a book, *New Principles of Gunnery*, in which he describes how he investigated the reason why musket balls and cannon balls, even on windless days, are frequently driven off their course by some force other than gravity. His results were the beginning of understanding one of the forces controlling the behaviour of a cricket ball in flight.

The musket balls were lead spheres fired from unrifled (ungrooved) barrels. Robins thought that the off-target curving might be caused by the spinning of the lead balls in flight. He set out to test his idea by firing from muskets, the last 3–4 inches of the barrels of which he had deliberately bent slightly to one side. The balls therefore pressed hard against the side of the barrel as they passed through the bent portion, and were slowed down on that side, thus emerging with a side-spin.

Robins' arrangement, with sheets of tissue paper at 50 ft and 100 ft, and a wall at 300 ft, is shown in fig. 4. The holes in the paper and the mark on the wall showed the curved path taken by the ball. His idea was thus proved correct; when the barrel was bent to the right the ball

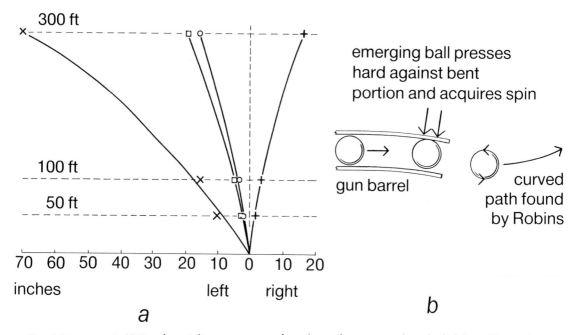

Fig. 4 Spin-swerve in 1742: **a** shows Robins arrangement of two sheets of tissue paper through which he could trace the curved path of musket balls fired with side-spin in different directions from point 0: **b** shows the bent gun barrel and direction of spin.

curved to the left, and when bent left the ball curved right.[1]

This phenomenon is usually called the Magnus Effect, named after H. G. Magnus, a German physicist and chemist, who did not publish his work until 1853, more than a century after Robins. Magnus has no real claim to association with ball games: he failed in his work with spheres and obtained his results from rotating cylinders. For these reasons Robins will be accorded his due honour throughout this book.

Present-day sports people are constantly reminded of the Robins effect in games like tennis, golf, baseball, softball and soccer, but nowhere is it more marked than in table tennis, where the lightness of the ball, in comparison to the Robins Force on the surface, gives rise to quite dramatic effects. The topspun ball will dip sharply downwards; the underspun (i.e. back-spun) ball will perhaps climb a little or at least not fall so rapidly under gravity; the ball given a sideways hit will curve to the side opposite to the direction in which the bat is moving across behind it.

The basic Robins movements, applying to any ball, are shown in Figure 5. These take place vertically (Fig. 5a) or horizontally (Fig. 5b), but a combination of the two is both possible and common in sport.

What causes the Robins Force? The answer can be seen in Figure 6, showing the air flow around a spinning baseball. The lines of smoke injected into the air stream show the layer of air close to the ball — the boundary layer — behaving differently on the two opposite sides. On top, the part spinning towards the airflow, the boundary layer can be seen leaving the surface quite early, whereas at the bottom, the side spinning away from the air flow, it clings on longer, not leaving the ball until it is a little distance around.

The different amount of 'clinging on' on the opposite sides distorts the air flow upwards. Because the ball has made the air rise, the ball must experience a reaction in the opposite direction, downwards.

So far so good; but why does the air stream come off the ball earlier on one side than on the other? It depends on the amount of disturbance or turbulence in the boundary layer. The turbulence depends not just on the roughness of the ball, but also on the air speed. In Figure 6 the air speed

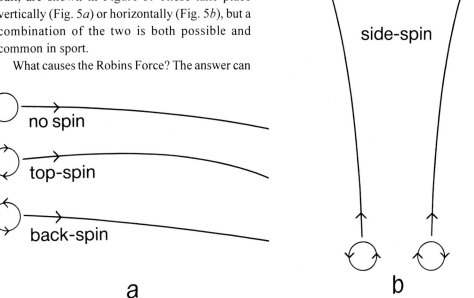

Fig. 5 Spin-swerve resulting from the Robins Force. The effect of spin on the flight path is shown in side view (**a**) and top view (**b**). These are all positive Robins effects. Under certain conditions the force is in the opposite direction—the negative Robins Force.

across the top, spinning toward the air, is obviously greater than across the bottom, which spins away from it.

The importance of where the air layers separate from a ball is by no means confined to the Robins effect; it underlies the whole of what cricketers call swing. We shall return to swing in the next chapter.

In the meantime we should note some fascinating and vitally important facts about how roughness, or rather the different turbulence caused by difference in air speed across the top and bottom of the ball, affects air layer separation. Whereas an air stream across a shiny, very smooth, surface leaves early, it also leaves early if the surface is quite rough; and from a surface that is dull or very slightly coarse in texture, it will cling on longer! We come back to this when we look at swing.

How rough is a spinning ball to the air stream, and what if the roughness varies over the surface,

such as the stitching and seams, major and minor, around a cricket ball, and the figure-of-eight seam around a baseball? Spinning baseballs behave like Robins' cannon balls, but some apparently smooth balls, such as smooth experimental golf balls without dimples, gave a deflection in the opposite direction as a result of what is called a 'negative Robins effect'.

While published studies of the Robins Force on tennis balls, dimpled golf balls, baseballs, softballs and table tennis balls all show positive Robins behaviour, my own work has shown that cricket balls at particular speeds, spin rates, and angles to the wind will, as has been found with some plastic balls, and as Macoll[2] found with wooden balls, 'go negative'. This mixed behaviour of cricket balls is explainable, since they possess both rough and smooth areas, each quite large in extent, more so than on baseballs.

Sports books are often wrong when attempting to explain the Robins effect. One simple but

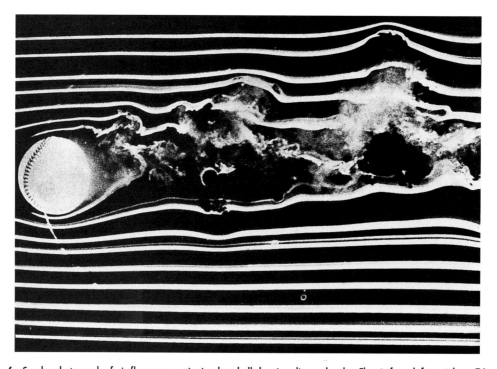

Fig. 6a Smoke photograph of air flow over a spinning baseball showing diverted wake. Flow is from left to right at 76 km/h (47 mph). Spin is counter-clockwise at 15 revs/sec. (Photograph taken by F. N. M. Brown, courtesy of the University of Notre Dame.)

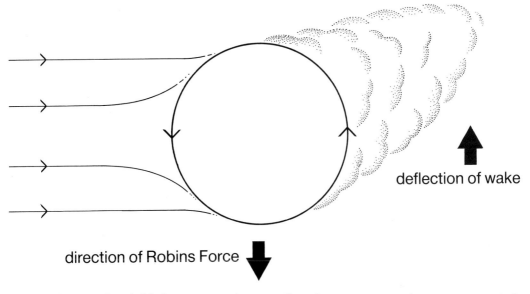

direction of Robins Force

deflection of wake

Fig. 6b Air flow around any ball feeling a positive Robins Force. The surface spinning against the oncoming air acts in the same way as the smooth side of a swinging cricket ball.

incorrect description states that if the top side of the ball rotates against the oncoming wind it will experience a stronger wind force on the curved surface facing the wind than on the bottom side rotating with the wind, and that this force will push the ball downwards. Apart from all the other knowledge about air layer separation, more of which we shall come to later, the mere existence of the negative Robins effect is enough to disprove this explanation. In the 'negative' situation the air is still pressing against the top half of the ball. Therefore if the common explanation was correct the ball should never feel an upward force, but, in the 'negative' situation, it does.

Because swing and Robins behaviour are basically the same phenomenon, it follows that small-scale (micro-) atmospheric turbulence which reduces swing will also reduce the Robins Force. The conditions of low turbulence discussed in Chapter 7 which favour swing will also favour Robins spin-swerve.

Fieldsmen and wicket-keepers will be very aware of the Robins Force. A return from the out-field, especially a return from alongside the body, will normally carry a good deal of side-spin. A right-handed fieldsman would most likely release the ball by sliding his fingers off the left side of it. In that case the ball would swerve to the right. In conditions favouring Robins spin-swerve i.e. low microturbulence, and/or more air to pass through, i.e. against the wind, returns could swerve well off line.

3
SWING: UNDERSTAND IT TO USE IT

The winning ball in many sports is the spun ball, spun to make it curve through the air. But cricket is unusual; the cricket ball will curve in flight without any applied spin whatsoever; behaviour which demands a new name, swing.

More correctly we should say that the ball *may* swing, and let Bernard Hollowood, writing in *Cricket on the Brain*, help bowlers keep their feet on the ground:

> I have watched Trueman on numerous occasions, but only once or twice has he been able to bowl his famous outswinger consistently. The radio and TV commentators (some of them, anyway) are ever ready to ascribe marvels of cut and swerve to a successful trundler. 'That was his outswinger,' they say. 'A beautiful ball — it swung late and then cut back off the pitch.' Well, yes, it happens. Not often though.

> There would be few batsmen with averages of thirty and more if bowlers were able to achieve the miracles of flight and turn claimed for them. In my experience the vast majority of fast bowlers deal chiefly in straight stuff and achieve cutters and swervers only rarely.[1]

Nevertheless, many a batsman has had to watch helplessly as the swinging curve takes the edge, or worse, finds nothing at all blocking its passage to the stumps.

There are reasons why a ball swings and there are reasons why it does not. In the swinger's dream the ball can be swung at will to one side or the other, all under good control. Not quite the dream however: in the dream the swing appears to occur late in the flight, just when the batsman thinks he has it nicely lined up.

To understand swing we must look back to the

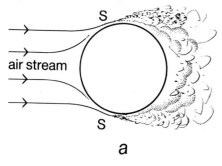

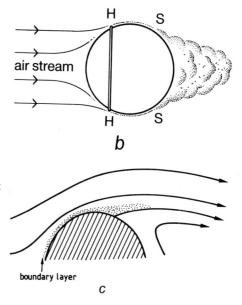

Fig. 7 Air going around a ball, based on wind tunnel photographs and using smoke to make the flow pattern visible: **a** is a smooth ball and the air layer near the ball leaves the surface at S; **b** is a smooth ball fitted with a hoop H behind which is formed a thin turbulent air stream which clings to the surface of the ball until it reaches point S; **c** general picture of the air layer close to the ball (the boundary layer) separating from the surface. If the separation point is different on opposite sides of the ball it will swing or swerve.

days when the invention of the aeroplane stimulated investigation into the behaviour of air flowing over wings and surfaces of all shapes. In 1914 a German aircraft engineer[2] published photographs showing how a wire hoop tied around the front of a sphere influenced the shape of the wake behind it (Fig. 7).

The hoop had the opposite effect to what might have been expected: instead of causing the air stream to fly off the surface of the ball and form a wider turbulent space behind the ball, it narrowed the wake. The hoop, in fact, made the ball more streamlined. This was because the hoop delayed the separation of the air stream from the ball. Stated another way, the hoop (Fig. 7*b*) caused the air stream to go around the ball a little further before leaving the surface past the bulge between H and S. Dimples on a golf ball have exactly the same streamlining effect and therefore allow a shot to go much further.

There is no such thing as a perfectly smooth solid surface; viewed under a powerful microscope, all solid surfaces are more or less rough. Air molecules passing over the supposedly smooth surface of a cricket ball would resemble a cloud of fine dust blowing across a series of mountain ranges, colliding with them and swirling around in eddies. This means that close to a solid surface there is no such thing as smooth air flow.

Across a cricket ball therefore, all flow is turbulent. But the turbulent layer varies in thickness from one surface to another. Across the smooth shiny area of the ball the turbulence is shallow, but across the seam or a worn patch it is deeper. Roughness is not the only factor: equally important is where the roughness is situated. The area where roughness has the most influence on where the air layer separates from the ball lies between H and S (Fig. 7).

The seam, as in Figure 8, because it lies near the front of the ball, has less influence, but still enough to produce a thin layer of turbulence which washes back over the ball causing the air layer to cling longer to the surface. But too much turbulence, say from a thicker hoop, has the opposite effect because the thicker turbulent layer flies off the ball earlier rather than later. If the seam was pointed further around towards the bottom of the ball in Figure 8 it would have a very big influence, so much in fact that the air stream would come off much earlier, as if 'ramped' up off the surface. The collapse of swing at very high seam angles (50–70 degrees), as seen in the 'swing pictures' in Chapter 4, is the result of this overturbulence. At those angles the seam is right around into that critical area. This influence of major roughness is also the basis of the so-called 'reverse swing' which will be discussed in Chapter 5.

In the normal situation, illustrated in Figure 9, the extra turbulence resulting from the stitching, positioned at an angle near the front of the ball by the skilful bowler, hangs on to the ball a little longer than the smoother air streaming off the ball on the shiny, non-seam side. Not a difficult picture to grasp once we realise that the turbulent air, provided that it is only a very thin layer of minor turbulence, has lost some speed and therefore has less tendency to fly off the surface. The over-all result is a deflection of the wake to one side behind the ball. The ball, having deflected the air, must itself be deflected in the opposite direction, i.e. it will swing to the side (Fig. 8).

Forty-one years after the experiments with wire hoops, J. C. Cooke, in the first published scientific analysis of swing,[3] applied to the cricket ball the discovery that a wire hoop increases streamlining. He pointed out that the seam could, as described above, act in the same way as a wire hoop that reached across one side of the ball only. If the seam is on one side of the ball facing the air flow, then, as Cooke stated, the delayed separation will take place only on that side (Fig. 8).

Cooke did not carry out any experiments with cricket balls; his work was nothing more nor less than speculation. But all the work done by others since that time has shown what a fine piece of speculation it was. Numerous photographs, and measurements of the flow and pressure patterns around cricket balls, have fully supported his general idea.

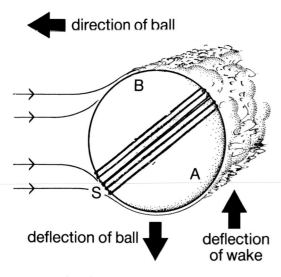

direction of ball

B

A

S

deflection of ball

deflection of wake

Fig. 8 Looking down on an outswinger; the seam pointing towards slips. The air striking the seam at S increases the turbulence of the air passing around the ball so that it clings longer to the ball. On the other (smooth) side there is no increase in turbulence and the air stream leaves the ball earlier, at B. The result is a deflection of the wake behind the ball, to one side. The ball must therefore be deflected in the opposite direction.

Two years after Cooke's paper, R. A. Lyttleton published an article[4] repeating the wake diversion idea, but still without testing it experimentally. Lyttleton went much further than Cooke, discussing related topics such as late swing and the effect of weather on swing. But speculation had gone too far and his assumption that flow around a cricket ball changes suddenly at a certain speed, and that this may account for late swing and swing in a humid atmosphere, has not been supported by subsequent work. Don Bradman published part of a talk given by Lyttleton on the BBC at that time, in his classic *The Art of Cricket*.[5]

Bowlers have swung the ball for about a century, building up a fund of knowledge which they pass on to the next generation. But even the best of them don't claim to understand many of the things they see happening on the field.

Not surprisingly, there is a limit to the knowledge of swing that can be gained during actual play. There are too many uncontrolled and unmeasured factors; different bowlers, different

air currents, different balls, different wear on balls, different seam angles. If anyone thinks that reliable measurements in a wind tunnel, where all these factors are under strict control, will destroy some of the mystique of cricket, they should think again. Cricket is not played in a laboratory, and cricket in the middle will forever carry its full and fascinating load of uncertainty.

A few cricket enthusiasts, lucky enough to have access to a wind tunnel, have carried out useful work in their leisure time. In other cases the projects have served to train students in the techniques of investigation. I spent nearly every weekend and holiday for six months making thousands of measurements in pursuit of my own work.

To the Australian, N. G. Barton, goes the credit for publishing the first measurements of the swing force.[6] He used two methods, one involving a ball skewered on a pendulum hanging at the exit air stream of the wind tunnel. From the amount of sideways deflection of the pendulum with the seam at a few different angles to the wind, he could calculate the swing force. The other method, which had been used 23 years earlier in a study of base-balls,[7] involved dropping balls through the air stream with the seam at various angles and measuring the position where they landed. If there was no sideways force the balls would drop straight down. But in actual fact the falling balls found themselves, for the fraction of a second that they took to drop through the air stream, in the same situation as a ball hurtling through the air towards the batsman. The air pushing past the ball was no different from the situation in which the ball was bowled through the air. The result was that the falling balls were diverted sideways by an amount which was measured from the mark they made hitting the floor. The swinging balls were of course pushed ahead a little as well, because of their drag, but the sideways deflection was easily measured. In fact the balls were not just dropped, but rolled down a ramp set at various angles to the air stream. In this way the back-spin, applied by the bowler as the fingers travel down

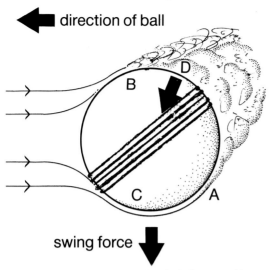

direction of ball

swing force

Fig. 9 Pressure difference makes the ball swing. Adding to the picture in Figure 8. Because the air stream clings longer on the rough (seam) side, leaving the ball at point A, whereas on the smooth side it leaves earlier, at B, there is a faster air flow across the region between C and A than there is between B and D, (the BD area being under the wake at the back of the ball). Daniel Bernoulli, a Swiss scientist, noticed in the eighteenth century that the pressure is least where the flow rate is greatest. This means that the pressure in the BD area is greater than the pressure in the AC area, thus causing the sideways swing force.

the back of the ball during release, is imitated. The spin was regarded as stabilising, like a gyroscope, the position of the ball in flight.

Barton found swing forces increasing from 10 per cent to 40 per cent of the weight of the ball as the air speed was increased from 55 to 108 km/h (34 to 67 mph), and the seam angle held at 30 degrees. As well as having to cope with a certain amount of uncontrollable seam wobble as the balls rolled down the ramp, Barton had no way of knowing what fraction of a second it took for the diverted wake flow pattern to develop around the ball as it fell through the moving air.

Using smoke in the air stream he confirmed the diverted wake explanation of swing (Fig. 8). Seventeen balls were used in the study. Worn balls generally gave lower swing force values. These methods established approximate values for the sideways force in a few of the situations encountered in swing bowling.

Shortly after Barton published his pioneering work, a study[8] was published by a group from London which used the same rolling and dropping technique that Barton had employed. A new measurement carried out by this group found the pressure differences around the surface of a fixed ball. For this they inserted tubes into the ball connected with small holes on the surface. The fast-moving air stream which clings longer to the ball on the seam side creates a low pressure area which is not matched on the opposite side of the ball. This pressure difference causes the ball to swing towards the seam side, as illustrated in Figure 9. This rounds off the diverted wake picture of swing.

About this time a brief study[9] showed that a ball mounted in a wind tunnel experienced drag and swing forces similar to those on a sphere fitted with a trip wire, and that there was no sudden drop-off at higher speed.

For my own work in New Zealand I had access to a high quality wind tunnel[10] and was able to develop methods which were sensitive and versatile.

The arrangement for swing force measurement is shown in Figure 10. The balls were mounted on the end of a thin rod coming up into the wind tunnel through a hole in its floor. The rod was pivoted and joined by another rod at 90 degrees (i.e. horizontal), the end of which rested on the pan of a sensitive electronic balance. A sideways (i.e. swing) force on the ball[11] thus registered as a change of weight, to an accuracy of one hundredth of a gram, without movement, on the balance pan. The method used was well designed for uncovering the detailed behaviour in many different circumstances connected with both static and spinning balls.

The spinning balls were mounted on a hollow column through which was inserted a thin flexible cable turned by an electric motor to supply the spin (Fig. 10b).

Imagine a fast bowler coming in to bowl with the ball cupped in his fingers, and delivering it merely by pushing it straight ahead without any

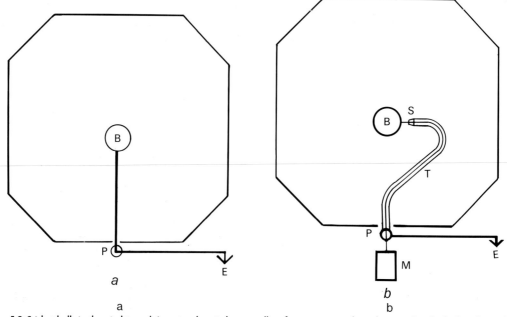

Fig. 10 Cricket balls in the wind tunnel. Imagine the wind as travelling from your eye along the tunnel to the ball: **a** shows the view along the inside of the wind tunnel of a ball mounted on a rod connected to point P and electronic balance E: **b** shows a similar view of the mount for studying a spinning ball set at any angle for swing. The ball is mounted on a thin shaft (S) at the end of metal tube (T) through which passes a flexible cable to convey rotation from a variable speed motor (M). (Wilkins 1985)

of the normal final downward flick of the fingers. This would not be his fastest delivery because that final wrist and finger action is known to be the source of about 5 per cent of the ball's speed. However, it is an uncomplicated delivery and for that reason was the first type I studied in the wind tunnel.

The ball fixed on the rod in Figure 10 is twisted around through the range of angles from 0–90° and the swing force measured at six wind speeds from 55 to 130 km/h (34–81 mph). Fast men have been timed at 153 km/h (95 mph) or more, but the few bowlers capable of such awesome speed appear to use it sparingly. For later studies on so-called 'reverse swing' of deliberately damaged balls I included higher speeds.

That Sunday morning, turning up the wind and calling out the force figures to my son Damien, who wrote them in a notebook, was an exciting time. The wind tunnel is somewhat more than half a cricket pitch in length and makes quite a noise. Air flung out of one end by a powerful fan flows back through the large room and is sucked into the other end. A seam angle of zero is chosen; the seam points straight down the pitch. The knob is turned, the wind builds up; slow, slow-medium, medium, fast-medium, fast — name your hero appropriate to the pace. The rising howl of wind and machinery drowns all conversation. But inside the working compartment of the tunnel, behind strong plastic windows, the air flow is known to be beautifully smooth, as on a dull windless day, the hallmark of a good instrument. We are now at the top of the range. The returning air scatters paper from the table.

Inside the tunnel the ball may well have just left the hand of a warmed-up fast man letting it go at a lively pace. But what's happening? Ball and rod begin to vibrate uncontrollably, the readings on the electronic balance fluctuate wildly, making no sense at all. Quick, turn down the wind; slow-medium, not much improvement. Stop; start up again at two other seam angles, 2.5° and 5°. The same problem, but less at 5°. This can't go on; our equipment will fly to bits. Try 7.5°; yes that's much better. Now everything settles down, no more problems all the way to 90°. No problems with *this* ball, but with other balls, old and new, some spectacular collapses, unstable behaviour and reversals of swing force were encountered, and not only at low seam angles.

Later I came across work by a German[12] and a Japanese[13] who had seen it all before. Flow around spheres, they found, was basically unstable. Their smoke photos showed wakes oscillating in all directions behind the spheres and creating a wavy pattern.

Our cricket ball at low seam angles had been experiencing a similar rapidly changing force. In this case, because the seam lay at or near the

Fig. 11(i) Seam angles as they appear from behind: **a** 0°; **b** 7.5°; **c** 15°; **d** 25°; **e** 45°; **f** 70°.

middle of the ball as it faced the on-rushing air, the force was first to one side and then to the other, hence the violent vibrations. Nothing new here for the observant bowler, I'm sure. Most bowlers are candid enough to admit that the ball can do strange and unpredictable things. Maurice Tate, one of the great medium-pace bowlers, confided many years after his retirement that he was unsure of which way the ball would move in the air.

Ray Lindwall has said that one of his chief joys in England was to wait and see which way the ball moved after he had bowled it.[14] If confirmation of this was needed, it comes from motion pictures taken by Imbrosciano, who used high speed photography to study the Australian left-handed swing bowler Garry Gilmour.[15] Close examination of the pictures indeed show sudden changes of direction, where loss, gain, and reversal of swing had occurred.

However much the literature of cricket might be enlivened by stories of the weird and wonderful behaviour of cricket balls in flight, this basic fact, the instability of the air flowing past a ball, is always likely to be one of nature's manipulators.

The wind tunnel incident, the experience of bowlers, and the photographs, should remind bowlers of the benefits to be gained from pointing the upright seam straight, or more or less straight, down the pitch. Useful, unpredictable swing, including late swing, may be there for the taking, and even more likely if there are variable wind currents around, which effectively and unpredictably change of the angle of the seam to the air flowing past. But bowlers should know that if they do anything to make one side of the ball aerodynamically different from the other side, for example by shining or by damage, they have, at the same time, reduced the possibility of unpredictable low seam angle swing.

Before we come back to this in the next chapter, where we uncover the picture of swing, it is worth the bowler's while to study Figure 11, and get to know what the various seam angles look like.

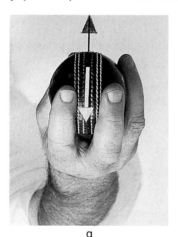

g

h

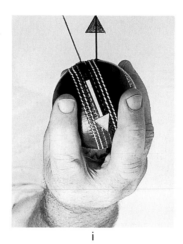

i

j

Fig. 11 (ii) Various grips and angles for swing: **g** 0° (may give unexpected swing if the ball is shiny on both sides); **h** 10°; **i** 20°; **j** 30°.

4

SWING UNDER CONTROL

Swing is about sides; not the top or the bottom. No sports ball is so clearly divided into two hemispheres as is the cricket ball. Only what happens on the sides can make the ball move sideways. What happens on the top or bottom can only nudge it up or down. Air pushing against the front slows the ball a little, but the only way the front can affect the side is when the seam is near the front and a little to one side creating turbulence which 'washes' back around the ball on that side.

Swing is also about air; air and the ball, nothing more. Swing has nothing whatsoever to do with the pitch, except of course that the pitch will wear the ball and ultimately destroy the swing.

The skill of the swing bowler is to send the ball out 'frozen' in a fixed attitude so that the air 'sees' one side hemisphere as different from the other.

Assuming that the ball has not been deliberately or accidentally damaged more on one side than on the other, the only way to achieve this distinction between the two sides is to employ bowling skill to point the main seam at some angle across the line of flight and ensure that it stays there.

While it is relatively easy to bring the fingers straight down off the back of the ball during release, and thus point the seam straight, this zero angle is not normally the best angle for swing, although, as we saw earlier, its unpredictability has some attraction. The more usual, and more difficult, task is to release the ball at some angle to the flight path while at the same time keeping the seam vertical. The greater the angle which is attempted the more difficult is the task. Fortunately, we can see from the 'swing pictures' that there is no need to go above 35° and, in the absence of cross wind, any angle within the range 15–30° is effective.

Then the backward rotation of the released ball ensures that what is on the left side, when it is delivered, will stay on the left all the way down the pitch, and what is delivered on the right will stay on the right. The back spin also ensures that because both sides are turning in the face of the oncoming wind, the wind does not 'see' a face as 'fixed' but 'smeared out'. Thus any grooves, such as that from the minor (quarter) seam, or marks, or any other damage will be 'averaged out' because the ball will normally have made a number of backward turns, on its way down the pitch.

Our first 'swing picture', Figure 12, is the simplest possible example. It is a new, non-spinning, two-piece ball and therefore uncomplicated by the minor seam that makes a small groove across the two leather faces of a four-piece ball.

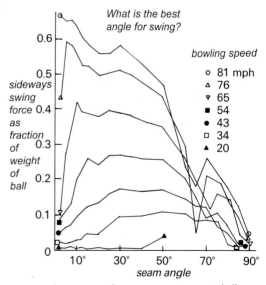

Fig. 12 Sideways swing forces on a new two-piece ball at any angle and any speed. (Wind tunnel work, Wilkins 1985)

The air on one side 'sees' a smooth shiny leather face, and on the other the seam curving across the face. It shows that swing is obtainable right down to the speed of a very slow bowler and that it gets progressively stronger right up to the highest speed tested, 130 km/h (81 mph). There is no collapse of the swing force at high speeds, as had been predicted by some. As for the best seam angle, no great differences are seen at any speed in the range 10–30°. Although we cannot bowl at much higher seam angles, a strong cross wind could make the angle at which the air crosses the ball different. The 'swing pictures' also provide information about how roughness, in this case the seam, affects air flow at high angles.

Higher air-to-seam angles can only occur in a strong cross wind.

The collapse around 50–75° results from the air hitting the seam more side-on than when the seam is nearer the front of the ball. This makes the air stream fly off the surface, like a ski jumper, rather than clinging on longer, as it does with less roughness and less turbulence. The seam, in the 'zone of collapse' also happens to be in a favourable position, near the bulge in the ball, where air layer separation is more likely to occur anyway. The two things to note about roughness are: how much and where? Roughness, including the seam and any wear, has more effect when it is on the outer third, A or B, in Figure 13b. We will come back to the effect of major roughness near the outside bulge of the ball when we look at 'reverse swing'.

How far would the ball in Figure 12 swing? If everything was ideal, and that means no 'wobbling' of the upright seam, no significant turbulence in the surrounding air, no crosswind or headwind, and if the swing force operated all the way from the bowler's hand for, say, 17.5 m (19 yds), the sideways movement in the air would be about 60 cm (2 ft). But, by firing balls from a ball gun in a laboratory, with the seam upright at various angles, we find that the actual swing is less than this; usually about 60–80 per cent of the full amount. This is because the full swing force does not operate instantaneously and the air pattern around the ball takes a little time, a fraction of a second, to build up the full sideways push. However this finding does not lessen the value of the 'swing pictures' found by fixing the ball in a wind tunnel and measuring the steady swing force; much new and valuable information has been obtained from these 'trapped' balls. Later we will see that the time delay during which the swing develops is the reason why faster bowlers generally get less sideways deviation from swing.

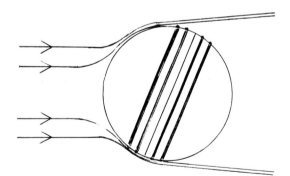

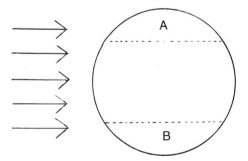

Fig. 13a Seam at 65°: major roughness near the critical bulge pushes the air away from the ball: the reason why a large seam angle would be bad for swing; compare with Figure 8 where the roughness of the seam is around near the front and has the opposite effect. Compare also with Figure 7b where the wire hoop has less effect than the seam.

Fig. 13b Zones A and B where any roughness, from the seam, or from wear, or from water-swelling, has most effect.

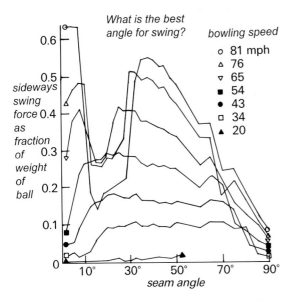

Fig. 14 Sideways swing forces on a new two-piece ball with a coarser leather than that used for Figure 12. (Wind tunnel work, Wilkins 1985)

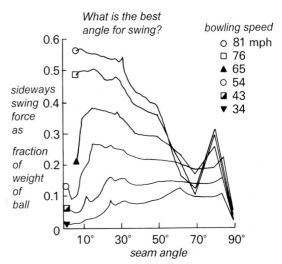

Fig. 15 Sideways swing forces on a new four-piece ball which has the minor seam on the smooth side in line with the air stream. (Wind tunnel work, Wilkins 1985)

The great sensitivity of swing to minor surface roughness is shown in Figure 14, which depicts another two-piece ball apparently the same as that used in Figure 12. The collapse of swing force between 10° and 30°, and at higher speeds, was only explained when a close examination of the surface showed a slightly coarser texture in the leather in the second ball.

Setting up a new four-piece ball so that the groove of the minor seam is in line with the air stream gives an almost identical 'swing picture' (Fig. 15) to that given by the two-piece in Figure 12. The air stream 'sees' along the groove and can ignore it.

Figure 16a, a four-piece ball from a forty-over game on a grassy pitch, only moderately worn and with no shredded leather, gave interesting results. The minor seam lies across the air flow, while in Figure 16b it lies in line with the flow. The slightly opened groove in the leather is enough to reverse the swing at most speeds in figure 16a.

Figure 16b, with the minor seam in line with the air stream, is not greatly different from the new four-piece ball pictured in Figure 15. This

shows the moderate wear as having little effect. However, in case this information on swing reversal has bowlers itching to get their hands on the nearest four-piece ball, they must be reminded that the graphs are 'frozen' pictures, designed to provide inside information on a ball that is not spinning backwards, as it would be if actually bowled. When bowled, the ball's rotation would 'smear out' the groove so that air would not be across it all the time as in Figure 16a, but only for an instant during each rotation. The overall result, some combination of Figures 16a and b, confirms what bowlers have known for many years: that the two-piece swings more than the four-piece. Although the minor seam is turning around on both sides of the ball, it is more exposed on the non-seam side facing the wind, and, because it serves to make the smooth side a little bit like the rough side, it reduces the difference between the two sides and therefore reduces the swing a little.

Other questions to be answered are: what exactly is the final swing force on a rotating four-piece ball, and: does backspin help or hinder swing, and, if so, what is the optimum amount to use?

d   c

Fig. 16 Sideways swing forces on a moderately worn four-piece ball: **a** with the minor seam across the air stream (ball 16c) and showing the influence (in the 15–30° seam angle region) of the minor seam on the air flow to reverse the swing away from the direction in which the seam is pointing; **b** with the minor seam in line with the air stream (ball 16**d**). Assume that the air is flowing from the viewer to the page (this is the opposite direction from that normally used in this book, but it allows the minor seam to be seen). (Wind tunnel work, Wilkins 1985)

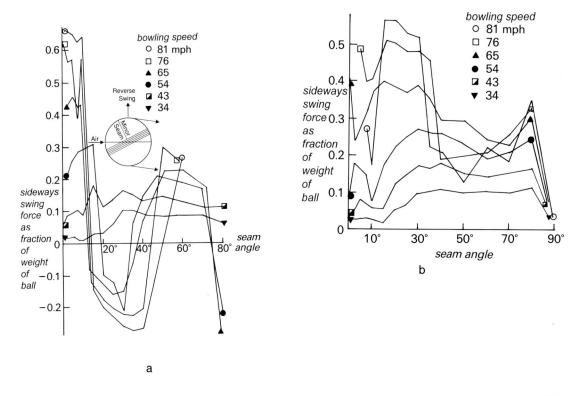

Two earlier workers, using the rolling and dropping method described in Chapter 3, came to different conclusions on this. Barton found that a back-spin rate of about 5 revs/sec was best for swing, but Bentley's group found 12 revs/sec to be best. My own work, carried out under more controlled conditions, showed that it did not matter how much back-spin was on the ball. It can be seen in Figure 17 that, at spin rates of up to 14 revs/sec, which seem to be around the highest

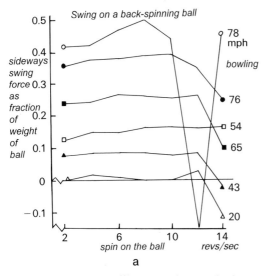

a

Fig. 17 Does back-spin affect swing? These results show that the answer is no. Seam angle 5° (**a**) and 10° (**b**) for various wind speeds and rates of spin. (Wind tunnel work, Wilkins 1985)

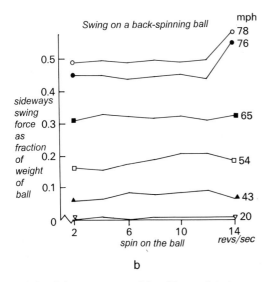

b

which cricketers are capable of imparting (except for the fastest delivery at a 5° seam angle) the swing force was virtually unchanged. Nor did the spin reduce the overall swing forces significantly. Back-spin is therefore not needed for swing, and we will see later that there is no need for back-spin to stabilise the ball like a spinning top.

Figure 16*a*, tells us that the slight roughness of the minor seam interferes when it is about 15°–30° forward of the position where it lies straight

across the ball, and loses its ability to interfere at about 40°. Normally the air stream will leave early from the non-seam side of a shiny ball. But the slight roughness of the minor seam, limited in area, makes the air cling a little longer; enough in fact to divert the air in behind the ball and enough to reverse the swing. More correctly, referring back to Figure 9, we should say that the air going further around the ball in Figure 16*a*, compared to the normal new ball pattern, creates a new low pressure area which draws the ball towards it, 'reversing' the swing. While this is revealing information, the bowler could only use it if he could merely push the ball out, rather than having it rotate and 'smear out' as it leaves the hand, as happens normally.

When wear is greater, such as in a four-piece ball used for a hundred overs, the two 'swing pictures' (Figs 18*a* and *b*) are so chaotic that the both the existence and the alignment of the minor seam are irrelevant. Nor is there any recognisable pattern, related to the major seam angle, over the whole of both faces. In other words the wear, over the whole of both faces, is more important than the major seam positioned near the front of the ball.

However, it should be pointed out again that while the 'frozen swing' pictures shown here are full of interesting information, the chaotic roughness, as far as the air stream is concerned, is 'smeared out' during backward rotation, on both sides of the ball, so that many of the positive and negative swing forces will largely cancel each other out. In this case the presence or the position of the minor seam is less important. But we shall see in Chapter 5, that although the minor seam is normally of no consequence in cricket as played according to the Laws, it has, in the hands of some players, taken on a somewhat sinister role as a point of entry for water, fingernails, and any sharp object that might be at hand.

Another hundred-over ball, in Figure 19, shows that swing has practically disappeared.

Because swing depends on two sides affecting the air differently, it is not surprising that extensive

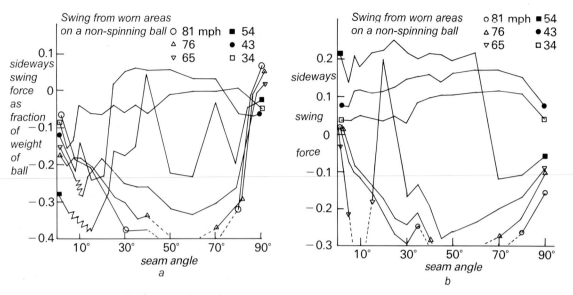

Fig. 18 Sideways swing forces on a well-worn four-piece ball: **a** minor seam across air stream on the non-seam side; **b** minor seam in line with the air stream; but the minor seam is of little importance because the wear dominates both pictures. (Wind tunnel work, Wilkins 1985)

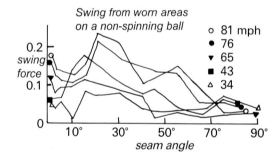

Fig. 19 Swing on a hundred-over ball. Air stream separations on opposite sides of the ball have practically cancelled each other out and nullified swing almost completely. (Wind tunnel work, Wilkins 1985)

wear over the whole of both faces of the ball overcomes any effect from the roughness of the seam. This makes the angle of the seam irrelevant, and equalises the effect over the whole ball so much that swing becomes impossible.

To emphasise the fact that, on a worn face, the minor seam is merely one more bit of roughness among many, the swing reversal in Figure 20 happens on a ball that has no minor seam.

Earlier we talked about the amount of sideways movement from swing. Why do we generally see less swing from the fastest bowlers if, as we have seen in our 'swing pictures', the swing force in a faster delivery is greater? For a ball to swing it needs both a swing force and sufficient time for

that force to have its effect in pushing the ball sideways. Since the faster ball arrives at the other end sooner, it has less time in which to feel the effect and will therefore deviate less than we might expect. But there is more to it. If we take this to be the only factor, some simple calculations show that all bowlers will swing by about the same amount. However, this cannot be true: we know that fast bowlers swing less. What is happening here?

The effective length over which a ball swings between the bowler's hand and the bat is probably no more than about 17.5 m (19 yds). Table A shows the amount of sideways deviation seen by the batsman, calculated using the average swing forces for seam angles of 10° to 30° taken from

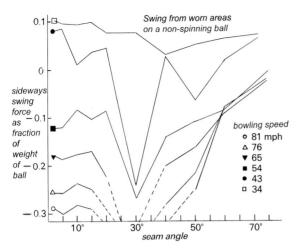

Fig. 20 The minor (quarter) seam is not necessary for 'reverse' swing. Reversal of swing forces on a worn two-piece ball. What the wear is doing to the air stream makes the position of the main seam irrelevant. (Wind tunnel work, Wilkins 1985)

Figure 15. But since it is impossible for the air flow pattern which provides the swing force to develop instantly, there must be a delay, and a period at the beginning of the ball's flight during which it is not swinging at all. No one, as far as I am aware, has measured this delay — more correctly described as a build-up period — but I have included in the table figures to show how the amount of final deviation would be affected by delays of one tenth and one quarter of a second.

With no time delay, all the bowlers in the fast and medium range, say down to 77 km/h (48 mph),

achieve about the same amount of swing. As the delay increases, the fast men achieve less swing in comparison to the medium pacers, until a delay of 0.25 seconds reduces their swing to nearly half as much.

The idea of a 'no swing' period suddenly giving way to a 'full swing' period is just a convenient way of coping with what is more likely to be a gradual build-up in swing force. Although swing will vary tremendously, depending on the state of the ball, the atmosphere, and the skill of the bowler, the common experience of cricketers indicates that the results of the time delay concept are in broad agreement with the real situation. Sideways movement measured from the impact of balls fired at a polystyrene target from a ball gun confirm the existence of time delays of 0.1–0.2 seconds.

The faster the delivery the further a ball will go before any swing is visible. The curves plotted by Imbrosciano from the photos of Gilmour's bowling show little or no curvature at the beginning of the flight paths. Late swing will be discussed in Chapter 6.

Baseball pitchers use this combination of increased speed and consequently later curve in the slider ball, probably the most effective ball in their repertoire. Although the stitching pattern around a baseball differs from that around a cricket ball, the forces causing baseballs and cricket balls to swerve or swing arise for essentially the same reasons.

Table A Why do most of the fastest bowlers swing less? Sideways movement from bowlers of different speeds.

Bowling speed (mph)		Time in air for 19 yds flight (secs)	Calculated sideways movement (inches)*		
			No time delay	Delay 0.1 sec	Delay 0.25 sec
33	Slow	1.18	14	11	9
43	Slow	0.92	22	17	11
54	Medium	0.72	24	18	10
66	Medium	0.59	25	17	8
76	Fast	0.52	25	16	7
81	Fast	0.48	24	15	6

* Using the relationship between the sideways deviation (Δ), the acceleration (α) and the time (t): $\Delta = \frac{1}{2}\alpha t^2$

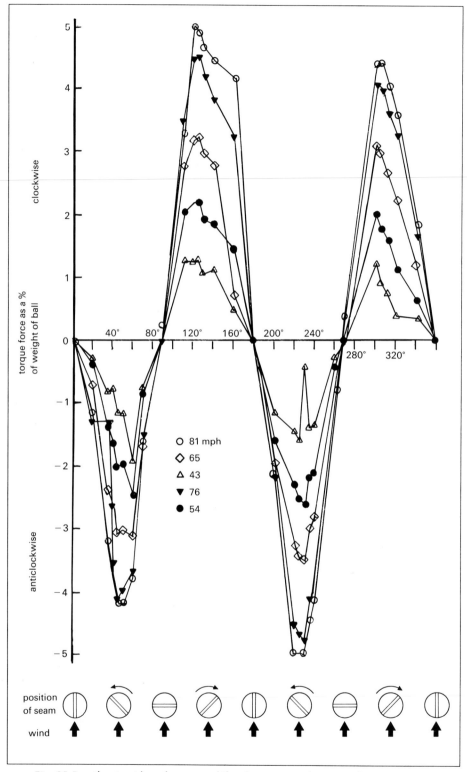

Fig. 21 Does the air catch on the seam and if so, how strong is the twisting force (torque)? Yes it does but the torque force is weak. (Wind tunnel work, Wilkins 1985)

It has been claimed that back-spin is good for swing bowling because, like the spinning top that will not fall over, the backward spinning ball will be better able to remain at a fixed angle as it travels through the air. Why would it change its angle? If it was a perfectly smooth sphere it would not. But, as we have seen in our examination of swing, the seam gets in the way of the air and changes its flow pattern. The seam side of the ball must therefore tend to be pushed around or twisted by this frictional effect of the air stream. Since a few authors have mentioned the probable existence of this twisting (torque) force, and since no one had ever measured it, I decided to do so with the aid of a delicate lever system connecting a new four-piece ball to the sensitive electronic balance.

Figure 21 shows the basic twisting process and the results of the torque measurements. It proves that there is torque and that it varies markedly with the angle of the seam to the air flow. At seam angles where the wind 'sees' no difference in roughness between one side of the ball and the other, i.e. at 0°, 90°, 180° and 270°, there is no torque. Between these positions the torque force rises to a very moderate amount of push around the equator, depending on wind speed. However, at the seam angles used by medium and fast bowlers, i.e. up to about 30°, these forces are halved.

Small torque forces such as these are unlikely to twist the ball around during flight. Even if the seam angle did change a little during flight, perhaps in deliveries carrying little or no back-spin, the results need not be all bad since it might blunder into a region where swing is better, or where catastrophic collapse and reversal of swing force may yield an unexpected bonus when it 'goes the other way'.

Another oddity that has been mentioned by writers is the possibility of the spinning and twisting ball behaving like a spinning top, displaying a sort of slow, weaving, circular movement known as gyroscopic precession. A calculation on this gives a time of 12 seconds for one complete rotary motion of the axis. The ball — by this time, possibly back in the bowler's hand for the next delivery — would unfortunately not be able to complete this complex dance to nature's tune.

Jack Massie (1890–1966) must have been one of the best Australian bowlers never to play for his country. He was wounded in the First World War and played no more first class cricket. In 1926 he wrote a coaching booklet full of good practical advice. Unlike many earlier writers he recognised the difference between swerve and swing. But, limited by the knowledge of those days, he thought that if more back-spin was applied to a ball it would swing more. However, as we saw earlier, it appears to have no effect.

5

TAMPERING WITH SWING: FORWARD AND REVERSE

When certain bowlers began to decimate top batting line-ups by swinging the old ball, the cricket world became curious. For a century bowlers had been required to spend years mastering the art of swing. But what we were now seeing was different.

No longer was it necessary to release the ball after a carefully organised set of movements designed to keep the seam upright, but holding a steady pointing within a fairly narrow range of angles slightly across the direction of travel. For all to see, the new practitioners simply delivered the ball from fingers coming more or less straight down the back of the ball in the simplest possible manner.

It is an easy delivery and it betrays none of the tell-tale actions that alert a good batsman as to which way the bowler might be trying to swing the ball.

At the same time were seeing, and are still seeing, the clear demonstration of an insatiable desire on the part of many players to apply bodily fluids to the ball. Sweat, and especially saliva, is applied by anybody and everybody — not only bowlers but fieldsmen as well — anywhere and at any time: cricketers programmed for an interminable process that is quite beyond the traditional light moistening of the bowler's fingertips for grip; now a chronic ball-wetting, a sort of grand reverse thirst.

Why the swing; and why with the old ball? Citizens of the twentieth century who trust their lives to the wings of a jet aeroplane could be expected to assume that someone knows why they don't fall out of the sky. Talk of 'the mystery of reverse swing' suited the old ball swingers, but the sceptics were bound to start asking questions sooner or later.

Strange things were happening to balls. Umpires inspecting the ball at Melbourne, during the interval in a game between Victoria and Pakistan in 1990, discovered 'unnatural marks' as if one side of the ball was being prepared for a game of noughts and crosses, whereas the other side was shiny and unblemished.[1] Imran Khan has recently admitted that he damaged balls as far back as 1981. Apparently that was in the days before umpires suspected anything. The 1990 incident which, as far as I know, involves one of the earliest records of the actual state of the ball, is a good place to begin to understand one of the two routes to 'swing-from-damage'.

While we must not presume that one country or group of cricketers had a monopoly on such tricks, the historical record tells us that Pakistani bowlers had been achieving unusual feats of swing with old balls since 1977, fourteen years prior to the Melbourne incident. Whether or not they received advice from someone with access to a wind tunnel, we do not know. But they must have learned something, even if only by trial and error, during those fourteen years.

What the umpires found at Melbourne agrees with what we know about swing: it is no mystery, and it tells us that there is profit for those who damage the ball on one side.

The marks were not on the main seam, nor was the main seam 'picked', as bowlers have always done, either to give themselves a better grip in their fingers, or to enhance the grip of the ball on the pitch, or both. We know, as did the Pakistanis, that swing depends on the state of the two leather faces and is less influenced by whether or not the main seam is 'picked'. The two leather faces on either side of the ball rotate backwards at a fixed angle and the swing comes about when the air stream comes earlier or later off one face than the other. (Fig. 13b shows the areas of the ball which are most sensitive to damage.)

Therefore they scratched only one face. Lines going in different directions across an area of the leather ensured that a major part of the air flow near the surface was made more turbulent on that side. If the other side was shiny it must have been fairly early in the innings, or the pitch surface was not very abrasive, or both. Even the most vigorous polishing cannot prevent balls from wearing. Depending on the abrasiveness of the pitch the normal wearing process might not go beyond the dull stage, or it might ultimately go a long way further and get there quicker. In any case, rubbing is needless time-wasting and should be stopped except by the bowler who frequently has a genuine need to clean the ball and the stitching in order to obtain a better grip.

Which way will I swing it this time? This is a one-day game; no slip, not much point in bowling the outswinger. I grip the ball, seam pointing straight, with the scratched side on the right, facing leg, and let it go fast and straight. No swing skill is involved. Nice inswing. If I don't get an lbw, a stump might go down. To keep them guessing I occasionally turn the ball around 180° for the outswinger, and if I'm bowling to a lefthander I keep it that way most of the time to swing the ball back in. I'm happy if some onlookers think that my so-called skill in 'reverse swing' helps me to swing in but not out; the less they understand the better.

If it is not a one-day game, and I am bowling with slips and a gully, I expect to embarrass batsmen by frequently changing the damaged side from left to right in my grip and getting both outswing and inswing with no change of action.

What exactly happens around a ball that has been interfered with like the one at Melbourne? The scratching has the same effect that the seam would have if it was pointing to that side: the normal technique we looked at in Chapter 4. The air flow that makes the scratched ball swing, comes

off the ball early on the shiny side and late on the scratched side. In other words the scratches relieve the bowler of the job of pointing the seam as in normal swing bowling. Because the scratches are right on the face, the centre of action, they can produce the same turbulence without needing to be so prominent.

This, pictured in Figure 25b(i), is the simplest type of interference that removes the need for skill in swing. Note that the damage was minor, no more than a few scratches; not the wholesale mutilation of leather that we have seen since then, and which gives rise to the second type of 'tampered' swing which we shall look at later. It is minor damage that is an essential feature of this first form of tampering. This being the case, there are other, easily accessible tricks, that can do the same job. A quick finger nail into the minor seam to raise the edges, even if only a little, will be just as effective as scratching, or a quick claw at water-softened leather.

The damage might be minor but the consequences are certainly not minor. Imitating the seam in this way, and in doing so, by-passing the need for skill in swing, while removing the tell-tale action signs picked up by good batsmen, is cheating.

Because the ball still swings towards the rougher side, as with a 'normal' seam-based, skill-based, swing, we cannot call the tampered swing 'reverse'. If we use 'reverse' in this way we will be unable to distinguish between the two types of tampered swing. I suggest that this type of interference should be called *assisted swing*. The resulting swing could be called 'swing-from-damage-that-imitates-the-seam', but I doubt whether such a name, which describes it all so nicely, will enter the vocabulary!

The only situation where damage leading to *assisted swing* could take place legally would be when a ball, at least moderately shiny on one side, has been accidentally damaged on the other side. In this case the bowler merely places the damaged side facing the intended direction of swing. Even if he points the seam a little the other way the damaged side may still win out. If a bowler is given a ball that has been accidentally damaged on one side he should get the best out of his good fortune by always pointing the damaged side to the intended direction of swing. He may find that he doesn't even need to go to the trouble of pointing the seam in that direction although, if the damage is very minor, or too near the main seam, it may help to do so. However I believe that the batting side has a right to object to this use of a damaged ball.

Although there is no evidence that water was used in the Melbourne incident, water is implicated, in the form of sweat, or saliva, or any other form, as a major culprit in the whole 'swing from damage' business. But, to start with, I will describe how water, in one of my experiments, can bring about the 'seam imitating' swing situation like the one in Melbourne.

Place a slightly worn four-piece ball in water about an inch deep, for a few minutes. It must be a little worn because otherwise the lacquer prevents the uptake of water into the leather and into the crack of the minor seam. Take it out and dry it. Where each of the totally concealed stitches in the minor seam runs across under the smooth leather face, there is now a distinct little bulge, which, surprisingly, does not disappear even when the ball is dry. Even after years of storage following immersion this ball retains enough water-induced roughness along the minor seam to cause it to swing towards that side when bowled by a medium pace bowler at zero seam angle.

As long as one side has been altered even a little bit, the instability and the uncertainty that Ray Lindwall (Chapter 3) noted, when he delivered the ball with the seam pointing straight, has been removed. Today's bowlers, constantly polishing one side of the ball, should be conscious of this loss.

The 'seam imitating' situation is mimicked in a striking manner in Figure 22, where a plain smooth hockey ball, sandpapered on one whole side with a moderately coarse sandpaper (80 grade), will experience a large sideways swing,

larger than that normally found on cricket balls, and increasing steadily over the whole range of speeds (up to almost 145 km/h (90 mph)) in the wind tunnel.

We can now give directions to the apprentice tamperer: the bowler himself, or his accomplices. The following sequence of actions can be seen on many cricket fields these days, but nowhere more clearly than under the prying lens of the TV camera. No need to slobber; just keep placing sweat or saliva on the minor seam on one side. Impact on the ball has already opened the gap a little. Rub the hand across the surface to force the water into the gap. Now comes the tricky stage. Holding the ball in one hand to hide the action as much as possible, quickly run a thumbnail or fingernail of the other hand along the partly opened gap. If the previous work has been carried out properly, the leather on either side of the gap will have been softened allowing it to be raised on either side to open it a little. This is enough. If umpires carry out an inspection at the end of the over, press down the leather and raise it again later.

Is such interference with the natural aerodynamics of a cricket ball legal, and

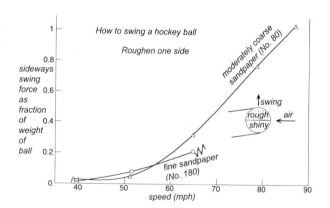

Fig. 22 Even a smooth shiny hockey ball will swing if you tamper with it. The sideways forces on two hockey balls which have been roughened on one side. When the roughness is only slight (fine sandpaper) the air at 105 km/h (65 mph) does not 'see' enough difference in the two sides to give a steady sideways force. (Wind tunnel work, Wilkins 1996)

compatible with the spirit of the Law? Of course not. But there is a lot more in this bag of tricks. Our apprentice tamperer will find that when the 'fairly shiny' side wears to 'slightly rough', his tampering no longer works. He now has late air separation on *both* sides, and little or no swing. This is when he needs to pull out tricks labelled 'reverse swing'.

'Reverse' swing; the reverse of what? I have in my desk a fat file of cuttings and other printed material about swing. I apologise to the reader if I sound arrogant, but the majority of this material is so packed with confusion, half-truths, and straightout error, that I have given up on an idea that I once had of answering every one of those well-meaning authors and trying to put them right. An example is a book entitled *Tampering with Cricket* which is spoiled by a lack of basic understanding of the subject.[2]

If cricketers are uncertain about 'normal' swing there must be little hope of their being able to cope with its two back-alley cousins.

Qualified researchers in close contact with cricket, reporting on their own work and distinguishing carefully between fact and speculation, are normally reliable. I would hope that readers of the previous two chapters are now as well informed on swing as most.

At the risk of tedious repetition, a quick summary will help us move on to the second type of 'tampered' swing. Swing, as used by bowlers for nearly a century, depends on roughness on one side of the ball. It is the roughness of the main seam, and its use depends on the skill of the swing bowler. Years of practice with body, arm, wrist and fingers enable him to release the ball so that it travels 'frozen', with the seam upright and pointing to one side, all the way to the batsman.

The roughness is therefore near the front of one side, and, as we saw earlier, the turbulence which washes back from that roughness causes the air to cling longer. But on the other side, not behind the seam, the air stream near the ball is smooth and leaves the ball earlier. The result is swing. 'Reverse' therefore must be about air streams

behaving differently from this.

The answer to the question: 'the reverse of what?' where mutilation is more serious than in the Melbourne example, is simply that instead of swinging *toward* the rougher side, as is normal, the ball 'reverses' to swing *away from* the rougher side. If it swings away from the roughness, something different must be happening. It is not just whether or not the ball has been damaged, but where and how much it has been damaged.

Reverse swing depends on three factors; amount of wear (less effective near the main seam), wear relative to the other side of the ball, and the speed with which it is bowled.

The cricket field is where it counts, but the cricket field is not a reliable place on which to sort it all out. The wind tunnel and the 'ball gun' offers better control.

Air flowing around balls of different roughness has been studied in detail as part of the work needed to understand how radioactive balls in atomic reactors give up their heat to air flowing past.[3] In 1974, three years before the Pakistani bowlers are recorded as having obtained swing from roughness, a German scientist found where the air stream leaves the surface of balls in different situations. He studied a much bigger range of air speeds, but his results, as they apply to cricket, are shown in Figure 23. He roughened the surface by glueing small beads of various sizes to the whole ball. While the balls were nearly three times larger than cricket balls, it is possible to calculate so as to allow for this.

Looking at Figure 23 we see the following pictures: from a smooth ball, nature decides that the air stream leaves at 82°, i.e. before it gets halfway around the ball. This is about what one sees in the published smoke tracks of air coming off the smooth faces of cricket balls.

From a slightly rough ball, the equivalent of 0.18 mm roughness on a cricket ball, the air comes off later, and later still when the air speed is greater.

Increasing the roughness to 0.9 mm changes the picture. At slower speeds the increased roughness has little effect. At faster speeds it starts

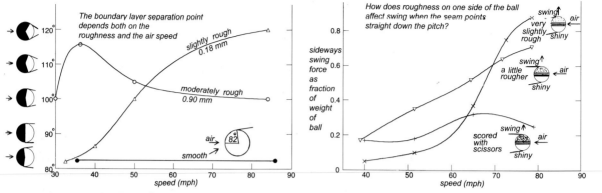

Fig. 23 How air behaves; from German atomic reactor research (Achenbach 1974) to find where the air leaves a sphere. It depends both on the roughness and the speed. All swing, legal and otherwise, and all swerve, depends on air leaving the ball earlier on one side than it does on the other side.

Fig. 24 Roughness and speed controls the air around a damaged cricket ball. (Wind tunnel work, Wilkins 1996)

coming off earlier and earlier, but never as early as from a smooth surface.

To summarise, smooth sides make the air come off early; slightly rough sides make it come off a good deal later; and from quite rough sides the air comes off somewhere in between these two extremes. This 'quite rough' surface is what distinguishes the true 'reverse' swing, our second class of 'tampered' swing. It may be useful to think of the extra roughness as making the air fly off the surface as from a lot of little ramps, but moderate roughness has the opposite effect (Chapter 3).

Roughened cricket balls confirmed the broad truth of this picture at speeds up to nearly 129 km/h (80 mph), as shown in Figure 24. The lines coming off the diagrams of the balls are based on the measured sideways forces. None of these balls 'reversed' at the speeds studied, and with those roughnesses.

It can be seen that a slow medium bowler bowling at 105–113 km/h (65–70 mph) would not notice any difference between a slightly rough ball with no more than a distinct dullness to the surface, and a somewhat rougher ball, without any raggedness but a little coarse to the touch.

However, as shown in Figure 24, a ball scored heavily across the leather would swing a good deal

less because the early-leaving air on the smooth side is now being opposed by the early-leaving air on the very rough surface.

Here is one reason why the reverse swing merchants wait until the smooth side is at least a little bit worn before they get the best return from their mutilation. (The other concerns waiting for the lacquer to wear off, and the minor seam to open up a little, to allow wetting and picking). I created this 'ideal' situation in the wind tunnel. The swing picture for it is the furthest left-hand curve of the seven swing pictures illustrated in Figure 25, and redrawn in Figure 25*b*(ii). By waiting for the 'shiny' side to get just a little rough — and maybe, by much rubbing, warding off to a minor extent the effects of normal wear — while continuing to mutilate the rough side, the reversers have been able to get both air streams working together; the most favourable result from their efforts.

Contrary to some opinion, this can happen at any speed over the whole medium and fast range. Remember that under normal cricket circumstances, the ball would have worn to some extent on both sides, and it would normally have worn evenly. No swing would have been possible. Only by introducing significant new roughness on one side to induce comparatively early air stream separation on that side, can the bowler get any advantage from the tendency of the slightly worn other side to retain the air stream.

The fascinating picture revealed in Figure 25 shows how increasing roughness on one side, relative to the roughness on the other side, begins the reversal of swing at progressively lower speeds. Excepting the ball scored with a scissors point, the roughness came from powders and grains of known size, attached to the surface.

Some writers have claimed that 'reverse' swing happens only at the highest speeds, speeds attainable only by a few of the top bowlers. The results shown in Figure 25 disprove this. The best 'reverser', the bottom lefthand curve in Figure 25, was verified by firing that ball from a ball gun and measuring the amount of sideways deviation.

It is worth noting that the maximum sideways forces found here are higher than those found in orthodox situations at normal seam angles and with undamaged balls: confirmation of what we see on the TV screens, when some fast bowlers known to be associated with ball tampering are able to get sharp swing and at pace. As described later, I have shown that this illegal swing is unaffected by the atmospheric microturbulence that interferes with normal swing and swerve.

It has been recorded that bowlers who interfere with balls don't always get the results they expect. Assuming that the air is favourable, we can get a clue as to why this may be so from Figure 25. Say, for instance, a bowler knows that he normally bowls at 120 km/h (75 mph). If the roughness is 0.2 mm or less, the swing will normally tend towards the rougher side; but if it is 0.3 mm or more, or if the smoother side has been roughened a little more than dull, the swing will reverse. It is no wonder that the spoils of wrongdoing are not always there for the taking. When Mike Atherton was spotted at Lord's with dirt in his pocket he qualified as fit to join researchers like the German mentioned earlier, and myself, and all the others who recognise that powders attached to a ball can change the air flow.

Normally a new cricket ball, two- or four-piece, turning backwards in the air as released by a good swing bowler, will not reverse the air flow at any speed or seam angle. The minor seam alone does not reverse the swing. The groove is not fixed in one position but turning over and over, and has little effect. But bowlers know that the two-piece ball does swing more than the four-piece when new, and that the four-piece ball 'wears' more

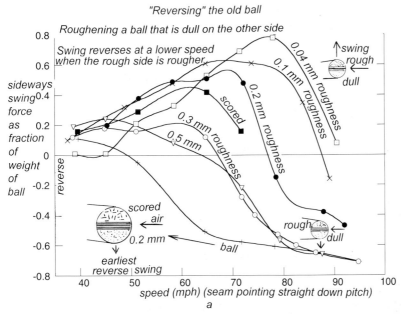

Fig. 25a Cricket ball mutilation: the big picture.

Sideways swing forces across a wide range of speed and roughness for balls damaged on one side, except for the lower lefthand curve which is for a ball altered on both sides. (Wind tunnel work, Wilkins 1996)

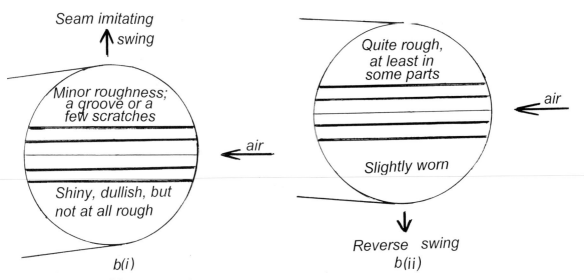

Fig. 25b pictures of the two 'tampered' swings, (i) involving 'seam imitation' and (ii) a combination of minor wear on one side and a much rougher surface on the other, which is the true 'reversing' pair.

quickly, because of the opening up of the minor seam on both sides. The turning minor seam adds a little to the general roughness of the side not behind the seam, and so reduces the swing slightly.

I should add here that one new (English) four-piece ball, out of the many, mostly Australian, balls I have studied, did reverse at high speed. This was caused by an unusually rough 'smooth' side, where the leather was squashed-up and heavily embossed, and quite rough around the minor seam. It was the type of ball that would be difficult to swing well by the normal technique: the sort of ball that bowlers should avoid.

Do players perhaps use the word 'reverse' to describe a ball that starts swinging one way and then goes the other way? I don't think so. Air drag on a cricket ball can slow it by about ten per cent. Look at Figure 25 and consider whether slowing by that amount will take the swing down into 'reverse'. Some balls may be starting to do that by the time they reach the batsman, but I doubt whether it should worry anybody. When we look at late swing in the next chapter we will find other possible reasons why this can happen; but it is almost always likely to be uncontrollable.

We have talked about 'reverse' as it applies to balls delivered with the seam pointing straight down the pitch. That is the way most bowlers seem to use the deliberately damaged ball and it has allowed us to advance our understanding in wind tunnel work.

When we start talking about damaged balls delivered at various seam angles, balls which may have uneven wear on each side, we then have two competing roughnesses, the roughness of the seam (plus any wear) on one side, and the wear on the other side. Which side wins 'the battle of the roughnesses' depends both on any difference in the roughness, and at what angle the bowler can deliver the seam. The further around it is, the greater is the turbulence produced by the seam.

The situation is obviously unpredictable, with swing possible either way. But, whatever happens, if it is the wear that produces the swing, then it must be uneven wear, and such wear is almost certain to have been inflicted illegally.

To some people, four-piece balls are essential to the 'reverse' story, but they are wrong. The groove of the minor seam is merely one source of roughness among many rotating with it during flight. The true reason for the connection is nothing more than the greater ease with which that groove allows the human interference previously described. If you are bent on mutilation it makes

44

little difference whether the ball is four-piece or two-piece. My wind tunnel work showed reverse behaviour to be just as common in damaged two-piece balls as it is in four-piece.

Reverse swing, like normal swing depends therefore on the interplay of a curved surface, an air stream and the varying roughness of that surface, with speed a factor in some situations.

The most bizarre and nonsensical idea in this 'tampering' business is the claim that the cause of the swing we have been talking about is the decrease of weight when leather is gouged out of one side, and/or the increase in weight from wetting the other side. It betrays that its advocates have not even begun to grasp the rudiments of the interaction of air with a cricket ball. It does reveal however, that gouging, at the hands of some is no gentle matter.

When it comes to linking wetting with roughness, and therefore with swing, anyone who

has tried to polish a pair of water-saturated boots can provide the answer. Wetting, in the opinion of some, is connected with polishing. While this may be true in the very early stages of wear, the truth is in fact the opposite.

Fingernails or other sharp objects on the softened leather: screwing one side of the ball into the concrete as the ball is recovered from the boundary ditch: the possibilities for attack are unlimited. If the ball is damaged on one side by a fielder trapping it under the boot spikes it should be replaced immediately. Teams involved in this form of cheating must be careful to do it to one side only, otherwise they may bring about opposing and cancelling effects!

The Law enforcers have apparently opted out. One can't blame the players striving to keep up with their rivals. Some leading bowlers, liberally wetting the ball between overs, don't even bother to go through the action of appearing to polish it.

A Quick Guide to Rough Swing

Seam pointing straight down the pitch. Roughness can only be described approximately: both its depth and extent are relevant.

State of the Ball		Swing	Comments		
One Side	Other Side		'Reversal'?	Legality	
Shiny	Shiny	Unpredictable	Does not apply	Legal	
Shiny	Dull	To dull side	No 'reversal' on well-made balls	Could happen naturally with polishing but usually only early in innings	
Shiny	Moderately rough or grooved	To rough side	No 'reversal' on well-made balls	'Seam imitating' swing Almost certainly requires tampering including groove opening	
Shiny	Very Rough	To rough side: but swing is weak	May 'reverse' at highest speeds	Must have been caught under mower	
Dull	Moderately rough	Mostly to rough side	'Reverses': depends on wear. See fig. 25	Tampering underway	
Dull	Very rough	'Reverses' to dull at most speeds	Almost the 'best' 'reverse' product	Unnatural: rough also on batsmen	
Moderately rough	Very rough	'Reverses to moderately worn side at all fast and medium speeds	Top 'reverse' anti-batsman product	Could become a collector's item	

We know that quite small changes of surface roughness, inflicted more on one side than on the other, can give bowlers a lethal advantage. When the makers of Law 42.5 stated that no artificial substance is to be used in polishing the ball, and that no one shall rub the ball on the ground or use any artificial substance or take any other action to alter the condition of the ball, they did not have the advantage of the knowledge that is available to us now. But water, a natural substance, lies behind most of the aerodynamic havoc that has tarnished cricket. In comparison, the old Brylcream, or whatever oily concoction the bowlers of the past have used to keep some shine on the ball, is positively benign. Yet these are the substances targeted by the Law, while water, a substance capable of causing more profound effects, goes free.

It should not be impossible to ban all rubbing (except by the bowler) and the application to the ball of water in all its forms except moistening the fingers for grip. Umpires, who in the normal course of their work monitor all sorts of actions, should have no difficulty distinguishing this from wetting the leather face of the ball. Irregular inspection, which is now recommended, should deal with the rest, including the infliction of seam-imitating damage to one side. If substitute balls are required during a game, to replace those which are, for any reason, significantly different on one side compared to the other, the replacements should be heavily worn on both sides. These balls will not swing, nor will they respond to any further attack. However they will come off the pitch significantly slower: not a happy situation at all. It is better to prevent it getting to that stage.

If some brands of ball respond more to wetting than others, the reason could lie in different waterproofing substances incorporated into the leather during manufacture.

When a fast ball hits the pitch the force on the leather where the contact is made can be up to 227 kg (500 lbs). Under normal circumstances and on most pitches, balls wear steadily, and they wear equally on both sides. No amount of polishing can stem this inevitable process.

Of all the wrong notions connected with reverse swing, the one that calls most into question the honesty of some of those involved is the claim that on hard, moderately abrasive, pitches, one side of the ball can be kept smooth by some sort of legal treatment, while the other becomes quite rough *on its own*. If one side becomes quite rough on its own, all the polishing in the world cannot keep the other side smooth. The truth almost certainly involves human interference on the rougher side. The existence of balls that have been moderately worn on one side and heavily mutilated on the other attests to the lengths certain players can go to obtain illegal swing after normal wear.

In Chapter 13 we will see how uneven wear inflicted on a ball by human interference can, depending on what part of the ball contacts the surface, unpredictably influence the pace at which it leaves the pitch; another unfairness to batsmen. This amounts to an artificial introduction of a two-pace effect, depending on which side the ball lands on; a grossly unfair intrusion.

We should be careful in our use of the term 'reverse swing'. Careless language confuses rather than clarifies. Some commentators have already lost the respect of many people by applying the name 'googly' or 'wrong un' or 'mystery ball' to any delivery that does not turn, when bowled among those that do turn. TV viewers, now being given a clear picture of the ball rotating in the air, know that the true reason is that many deliveries simply fail to grip. If 'reverse swing' is to have any use in describing a certain type of swing, it must be confined to balls in the state which produces air flows of the type described in the negative region of Figure 25.

It is not correct to assume, for instance, that because Wasim Akram is swinging the ball in the last stages of a fifty over one-day game, that he is employing 'reverse swing'. Yet this is what was claimed by a commentator in Melbourne when Australia played Pakistan in a one-day game early in 1997. Slow motion showed that the seam was not only upright but pointing across the line as normal. In other words Wasim was applying the classical skills of the great fast bowlers, as he had been doing in the early overs of that innings when he swung the new white ball very effectively. Plenty of balls are only slightly worn after forty overs. This, and the fact that it was the night hours of a day-night game, and therefore the most favourable of conditions for swing, made legitimate swing wholly feasible. All this, coupled with the absence of any detailed knowledge of the state of the leather on the opposite sides of the ball, should have precluded any claim that Wasim was 'reversing' in the true meaning of the term. However it should be added that two days later, Waqar Younis was seen on close-up TV early in one of the finals games against the West Indies, to be carrying out actions which looked suspiciously like picking at the white ball.

In the next chapter, when we look at late swing, we will see how wind can effectively change the seam angle so that the swing appears to be 'against' the seam. Because this normal new ball behaviour has nothing to do with damaged balls, it cannot be linked in any way with the modern 'reverse' delivery.

It is unfair to pick out any particular team or individuals. Television watchers in New Zealand, during a recent tour, saw a clear demonstration of how players work together in ball tampering. The South African spinner Eksteen, after continually wetting the ball, was seen to pick at the centre of the smooth leather face and then hand it to De Villiers, who took a wicket with a swinger in the first ball of the following over. New Zealander Chris Pringle, admitted that ball tampering helped him to get seven wickets — the best figures in his career — in a Test in Pakistan.

Now that the truth about the more obvious form of ball mutilation is beginning to be recognised, it may be tried less often. Gross mutilation, at least where umpires are reasonably vigilant, is likely to become a thing of the past. However the more surreptitious but equally deadly 'seam imitating' form of cheating producing *assisted swing* will not be eradicated without clear understanding followed by firm action. Apart from the quite legitimate cleaning of the stitching by the bowler, there is no reason why any member of the fielding side should do anything at all to the ball except pick it up and convey it back to the bowler. Anything else is merely time-wasting or worse. Without bringing in any new Laws it would seem to be possible for captains who, under the existing Laws, 'are responsible at all times for ensuring that play is conducted within the spirit of the game as well as within the Laws', to inform the umpires that batsmen shall, under the eye of the umpire, inspect the ball at any time and may, in the event of their finding any irregularity, draw this to the umpire's attention. Such an irregularity need not have arisen from deliberate human interference; it may have been from accidental damage and it may, through being out on the leather face, be in a position to confer significant 'seam-imitating' swing. In this case the batsman would be perfectly entitled under Law 42 to request that the damaged ball be taken out of play and a substitution made.

There is no particular swing skill in 'seam imitating' or in 'reverse' swing. It devalues real skill in swing, it is at odds with the spirit of the game, and, if allowed to continue, it will make the game poorer by reducing the need for the genuine skills of spin and cut.

In the shadow of all this deceit it is not surprising that skill in unaided swing, at least in England, is said to be declining. Other causes may include the heavy diet of limited-over cricket and the roughness of some English balls (Chapter 15). Derek Pringle, a professional himself, has stated that 'the limits of fair play have been exceeded, even the most liberal of professional cricketers would probably consider it cheating'. Simple measures are available to root it out.

6

LATE SWING: TEMPTING THE UNCONTROLLABLE

The ball that swings late in flight is the Holy Grail of the medium and fast crusaders. But, as Bernard Hollowood reminded us earlier, such an awe-inspiring gift is more the stuff of legend than cricket in the flesh. Romance may take a beating at the hands of the sceptics, but enough unusual swing behaviour has been revealed in the preceding pages to convince us that something might be lurking behind the hype and the often careless ball-watching. We will attempt to coax *true* late swing out of its hiding place.

It is time for us to organise this knowledge and see where it can be put to use by the bowler. Until we get reliable information to the contrary, it would be rash to claim that bowlers have any control over late swing. At this stage the realistic goal for the bowler is to know as much as he can, and then start experimenting to find out how to make the unusual and the unexpected more likely to happen.

In a sense, nearly all swing is late swing, simply because the path taken by the ball generally increases in curvature the further it goes. Like the bend in a fishing rod pulling in a small fish, the parabola of a swinging cricket ball is usually of an unspectacular kind; J. B. King called his inswinger 'the angler' after its hooked curve.

The final amount of deviation varies tremendously from a frustratingly common nothing, to the 'big banana' or 'cartwheel' which are not the quickest deliveries and which are often wind-assisted.

Many factors affect the outcome of every delivery; the skill and pace of the bowler, the state of the ball and the surrounding atmosphere. Assuming that the ball follows a smooth parabolic path, most of the deviation occurs in the last 50 per cent of the flight, as shown in Figure 26 which is drawn from high speed photographs of a delivery from Garry Gilmour. A good batsman makes an early assessment of this curve, but a less able batsman may describe this perfectly normal swing as late.

Earlier we discussed the fast delivery that swings. Because it is fast it won't normally swing a great deal. But because of the combination of speed and the small amount of deviation over the earlier part of its flight, such swing as there is will always appear to be late. I cannot recall a bowler at the faster end of the range, in conditions where there is no wind from any direction to assist the swing, ever being described as swinging too early. In other words faster bowlers can probably always be described as swinging late. When the ball has been mutilated on one side, and the bowler is fast,

Fig. 26 Parabolic path of a swinging ball bowled by Australian left-hander Garry Gilmour (A. Imbrosciano, 'The swing of a cricket ball', Newcastle College of Advanced Education, 1981: an outswinger delivered from over the wicket.)

the larger sideways forces reported in the previous chapter for such balls make this combination a prime candidate for being described as late.

The genuine late swinger needs, for proof of its existence, an impartial judge. In the absence of a top-class batsman, a well-placed observer or a video would be required.

Can the bowler deliberately choose to make the ball swing late? Probably not. Can the bowler do things which make unusual swing, possibly involving late swing, more likely? Yes.

First we must rule out the existence of a critical speed beyond which swing was thought impossible, but below which the ball, slowed by drag, suddenly begins to swing. The evidence from research with cricket balls contradicts this explanation of late swing.

The easiest way for the bowler into to experiment with late swing is to bowl the new ball at a zero seam angle. Earlier we noted that this is an unstable situation; instability which made cricket balls in the wind tunnel vibrate wildly from side to side. To capitalise on this, the bowler merely releases the shiny ball pointing the seam straight down the pitch. For this instability to happen the ball must be exactly the same on both sides. Thus any treatment such as polishing one side, while allowing the other side to become rougher, will nullify the unpredictable swing.

But the angle of the seam to the air flow has a great deal more to offer us than merely trying for instability at a zero angle. We need to look at the other partner in the dance; the wind. In Chapter 7 we will see that, for swing, a friendly wind is not gusty or very strong, but smooth and steady, without small-scale turbulence. On a windless day a zero angle delivery will remain zero all the way. But what happens if, say, there is a wind from somewhere on the leg (the right). As every yachtsman knows, the seam is now pointing to the left of the air flow and therefore well set up for a nice outswinger. The same result in fact that one would get, in the absence of wind, from pointing the seam towards the slips. In the same way, a wind from the off (the left) could give the

bowler a nice inswinger without him needing to deliver with the seam at the normal inswing angle.

The essence of all this is the unexpected. With a little thought, we can see that the possibilities arising from the simple example described in the previous paragraph are as numerous as they are fascinating.

What if the wind is coming straight up the pitch against the bowler and he delivers at zero seam angle? No wind is totally steady in direction or strength. Within enclosed cricket grounds, behind trees and grandstands, it is even less so. Therefore the bowler can never be sure what the actual angle of the seam to the airflow will be. Without doing anything special the bowler might find himself delivering an unpredictable and bewildering series of inswingers and outswingers, as the ball 'sees' air coming from different directions.

What if the ball only begins to 'see' good air for swing when it is half way down the pitch? Or what if it started in good 'swinging' air and then ran into 'dead' air? Bowlers should experiment with various seam angles so as to enter these regions where wind-seam angle changes during flight can lead to sudden changes in direction.

The resulting changes of swing are partly dependent on wind strength and partly on wind angle. But the warning should be repeated that any treatment, legal or illegal, which alters one side of the ball will tend to negate this 'one-side-or-the-other' uncertainty in swing.

What if the wind is fairly steady from one side rather than the other? Does this cut out the chance of all uncertainty? Not necessarily. Say, for instance, the wind is from slips. The way the bowler could enter the zone of zero angle uncertainty is to point the seam towards the wind. Or with wind from leg, to point it to leg. Whether this works depends not only on the skill of the bowler but also on the bowling speed relative to the wind speed. Because one normally bowls much faster than the wind blows, it is the original seam angle that is usually the more dominant partner in the dance. A gentle breeze is 13–19 km/h (8–12 mph) and a strong breeze 40–50 km/h (25–31 mph).

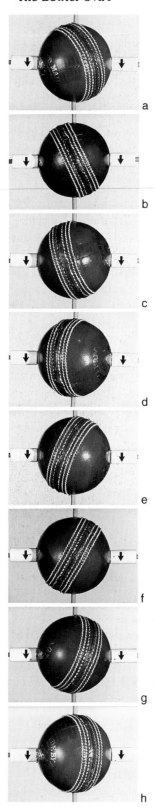

a

b

c

d

e

f

Fig. 27 A wobbling seam seen at different stages of the wobble. The wobble occurs because the axis of spin is not at 90° to the plane of the seam. The seam angle is seen to change constantly as the ball turns. Note how the minor seam of the four-piece ball changes its alignment to the oncoming air. Although a rapidly wobbling ball is unlikely to swing, a slow wobble has possibilities for late swing.

g

h

Therefore one would not normally point the seam around a great deal. The more the wind is across the pitch, the greater the angle that should be used.

The amount of swing also depends on whether the wind is against or behind. Against the wind it has much more effect because the ball has more air to go through to get to the other end.

A Wellington medium-fast lefthand bowler, Stephen Hotter, interviewed in January 1997 after getting a first class hat trick, said that the ball was swinging the opposite way to the direction in which he had pointed the seam. The interviewer, not very seriously, mentioned reverse swing; but the ball was new and it was a windy day, just the situation we have been looking at where it is not only the bowler's skill that determines what the real angle of the seam to the wind will be, but the wind itself.

There is a lot more in the bag of tricks labelled 'Variable Effective Seam Angle'. We haven't yet looked at how swing might change if the bowler could make the seam angle change during flight. The swing pictures in the previous chapters show numerous examples where quite small changes of angle can increase or decrease the swing, including taking it through a region where it may drop to zero and even 'go the other way'. We saw how, with worn balls, swing could collapse or increase following quite moderate changes of seam angle. Backwards rotation, as we also noted, 'smears out' to some extent the way the air 'sees' the worn areas and the minor seam (on four-piece balls). For this reason we are less likely to see, out in the middle, the dramatic changes in sideways force shown by balls fixed in the wind tunnel.

Nevertheless there always remains the possibility of swing changes from changes of seam angle during flight. In the absence of wind to do the job for him, how can a bowler arrange for the seam angle to change at some point after the ball has left his hand, say, half way down the pitch?

The task for the bowler is to achieve a slow wobble as seen in the 'snapshots' of the wobbling

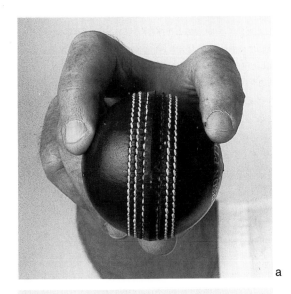

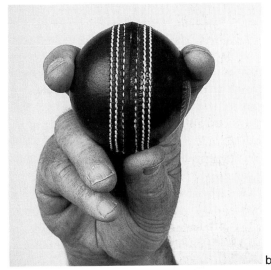

Fig. 28 Grips for experimenting with minimising ball rotation: the aim is to minimise the downwards movement of the fingers on the back of the ball during release and to maximise the simple 'pushing' action. These grips are also worth trying during experiments in learning to bowl disguised slower balls: **a, b**, and **c** are front and side views of grips with fingers splayed out wide; **d** is the palm grip ; **e** is the 'half-ball' grip where the hand feels as if it is going past the side of the ball during release.

51

ball in Figure 27 so that, at some late stage of its flight, the wobble happens to place the seam at a very favourable angle for swing, or at an angle that spoils swing that is already present. The same slow rotation, with or without seam wobble, may take the minor seam from a position where it lies *across* the air stream on the smooth side of the ball and interferes with swing, to a position where it is *aligned* with the air flow, and therefore allows swing to take place, late in flight.

To achieve the above 'late' situations, the bowler must minimise the back-spin applied to the ball. This is to ensure that the seam angles or minor seam positions, which are likely to cause or prevent swing, do not come and go too rapidly for the swing to develop or disappear.

Baseball and softball players pitching the knuckle ball rely on exactly the same principles as outlined here for the slow seam wobble as a cause of the baseball version of late swing. The knuckle ball is pitched with only a small amount of rotation and flutters unpredictably in various directions during flight. The effect of pitching with only a small amount of rotation is to bring the complex line of stitching into various different positions facing the air stream. Variable 'swing' forces result as the stitching comes around into the positions where it can affect the separation of the air layers from the ball.

It would be rash to assume that bowlers can achieve this slow rotation easily. Those attempting it should try releasing the ball with more of an outward push than a downward flick of the fingers. Merely holding the ball more in towards the palm of the hand is a normal method for releasing a slower ball. In the light of the present discussion there is more potential in such a grip than obtaining a change of pace. The 'half ball' grip is related to this. The ball is not only held in towards the palm but with about half of the ball clear of the side of the hand. As the hand moves forward the ball tends to be left to come forward slower with some slow side rotation which could effect changes in swing.

In minimising imparted rotation as for the baseball knuckle ball the aim is exactly the opposite of what a bowler should be trying to do when he cuts the ball. In cutting he wishes to maximise the 'back-and-slightly-to-the-side' rotation which is the essence of cut. In cut, the downward action of the fingers must be maximised whilst the grip of the thumb under the ball must be minimised. The purpose for late swing is the reverse.

There should be little or no feeling of the fingers sliding down the back of the ball. To achieve this (Fig. *b*) the three point contact should have the thumb as far forward and the pointed fingers as far back as possible. The fingers should not be in contact with the stitching but splayed out on either side of it. The 'width' of the wobble is chosen by the amount that the bowler grips the ball across, rather than along, the seam. Trials with a ball marked with chalk lines across the seam will show how much success has been achieved.

Because smooth non-turbulent air conditions favour swing, we have yet another possible source of late swing: the ball leaving a turbulent body of air and entering a smooth swing-favouring region of air nearer the batsman, or leaving swing-favouring air and entering turbulent air.

7
PICKING THE AIR FOR SWING

Every cricketer knows that there are periods when swing is rampant and periods when straightness rules. No one can overestimate the influence of swing and spin-swerve on the outcome of cricket matches. Can the modern cricketer afford not to understand why this happens? Put another way; can the modern cricketer afford to continue relying on a falsehood, especially when his opponents may be finding that superior tactical decisions can be made based on the truth?

You win the toss; do you decide to bat first or bowl? You have one or two bowlers who rely mainly on pace and you have others who rely mainly on swing. Do you understand the factors which are likely to allow one or the other to prosper? Do you understand that even in the course of just a few hours play a clued-up captain will be taking bowlers off and putting other bowlers on, at least partly under the influence of air conditions. And do you understand how that influence might change quite rapidly?

If the atmosphere is to be implicated in swing other possible explanations must be ruled out: better bowling, a better ball. With all this out of the way, what about the better swing when cloud blocks out the sun for a few overs? Atmospheric humidity cannot change as rapidly as that.

If there is one group of cricketers who can't have taken the humidity idea very seriously, it is those thousands of bowlers who have failed to swing the ball in conditions of high humidity. There will be plenty of examples to quote, but the best I am aware of is Brisbane, where, in humidity of around 100 per cent on a sunny day, the ball hardly swung at all.

If everybody had known the truth about *why* a ball swings, I doubt whether the humidity myth would ever have gained a foothold. *Swing is about whether a layer of air clings to the ball or not; whether it leaves the ball a little earlier or later.* Had cricketers known this, I doubt whether the presence or absence of water vapour would have counted for much.

Humid or damp air, often described as 'heavy', is in fact slightly less dense than dry air.

Part of the reason for the persistence of the idea may stem from the account of Daish[1] who, while dismissing the 'heaviness' concept for the reason given above, gave humidity a reprieve by suggesting that the stitching around the ball could swell in highly humid conditions, and thereby increase the swing force. Ten years later Bentley and others carried out the necessary experiment.[2] They placed two balls in a chamber at 75 per cent relative humidity for 48 hours, before measuring the swing force and the thickness of the stitching. No change was found in either.

Two papers have reported wind tunnel tests carried out in different humidity conditions. Neither showed any significant effect on the swing force.[3,4]

Since neither of the above workers used equipment as sensitive as that which I used for my own work, I decided to carry out a more rigorous test.

A passer-by observing me hanging wet laboratory coats on chairs and liberally splashing water around the wind-tunnel room may have been forgiven for thinking that they had stumbled across some ancient rite. Liquid water rapidly became airborne water vapour in the windy surroundings. Carrying out regular and accurate chemical analysis, I measured the humidity when it had settled to a steady level. Temperatures and barometric pressure were checked and the sideways swing force was measured precisely at three wind speeds and six humidities. The results given in Table C show that humidity has no influence whatsoever on swing.

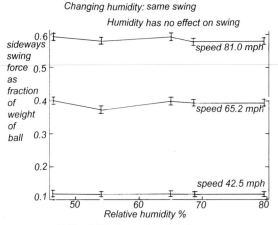

Changing humidity: same swing

Humidity has no effect on swing

Table C (Wind tunnel work Wilkins 1985)

The time has come for humidity to be handed over to the flat-earthers.

Getting rid of humidity is only the start. We must explain what cricketers have been witnessing, at least since swing came on the scene late in the 19th century, and find out how we can exploit this new understanding. It would also be interesting to find out whether the bowlers of the century before that, who did not swing, but swerved, noticed any effect from the atmosphere. Present knowledge suggests that they should have.

In 1982 Sherwin and Sproston, in a few brief lines at the end of their paper on trip wires and seams, suggested that enhanced swing under cloud cover may be due to lowered atmospheric turbulence which would interfere less with the smooth flow around one side of the ball.[5]

But we mustn't rush. What has turbulence got to do with swing, and what has the sun and cloud cover got to do with turbulence?

Turbulence can happen on any scale, large or small; from convulsions in the air massive enough to drive a hurricane or shake a giant aeroplane, to the sudden rustling of leaves, or the barely visible shimmering currents rising from a road on a sunny day. But put a cricket ball near the giant aeroplane in turbulence and the ball might feel nothing but a strong wind, and that, as far as the ball is concerned, is not turbulence. Turbulence requires that, on the scale of the object concerned, different portions of the air are moving at different speeds. The massive turbulence matched the scale of the aeroplane but not that of the cricket ball. Therefore if turbulence is to affect a cricket ball it must be small scale turbulence; microturbulence.

Aerodynamics experts know that a certain degree of turbulence delays boundary layer separation. In the case of a cricket ball this would delay and spoil the early separation of the air layer from the shiny side, an essential part of new ball swing. Stated in more general terms, appropriate for most swing and swerve situations, *turbulence would tend to blur the differences in the air layer separation on each side of the ball and thus nullify both swing and swerve.*

Cloud cover means no sun warming the soil and grass. No warming means no columns or spikes of warm air rising from the ground. Cloud cover means little or no microturbulence. Cloud cover therefore means swing. But does sun mean no swing? We are getting a bit ahead here, but the answer is that it depends whether or not the earth and/or grass is *dry enough* to heat up, and if it does heat up, whether it is *hot enough* to make the air in contact with it hotter than the surrounding air.

A lovely story, but where are the facts to back it up? Where is the evidence for the existence of these spikes of air that are claimed to be able to rise from dry earth or grass within minutes of the sun coming out from behind a cloud?

With the help of a meteorologist my search uncovered a most informative review of the subject of small-scale atmospheric turbulence.[6] It described what happened two metres above a field when the sun began to shine. Using sensitive instruments which could respond extremely rapidly to changes of wind speed and temperature, both vertical and horizontal air currents and how they fluctuated with temperature were measured. The picture uncovered was one of spiky rising air currents fluctuating rapidly, within seconds. These coincided with local and rapid fluctuations in air temperature resulting from the sun's radiation and causing local hot spots on the ground. Superimposed on this rising air was a moderate breeze of about 14 km/h (9 mph) which did not obliterate the microturbulence but carried it steadily across the field as the turbulence rose upwards.

Here then is a highly satisfactory proof of the existence of microturbulence, on the scale of a cricket ball, and happening rapidly enough to respond to sun and shadow.

Support for the idea that microturbulence destroys swing also comes from wind-tunnel work. Although Bentley and others were not investigating humidity, they found that turbulence deliberately introduced into the air stream reduced the swing force markedly.

Now the way is open to relate the necessity for low microturbulence to the false idea of humidity. The word 'humid' is often used along with 'heavy' or 'close' or 'muggy', to describe the uncomfortable feeling associated with a lack of air movement or poor ventilation. In other words *it*

describes the state of being in an environment of low air turbulence.

But if the surrounding air *is already quite hot*, then the heated air near the ground may not experience enough buoyancy to make it rise. Therefore on a hot day, not merely with bright sun, but with a high *air* temperature as well, this form of turbulence might not be present and the new ball will swing. This is why, assuming that the outfield is dry, the ball may swing well on hot days in Karachi, or at Adelaide. However on a sunny day in Hobart or Leeds, where the *air temperature might be cool*, the air would rise rapidly from the hot spots and create turbulence enough to destroy swing.

Mist at sea level is normally associated with relatively windless conditions. When the mist rises from a river near a cricket ground, such as the Trent in Nottingham, cricketers have explained the swing as being due to moisture. Since that is impossible, we get the right answer when we focus on the low turbulence rather than on the moisture.

We now return to the question of whether we can expect good swing on a sunny day. Putting the question another way, can we expect to get smooth, swing-favouring air on such a day?

Yes, we can, if the following two conditions apply: the wind should not be strong or gusty,

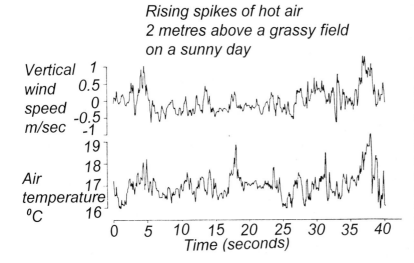

Microturbulence from the sun's heat
Rising spikes of hot air
2 metres above a grassy field
on a sunny day

Vertical wind speed m/sec

Air temperature °C

Time (seconds)

Fig. 29 What the ball must pass through, two metres above the ground, on a sunny day when the ground is dry enough to allow hot spots to form. The lower line shows the uneven temperature of the air and the rapid changes in temperature, while the upper line shows that each of these hot periods corresponds with a faster rising spike of hotter air.

because, at ground level, such larger scale turbulence will almost always be accompanied by some small-scale turbulence; and the sun should not be able to heat the ground to a temperature much above that of the air. Wet or damp soil and/or grass, following rain or dew, will aid cooling both by being a heat sink and by evaporation, and therefore reduce the likelihood of hot spots. A low sun will also be condusive to cooler ground temperatures. Always bowl if you have won the toss after overnight rain.

All these conditions describe exactly the first day of the New Zealand vs. Australia Test at Wellington on March 15 1990. The New Zealand bowlers swung the ball unusually well throughout the entire innings in the bright late-season sunshine as a light breeze moved steadily across the sodden outfield, and Australia, floundering on a slow pitch, were all out for 110 in less than four hours. A rain-saturated outfield at Lords in 1997 helped Australia to gain full value from the superb skills of Glen McGrath, 8 for 38 and England out for 77. Earlier that year, before the first Test, New Zealand vs. England at Auckland, it rained overnight and some of the England bowlers got good swing on a sunny first day, but they lacked the control needed to take advantage of the opportunity Mike Atherton had given them by winning the toss. A week later, for the second Test, at the Basin Reserve, an almost identical set of swing-friendly conditions prevailed: a steady light wind and a wet outfield soaking up the heat of a bright sun. English swing, this time well directed, humbled New Zealand, 6 for 56, in two hours of a rain-shortened day.

Why did New Zealand choose to bat after winning the toss? The reason appeared to be that they had chosen two spinners and wished to be bowling in the fourth innings. Unfortunately it was the *first* innings that determined the outcome of the game and there was *no* fourth innings. England won easily.

Microturbulence needs heat. Anything that sucks up heat will help swing and swerve. Therefore unless the wind is gusty, moisture in the outfield will help swing until the ball gets worn. Groundsmen keeping the outfield well watered are the best ally of the swinger and swerver. Night-time dew, or simply the natural moisture from soil and grass which has been out of the sun overnight, will ensure that the cooling effect operates at least during the first period of play. Captains should be aware of the reasons why drying may be fast or slow, thereby shortening or lengthening this period. Wind, hot sun and a shallow layer of grass all mean fast drying, thereby reducing the time during which swing might dominate. Sunless and still conditions, and/or a thick sward of lush grass, will extend the time for good swing and swerve.

Swing-favouring conditions should sound warning bells for one-day teams with good swing bowlers and playing under restrictive wide rules. A damp outfield, even on a sunny day, can raise the number of wides to a level that may make the difference between winning and losing. Unless a bowler has *practised* holding the ball in one of the many possible grips which prevent swing, including the cross-seam grip, he will not be willing to tinker with grip, especially when he is under pressure. The problem must be anticipated.

Seaside grounds have a reputation for favouring swing. Since, they are also frequently covered with a heavy dew early in the day, the cooling effect enhances swing, at least during the early part of the day. Another factor helping this could be the relatively clear pathway for a steady wind from the sea compared to the city wind which must negotiate a turbulent passage around and over large buildings.

The height of the sun in the sky is not only related to the season but to the time of day and the distance from the equator. All other factors being equal, we would therefore expect the lower sun, earlier or later in the day, especially later in the season when the sun is lower throughout the day, to interfere less with swing. On this basis captains should give more serious consideration to taking the second new ball late in the day. For the same reason bowlers should get more swing in the night phase of a day-night game, assuming that the surface of the white painted balls responds to the air flow in the usual way. Swing bowlers could be forgiven for feeling frustrated at the restrictive wide ruling in one-day games at the very time when conditions are best for swing. Similarly, spin bowlers should get more swerve.

How can this new insight be put to tactical advantage, helping us to win the next game? We will assume that we have a couple of bowlers who have learned the skill of swing. We also have spinners. The question may be asked; why concentrate on the effect of the atmosphere on swing when we know that the same conditions favour spin swerve? The simple answer is that swing at pace is normally a more attacking option at the beginning of an innings than is spin swerve, which is usually less pronounced than swing, and which gets its effectiveness mainly through its association with turn off the pitch. However, any bowler who has reached the heights of S. F. Barnes (see Chapter 16) should take the last sentence with a grain of salt.

Swing must be given its chance. If the weather is dull and the wind not too strong or gusty, or if it is sunny and not too windy or gusty, but the ground is damp, and you have won the toss, you want your own bowlers to be causing the havoc, not those of the opposition. But don't forget that the dampness can't be guaranteed to last all day. As an innovative captain you may alert your new-ball swingers to their likely recall to the bowling crease during cloudy periods on an intermittently cloudy day, assuming the ball is not too worn.

Another role for you is captain-astronomer-architect, where you look at the buildings or trees around the boundary and work out what time their shadows are likely to cross the pitch. Buildings are as good as clouds, provided that turbulence is not drifting from the sunny part of the ground. Shadows or a lower sun are likely to spell trouble for batsmen.

Weather forecasts are getting more accurate all the time. If you are a captain, you might have done a little homework on how the elements might cooperate with you a day or two ahead. Perhaps fine today; dry grass and soil; dull tomorrow: bat today, bowl tomorrow. Overnight rain: bowl. A heavy dew but the prospect of plenty of wind and sun to dry it out quickly: bat. Has the groundsman watered the outfield within the last, say 24 hours? How good has the drying been since he did that? Is wind predicted, if so, is it the swing-friendly steady breeze, or is it the turbulence-laden variety? In the bigtime you might even indulge in a little strategic team selection among your thirteen. We can work through this sort of scenario in the following example while at the same time reliving some cricket history.

Before the Test against England at Lords in 1972 the Australians needed to decide whether to include Inverarity, an all-rounder, or Colley, a medium pace swing bowler. Colley got the nod and swing won the game, although it was not Colley's swing but Massie's. On the day Australia chose their eleven the weather forecast was 'A depression will be slow moving north of Scotland'. In fact the depression remained in that area right throughout the game. Such a pattern of weather, being not uncommon, meant that when the team was to be picked, the selectors, had they chosen to find out, could have been aware that there was a high probability of a prolonged period of cloudy weather during the game. They apparently made the right decision for the conditions and Massie, with all his skill, and under the kindly blanket of cloud drawn in from the Atlantic, entered cricket history.

I do not know whether or not Colley's selection was influenced by the weather forecast, but if cricket strategists of the future are doing their jobs, they must take into account every factor that is likely to affect swing, including the short and long term weather forecasts.

Had the Australians indulged in some superior exercise in atmospheric prediction and relied on the widely held belief in humidity, they might not have selected any swing bowlers at all! On the first day, when Massie was just warming up with 5 for 75, the humidity was only 44 percent, and when he finished England off, ending with match figures of 15 for 122, the weather records of the time show that the whole match had been played in quite a moderate humidity.

The pitch for that game was described as hard and fast. Massie's feat should help to remove from cricket thinking the idea that dampness, apart from the outfield cooling process we have looked at, has anything whatsoever to do with swing. Swing is about air flow. *Nothing about swing requires us to link it to pitches, damp or dry.*

If, in the light of all this evidence that microturbulence is the enemy of swing, there are still some sceptics out there doggedly clinging to old ideas, I would like to have invited them to witness a dramatic demonstration that should put the matter to rest and let cricketers get on with the business of using this knowledge to their advantage. We fired balls from the ball gun, balls which swung beautifully; some (new balls) because of the angle at which we set the seam,

and others from the underworld of mutilation; these including both the 'seam imitating' type and the more heavily mutilated true 'reversing' type. The laboratory ceiling provided the ideal 'cloud cover': the laboratory air was not turbulent on any scale, large or small.

Then, using air blown out from tiny holes in long pipes under the flight path of the ball, *we made the air turbulent on a small scale.* Repeating the firings immediately, with the same balls but now in turbulent air, we found that *none of the new balls or the balls with the 'seam imitating' mutilation swung.* But balls with the heavy 'reversing' mutilation (see Chapter 5) did continue to swing, a finding that confirms what has been reported by cricketers. The significant roughness resulting from the heavy mutilation is obviously producing so much turbulence around the ball that the swing is not as sensitive to the turbulence of the surrounding air.

Perhaps it is unnecessary to add that during the above experiment, where we turned the air turbulence on and destroyed swing, and then got it back again immediately we turned the air off, there was no possibility whatsoever that the humidity was changing back and forth at the same rate!

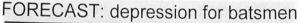

Fig. 30 Bob Massie and the weather join forces to make trouble for English batsmen at Lord's in 1972. The weather maps are those published immediately before and during the Test. Modern strategic game-planning can exploit weather forecasting.

8

TWO KINDS OF STITCHING: ONE FOR THE BOWLER

The four rows of external stitching going right around the ball are there for the bowler and for no other purpose. In Figure 31a they are seen going in and out through the leather case and having nothing whatsoever to do with holding the ball together.

They are there for no other purpose than to provide grip in the bowler's fingers, and, in the absence of any statement to the contrary from the early ball makers, grip on the pitch. As for swing, it would be nice to think that the artisans a hundred or more years ago, with their needles and thread, were designing a subtle aerodynamic object which would intrigue everybody for years to come, but I think we must accept that it was nothing more than a lovely accident.

Stitching is vital to the bowler's purpose even if it doesn't do half of the amazing things that many commentators give it credit for.

The word 'seam' is probably too entrenched in cricket usage to change its meaning now, but the wide strip, required by a British standard to be 19–21 mm wide around the ball, and which covers about 30 percent of its area, is not a seam in terms of the dictionary meaning of seam. In strict terms the seam is where the two edges of leather are held against each other by hidden or deeply embedded stitching, around the ball in the main seam and, in the four-piece ball, about half way around as the two minor, or quarter seams. Because all this true stitching is hidden it has no function other than to hold the ball together, although it may raise a smooth bulge in the leather around the main seam, and, in some balls, almost invisible little bulges at each stitch in the minor seam.

The true seams therefore have nothing to offer the bowler. We discussed 'picking the seam' earlier, in Chapter 5. Real knowledge and sympathetic understanding is required if we are to discriminate wisely among the various tricks employed by bowlers. Law makers have not always exercised this enlightened discrimination. But picking up the leather edges around the major seam, to produce a prominent and rough new leather ridge, introduces a very significant distortion of the original shape of the ball. Why does the bowler do this? The ball landing on the ridge might deviate, or 'fall off the ridge', this being sideways movement off the pitch without any skill being required from the bowler. Or it might kick up when the sharp leather bites on the pitch. Again it might simply be intended as a way of giving the bowler a better grip for spinning or cutting.

Whatever the bowler's intention, the grossly raised leather edges have the potential to take wickets without requiring skill. But we have a duty to think in a bowler's terms. He wants and deserves a good grip. He wants and deserves a grip that will allow him to show his skills. The fair sportsman does not wish to cheat by getting deviation off the pitch without needing to employ skill.

While raising a new ridge of leather around a ball is going beyond the bounds of fair play, I suggest that we should look to encouraging the bowler to find what grip he needs in the rows of external stitching designed for him.

Thread can be flattened in use, some more than others. Worse still for the bowler are the balls where, during manufacture, the threads are either compressed down quite flat and/or buried in shiny lacquer.

Soil picked up by a ball lies alongside the raised stitching and to some extent alters its effect on the passing air stream. In order to find the extent of this effect, I rubbed soil over the stitching of a new ball and measured the new swing force in the wind tunnel. Instead of protruding sharply, the stitches now showed a rounded profile.

For a new four-piece ball at seam angles of less than 10° the swing force was reduced by 30–50 per cent. At angles of 15–35° it was increased by about 20 per cent. If swing is the only consideration, this result is inconclusive. But since it is certain that a clean seam, at full height, will grip better, both in the fingers and on the pitch, there is no doubt that the present interpretation of cricket Law in which the bowler is allowed to clean

the stitching of any particles of grass or earth is wholly justified.

The grip in the fingers will benefit greatly from constant attention to this cleaning. If it is done thoroughly it will automatically counter, at least to some extent, the flattening that takes place on some seams, and provide a fully deserved retention of reasonable grip.

As long as we don't make the basic mistake of confusing 'fair' seam cleaning i.e. cleaning of the external stitching, with 'unfair' seam picking, i.e. raising of leather, there will be no misunderstanding. If there has been some misunderstanding in the past it appears to have arisen, at least partly, from a failure to make this discrimination.

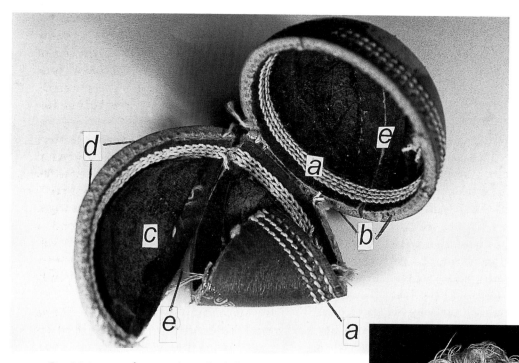

Fig. 31 Anatomy of a top quality cricket ball, the cover and the packing: **a** the stitching whose sole purpose is to provide a grip for the bowler, is clearly seen, going in and out through the leather, while **b** the stitching that holds the ball together, is almost invisible; **c** thin leather packing evens the contours where there is no stitching; **d** the major seam; **e** the minor (or quarter) seam; **f** string and cork inner packing provides rebound without too much hardness to damage bats (and cricketers!). Balls don't lose their bounce as much as is commonly thought.

9

RUN UP AND DELIVER

Slower bowlers tend to make their own rules; but fast bowlers, unless they try to match the great Australian all-rounder Keith Miller and bowl with explosive pace off just a few paces, must run in from 14–28 m (15 to 30 yards).

Bowlers are entitled to demand proper conditions underfoot. Occasionally a compromise must be made on less firm conditions in order to get play under way after rain, but a firm reliable grip, consistent all the way, not soft or spongy and not rising or stepping up significantly during the approach, should be the norm. Anything else acts against bowlers attempting to demonstrate their full range of skills under good control.

Interesting research[1] on fast bowling action comes from Perth, where Elliot, Foster and Blanksby worked with top Australian bowlers. Although their account of swing is wrong in parts, their analysis of what happens to a fast bowler is useful.

When recording run-ups they showed that Denis Lillee slowed appreciably while he leapt and turned side-on at the same time. Too fast a run-in, says Lillee, makes the jump-turn too difficult; too slow a run-in reduces the final delivery speed. The jump must be through the crease, not sideways, otherwise forward momentum will be lost.

Most bowlers use this side-on technique, which involves landing with the right (back) foot more or less parallel to the rear crease and shoulders pointing towards the batsman, while looking over the shoulder past the high left arm. But some of the best bowlers who, by the results they have achieved, have as much right as anyone else to be called orthodox, have done it differently. West Indian Malcolm Marshall and Australian Geoff Lawson, both successful at the highest level,

bowled quite front-on.

In front-on bowling the back foot lands pointing almost straight down the pitch, while the bowler faces more towards the batsman than with the side-on delivery. Note that in both types of delivery the shoulders and the lower half of the body are in the normal (standing) position in relation to each other, with no twist in the spine. In order to help prevent serious injury, researchers advocate that bowlers should avoid any delivery action that involves a twisted spine. They strongly recommend the adoption of either one type of action or the other, but nothing in between. By an in-between action they mean either the lower body facing the batsman while the upper body is side-on, or vice versa.

While this makes sense, it appears to leave unanswered the question as to whether there might exist a range of safe, 'in-between' types of action where, although the upper body is turned partly around, so is the lower body, at the same angle. Therefore the spine is not twisted. Although it would appear to be impossible to avoid at least some twisting of the spine in all bowling actions, these recommended techniques are obviously based on sound principles.

Measurements also showed that a side-on bowler, Terry Alderman, rotated his shoulders through approximately 105° in the delivery action, while a front-on bowler, Geoff Lawson, rotated his shoulders through 90°.

This research also showed that some of the various types of bowlers studied, especially among those who looked at least partly front-on, twisted their shoulders away from the batsman after landing but prior to delivery. This is regarded as dangerous for the spine.

How did side-on bowlers like Malcolm Marshall and Geoff Lawson achieve their pace without the initial turn and without the high shoulder rotation of the side-on bowlers? The measurements gave the answer. They showed that the front-on action does not require them to slow down in the final few strides as much as side-on bowlers who experience a slowing-down in the jump-turn. Because they maintain their run-up speed better right through the delivery, this compensates.

Although both types of action have been chosen by great bowlers, the front-on action must make it easier to bowl the genuine inswinger, i.e. without ball mutilation; and there is no evidence as far as I am aware that front-on bowlers have found any particular difficulty in bowling the outswinger.

To reduce stress on the body the front knee should be bent, at least slightly, to help absorb some of the impact when the foot strikes the ground. Stress is reduced by not suddenly cutting short the follow through but by gradually reducing momentum. Fast and medium pace bowlers choosing to run in at greater than normal angles should realise that, because they must change direction if they are not to run on to the pitch, this turning at speed adds to the stress on their bodies.

The Perth researchers sum up by emphasising a coordinated run-up followed by a rhythmic series of body movements. While appearing relaxed, the movements during delivery should be explosive.

Impact on hard surfaces is a matter of considerable importance, especially to faster bowlers. Sports medicine is in no doubt about the damage.[2,3] This is a painful and crippling set of conditions, including damage to soft tissues in the lower leg and stress fractures and compression damage to the lower leg bones. Practising and playing on artificial surfaces has added greatly to these problems.[4] Even on hard turf, impact-absorbing material should be used, whether it is part of the boot, or used as an inner sole, or in both. Although loss of firmness in the footing carries the risk of impaired control and balance during delivery, satisfactory compromises are possible.

How one should grip the ball has always fascinated cricketers. Their particular hero, photographed with fingers curling on either side of, along, or slightly across the seam, reveals the secret of his fame. Other photographs and diagrams may show his arm and body swing; different for the outswinger and the inswinger. But, as many a cricketer and coach have discovered, it is not as simple as that. Even more frustrating is the sudden loss of the ability to swing, a not uncommon problem among cricketers at all levels.

These problems arise because we have focussed too much on grip, and aspects of action, which in themselves do not guarantee that the ball begins its flight in a state capable of giving the best results. Instead, we should start with a clear picture of the ball on its way and, by careful experimentation and observation, adjust all the other complex movements of body, arms and hand, to achieve that end.

To begin with, a flexible action can deliver the ball at all sorts of angles, even though the grip is unchanged. Grip the ball with the seam running straight out, partly under, or partly between the first and second fingers. Merely by cocking the hand to one side or the other, the ball can be delivered at angles identical to those in frequently published photographs for the inswinger or outswinger. This does not mean that the usual grips are wrong, but it does mean that they are not in themselves a guarantee of success.

Neither is the arm action any guarantee. It is possible to swing the arm down across one side of the body, while at the same time having the hand cocked so that the ball leaves the hand facing the opposite way.

Finger action is the final variable. Precisely how do the fingers come off the ball at the instant of release?

A stranger to the game of cricket may well describe the task we are undertaking, for swing, as impossible. At the same time as propelling the ball straight down the pitch, the fingers must ensure a steady angle during flight, with the ball upright, but with the seam pointing to one side.

Gripped between the thumb and fingers, the ball is brought up to speed. Then, just before the moment of release, the hand opens. The thumb comes off the ball first, and the fingers, naturally reaching out further, are left to give the final push, which develops into a downward stroking of the back of the ball. This can be either straight down the back of the ball or, in varying degrees, to one side or the other. While all this might seem boringly obvious to bowlers, it is worth noting because it is the foundation of both swing and cut.

Whether the downward-moving fingers should both be on the seam, or one on the seam and one on the smooth leather, or even both on smooth leather, depends to some extent on the success or failure of one's own experimentation, and also on one's intentions.

If you intend to cut the ball off the pitch, with or without swing, then the backward spin carrying a significant amount of off- or leg-cut, must be the best obtainable. In that case the more grip or friction the fingers obtain as they move down the back of the ball, the better. At least one finger should therefore be on the stitching.

If swing is the sole intention, but with a minimum of cut-back in the opposite direction off a gripping pitch, then fingers on smooth leather are called for, provided you don't lose control on the slippery surface. An extreme form of this grip involves the fingers splayed wide on either side of the seam and propelling the ball from points nearer the outside bulges. Minimum back-spin will result from this technique which has also been employed to deliver a slower ball.

There is no such thing as a correct grip which will apply to every bowler, and no one type of body action can, on its own, guarantee success. Earlier we saw how the sideways swing force acts approximately at right angles to the 'wheel of the seam'. Therefore if the ball is tilted over to one side or the other the bowler will lose some of the hoped-for sideways movement as the ball tries to swing up or down. Some of these less efficient seam angles are shown in Figure 32.

The ball in Figure 32*a*, being at zero seam angle

to the line of flight, can swing either way, as shown by the two arrows. If it swings to the left, some of the swing force is manifest as lift and may cause it to over-pitch. If it swings to the right, some of the swing force acts downward, and the ball, while swinging less to the side, will dip into the pitch on a shorter length.

The other balls in Figure 32 will also 'waste' their swing. None of the angles is favourable for sideways swing and a good deal of the swing will be lost in other directions, including, as explained above, those that might have a bad effect on length. The round-arm slinger generally has a problem with length in any case, but for the reasons just explained, the high arm coming more or less straight over the top clearly offers a better launching site.

It is necessary to practise and experiment with an observer present to check on the position and behaviour of a marked ball in the air. Needless to say, all contact with concrete or wire or any other hard abrasive material on run-ups, such as crushed limestone must be strictly avoided. Modern practice facilities are decidedly unfriendly to swing and to the development of swing bowlers. If indoor facilities must be used, some ingenuity and careful choice of soft materials can overcome the problem. The banishment of batsmen from the scene will remove some of the danger. Make stumps from soft plastic piping. Re-lacquering of worn balls can also help. It is worth achieving this ball-friendly situation because the lack of sun-induced turbulence indoors is ideal for learning to swing, provided that care is taken to bowl at a lower pace and avoid the danger of coming down on unyielding surfaces.

If practising outdoors, a still, cloudy day is best for swing. A readily accessible and ball-friendly location is a grassy field, away from fences, with a simple back net, a few feet high and supported by two poles. The surface need not be perfect, since it is movement through the air, not off the pitch, that is the purpose of such practice. Regular cleaning of the stitching with the thumb-nail will be necessary.

Coaching books often underestimate the capacity of young bowlers to learn. I see no reason why a bowler learning swing should not, from the beginning, learn the different actions required for bowling both inswingers and outswingers. The sooner the better; there are plenty of other skills to get on with later.

Fig. 32 Some seam angles which are inefficient for swing. Any angle in which the seam is not vertical will waste the swing force because the ball will be pushed up or down to some extent and not purely sideways.

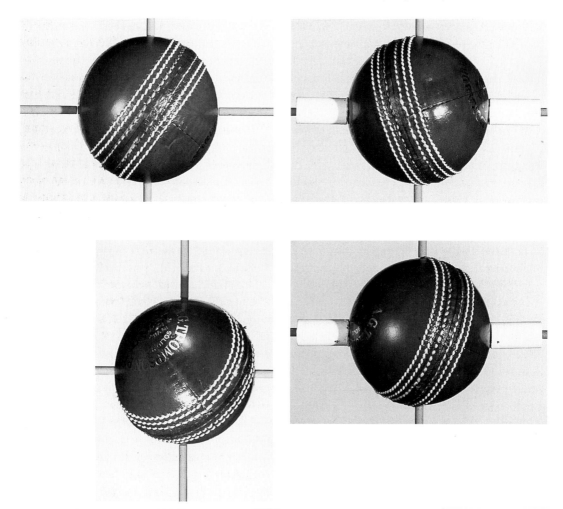

10

SPIN-SWERVE TAKES WICKETS

Spin-swerve takes wickets. Bowlers should know how it works and how to use it. 'Defend me from the swerver's puzzling flight' said the cricket poet. It is belittling to swerve to call it 'drift'; will we then call the bowler a 'drifter'? One would hope that it is also clearly recognised as quite distinct from swing.

In Chapter 2 we looked at the story of spin-swerve from cannon balls through to distorted air lines around a spinning baseball in a wind tunnel. All cricketers will be familiar with the many situations where spin-swerve adds an element of great interest to the game; the outward swerving off-spinner; the dipping top-spinner; the inward-curving leg-break; the frequently strange antics of the ball in the air after pitching; a list not complete without the greatest of all excuses from the slippery-fingered fieldsman, 'It just drifted away from me in the air'.

To study spin-swerve, balls were mounted in the wind tunnel (Figs 10a and 33e) and spun by means of an electric motor connected to a flexible cable leading to the end of a thin steel shaft inserted into the ball. Spin rates were varied up to 12 revs/sec, a rate which has been recorded for cricket balls in play.

The first ball studied (Fig. 33a) was prepared from a shiny plastic imitation cricket ball by carefully removing the imitation seam and lacquering the surface to produce a shiny but not perfectly smooth finish; in fact, a fair imitation of new ball leather. This ball did not show the negative forces found by Briggs for some balls, but gave a relatively uncomplicated pattern of positive Robins Forces, generally increasing both with spin rate and wind speed. It therefore served as a reference with which to compare the results obtained from proper cricket balls, new and used.

As mentioned earlier, the air flow involved in spin-swerve, i.e. separating earlier or later on one side than on the other, is no different from that produced in swing. Put another way, if the surface air stream separates differently on the two sides of the ball, a certain force is produced and it does not matter whether that separation is caused by spin, or by the seam, or by wear, or any combination of these. Conditions favouring swing will also favour spin-swerve. In my own experience one hits the pads with an inswerving leg-break more in indoor nets (conditions of low small-scale turbulence) than in most outdoor situations.

The roughness of cricket balls, with their seam and sometimes wear, made them behave quite differently from the smooth ball. Apart from a few readings out of the hundreds that were recorded, the maximum spin-swerve forces were only about half the values recorded for swing (Chapter 4), and a great many considerably less than that.

The new four-piece cricket ball (Fig. 33b) gave quite moderate Robins Forces which generally increased only slightly with wind speed. The new two-piece ball (Fig. 33c) plunges into the negative at about 97 km/h (60 mph). However, a well-worn ball such as the hundred-over four-piece ball, for which the results are shown in Figure 34, shows negative behaviour only at around 48 km/h (30 mph) which is probably too slow for competitive cricket. Nevertheless the prospect of negative behaviour by partially worn balls at higher speeds remains.

Most of the larger Robins Forces have shown up only in the high speed range and this should serve to remind faster bowlers of their usefulness.

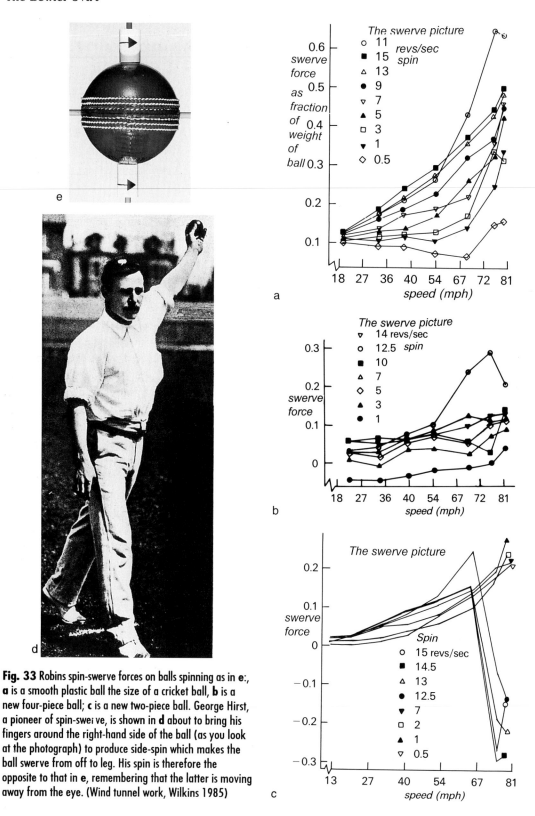

Fig. 33 Robins spin-swerve forces on balls spinning as in **e**:, **a** is a smooth plastic ball the size of a cricket ball, **b** is a new four-piece ball; **c** is a new two-piece ball. George Hirst, a pioneer of spin-swerve, is shown in **d** about to bring his fingers around the right-hand side of the ball (as you look at the photograph) to produce side-spin which makes the ball swerve from off to leg. His spin is therefore the opposite to that in **e**, remembering that the latter is moving away from the eye. (Wind tunnel work, Wilkins 1985)

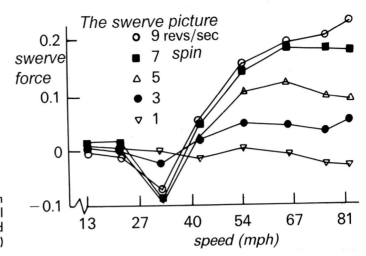

The swerve picture

- ○ 9 revs/sec
- ■ 7 *spin*
- △ 5
- ● 3
- ▽ 1

0.2
swerve force
0.1

0

−0.1

speed (mph)
13   27   40   54   67   81

Fig. 34 Robins spin-swerve forces on a worn (100 over) four-piece ball mounted as in Figure 33 e. (Wind tunnel work, Wilkins 1985)

However, in case the reader should regard this range of speed as being unattainable by a slow spinner, it is worth remembering that a ball delivered at, say, 64 km/h (40mph) straight into a 32 km/h (20mph) wind is experiencing a wind speed of 97 km/h (60mph). To be fully effective with his devastating side-spin-swerve from leg to off, Monty Noble needed a wind which was, at least to some extent, against him.

George Hirst, a good, fast-medium left-armer, became a truly great bowler when he learned how to swerve the ball from off to leg. Bowling with side-spin into a head wind, he was at his best exploiting the upper limits of the Robins Force. One bemused batsman demanded: 'How the devil can you play a ball that comes at you like a hard throw-in from cover point?' Recognising another of the characteristics of spin-swerve, Hirst was modest and candid enough to admit its unpredictability: 'Sometimes it works,' he said, 'sometimes it doesn't'.[1]

Monty Noble, one of the greatest Australian all-rounders, spun the ball on a vertical axis, from between his thumb and forefinger. Like Hirst he could take wickets on the best of pitches provided he had some sort of head wind. He also had a well-concealed quick ball and a penetrating off-cutter.

It was probably the spectacular curves sometimes associated with spin-swerve against the wind which prompted Jack Massie[2] to conclude,

wrongly, that although *swing* starts from the moment the ball leaves the bowler's hand, *spin-swerve* occurs only as the ball is dropping near the end of its flight.

So far we have been discussing balls spinning about the 'axle of the seam wheel', i.e. all the situations illustrated by the balls in Figures 33 and 34. But bowlers do not always deliver such 'pure wheel spin', and instead may spin 'across the seam,' as in Figure 35*d*. Any spin between 'pure wheel' and 'pure across' would produce a wobbling seam delivery.

Three balls were studied with the axis through rather than across the main seam, i.e. spinning 'across the seam' (Figs. 35*a*, *b*, and *c*.) A new four-piece ball (Fig. 35*a*) spun that way will not show very much spin-swerve at all; at least it offers the bowler a choice, and a method for delivering an uncomplicated ball: spin-swerve has been virtually eliminated.

A worn, 100-over, four-piece ball (Fig. 35*b*) showed a marked increase in force in the upper half of the speed range, and at quite moderate spin rates.

The new two-piece ball (Fig. 35*c*) showed little evidence of a Robins Force except for the startling rise at 5 revs/sec spin rate.

S. F. Barnes, with his trident of spin-swerve, turn, and pace, merits a chapter all of his own (Chapter 16). The cricket writer in the Melbourne

Argus, describing Barnes' historic bowling on December 30, 1911, said he was 'bowling a fine length and had a slight swerve'. It was a dull and cloudy day; the invisible carpet of low small-scale turbulence laid out to welcome the Master.

They hunt in pairs; swing and cut, spin-swerve and turn. Swing and cut have the potential for the spectacular. Spin-swerve and turn, when they decide to work together, can be just as effective — and a little sneaky.

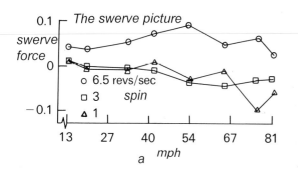

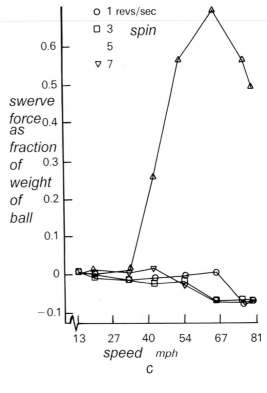

Fig. 35 Spin about an axis that goes in through the seam on one side and out through the seam on the other as in **d**. Graph **a** is from a new four-piece ball; **b** is a worn (100-over) four-piece ball; and **c** is a new two-piece ball. (Wind tunnel work, Wilkins 1985)

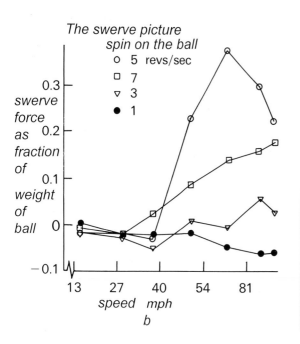

11

MIXING SWERVE, SWING, AND TURN

We have seen that when the ball diverts the air stream it will experience a force in the opposite direction. This diversion can be caused by the seam, or other surface roughness, or by spin. A combination of effects is possible. For example, in Figure 37a the outswing results from the air being diverted to the right behind the ball, in addition to which the top-spin diverts the air upwards. The combination results in air being diverted upwards to the right and the ball being pushed down to the left.

Downward force is of great potential worth in the bowler's armoury, since it makes the ball drop shorter than expected. Upward movement could never occur against the force of gravity, although the upward force is present. The upward Robins Force on a ball pulled down by gravity is, in fact, quite subtle. It is worthy of close attention from bowlers, and especially of batsmen, because of its effect of making the ball carry on further before landing.

How much does the Robins Force cause the ball to deviate in the air? The forces shown in Chapter 10 are smaller than swing forces. However, since spin is more often applied to slow or medium-pace deliveries which therefore have longer flight times, the Robins Force has more time in which to produce an effect. Taking the behaviour of the new four-piece ball in Figure 33b as an example, and selecting a spin rate of 12.5 revs/sec, the calculated sideways movement, assuming a delay of 0.1 sec before the force operates, is approximately 231 mm (9.1 in) for a speed of 72 km/h (45 mph), 250 mm (9.8 in) for a speed of 108 km/h (67 mph), and 150 mm (5.9 in) for a speed of 58 km/h (36 mph). These figures apply to a ball carrying 'pure' side-spin as in

Figure 36a and d. It is not an easy delivery to bowl as it requires the arm to be near vertical, and the hand bent back at the wrist at the moment of release with a leg-break or off-break type of action.

A much more likely version of the side-spun ball is the one in Figure 36b or e. Here the axes of spin, instead of being vertical, are tipped over to one side. The force acts in the directions of the arrows. For the leg-break action, a and b are producing side-spin-swerve and c has the addition of some dipping top-spin. For the off-break type of action, d and e produce away-swerve and f represents part away-swerve and part floating back-spinner.

It would be futile to attempt calculations of the amount of swerve and dip associated with these deliveries, because the possible angles and spin rates can vary so much. However, the underlying principles are not difficult to grasp. Any bowler neglecting them will be denied access to one of the most fascinating and productive areas in the art of bowling. Rather than complaining at having to cope with wind, bowlers should learn to exploit the increased possibilities it makes available both for spin-swerve and swing.

A simple rule describes the direction in which the (positive) Robins Force pushes the ball. The rule is as follows: *the force is in the direction in which the front face of the ball is moving across the oncoming air flow.*

When the axis of spin is horizontal, there is no sideways Robins Force; but even without it there remains swing, dip and turn; potentially a most useful combination. The ball carrying top-spin to make it dip, but not 'pure' top-spin (since the tyre on the wheel is pointing towards the slips), is an

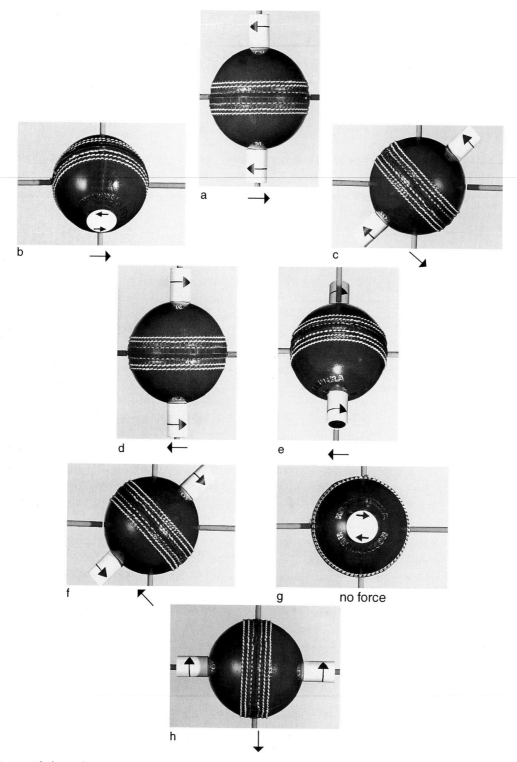

Fig. 36 Which way does the spin make the ball swerve? Arrows show direction of swerve. Note that the swerve is always in the direction in which the front of the ball is moving across the air stream.

a   b

Fig. 37 Photo **a** is an outswinging leg-break with top-spin making it dip; **b** is an inswinging off-break, also with top-spin.

example. This means that a certain fraction of the spin will go towards making the ball break from leg to off when it lands. Added to this, the delivery is an out-swinger since the seam is pointing in that direction. We therefore have an outswinging, down-dipping leg-break. Although this ball is not widely known and not recorded in any of the literature that I have read, I have noticed it occurring with my own leg-breaks occasionally. Figure 37a tells the story.

If an off-spin bowler, or, more easily, a left-hand chinaman bowler, delivers his version of that ball as in Figure 37b, it is an inswinging, down-dipping off-break. This is an exact description of Ian Peebles' googly which is recorded as having both swung in and turned in from off to leg.

Each of these two interesting deliveries has three barbs with which to sting the batsman: sideways swing, downwards dip, and turn off the pitch. If, for any reason, one of the barbs is missing; say for instance, the wicket is not taking much spin, the others remain to do their damage.

Two TV commentators I heard discussing the Indian leg-spin bowler Kumble underline the need to see behind the obvious. 'He's not getting much turn today' was the extent of their comment as they attempted to analyse the changed situation when Kumble came on to bowl. Yet it was obvious to viewers that the batsmen facing Kumble were not comfortable, and before long he had two wickets to prove it.

We must hope that commentators who are adequate to the task will know, even if they cannot see it from above and behind the pitch, that Kumble, like all bowlers of his type, begins to make the batsman feel uncomfortable with the dipping flight from the top-spin shortening the length compared to what they had previously faced, keeps them uncomfortable with the slight inward spin-swerve towards leg, and rubs it in with a little straightening or slight turn to the off, sometimes accompanied by a bit of extra kick in the bounce as the stitching catches the pitch. All this without any sign of the real turn that was required to impress the commentators!

The pair of deliveries discussed above combine swing, Robins dip and turn. Another interesting pair, well known to bowlers of all speeds for a century or more, but not now developed as a skill by modern bowlers, is similar. This second pair differs in the sense that it carries the back-spin normally associated with medium and fast bowling, and has inward or outward swerve to accompany the swing.

Figure 38a is an inswinging leg-break which will 'carry' a little further up the pitch before landing, as a result of the upward Robins Force. Figure 38b is an outswinging off-cutter which also experiences upward Robins Force. Whereas the first two (Fig. 37) swing in the same direction as their turn off the pitch, the second two (Fig. 38) swing one way and turn the other, making a more deadly pair.

In practice it is unlikely that any of the four deliveries discussed is quite as 'pure' as depicted in the diagrams. All four are likely to have received a certain amount of side-spin at the moment of delivery. The axes, instead of being horizontal, are likely to be tipped over a little as in Figure 39. Applying the basic principles, we can describe why each of these deliveries is a worthy addition to the bowler's art by consulting Table D which outlines the way in which the deliveries in Figure 39 behave.

Table D

	a	b	c	d
Swing	In and down	Out and down	Out and down	In and down
Spin-swerve	Out and down	In and down	Out and up	In and up
Turn on landing	Off-break	Leg-break	Off-break	Leg-break

The results from swing are best appreciated if it is realised that the wake in all the four cases is diverted upwards and therefore the swing is always downwards. Inswing *(d)* and outswing *(c)* is aided by the Robins in-swerve or out-swerve in both cases; but in *(a)* and *(b)* the Robins Forces oppose the sideways swing.

The relative strength of the swing force compared to the Robins Force depends on the state of the ball, the angles used and the amount of spin. All four balls illustrated in Figure 39 have the axes of spin tipped down at the back to obtain sideways Robins swerve, but it must be realised that if tipped over to any great amount, the ball will be less likely to land on the stitching than on the smooth leather, in which case the valuable turn off the pitch will be lost. Swing and Robins swerve on their own are useful of course, both as variations and as stock balls. In practising these it is useful to look at the mark on the ball after each delivery to find out its position on landing.

It is not only slower bowlers who can do damage with spin-swerve. Alec Bedser bowled Don Bradman for a duck in 1947. Bradman describes this ball, as delivered towards the off stump, swerving to pitch on the leg stump, then turning back off the pitch to take the off stump. Only the great are allowed to get away with tales like that, but what better example than this famous delivery for every bowler to study and master?

Bedser tells the story from his point of view:

A turning point in my career was to bowl Don for a duck in the Fourth Test at Adelaide with a ball which he generously described as the finest ever bowled to him. It started on the line of the offstump, swung late to hit the pitch on or about the leg stump, and came back to hit the middle and offstumps. My stock was boosted sky high and I gained considerable confidence. I had discovered my so-called leg-cutter, in which I actually spun the ball, during the Bradman-Barnes record fifth wicket partnership of 405 in the Second Test at Sydney. I was bowling to Barnes, who knew all about my inswing. To tempt him into error, I tried to make the ball go straight through without deviation. Allan Peach had taught me how to stop the new ball swinging by holding it across the seam in a leg-break grip. To my surprise, and that of Barnes, the ball went away from leg to off after pitching. Barnes' first reaction was to study the pitch with suspicion, and when he found it to be totally without blemish, he stared at me in disbelief and called out, 'What the hell's going on?' From that moment I knew I could spin the ball at a good speed, a considerable addition to my armoury.[1]

Bedser's so-called 'leg-cutter' reveals an interesting link with the great S. F. Barnes. At a somewhat slower pace than Bedser, Barnes' best ball was an in-curving leg-spinner.

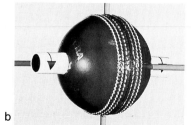

Fig. 38 Left: an inswinging leg-break with back-spin. Right: an outswinging off-break with back-spin. The Robins Force is upward in both cases.

a

b

Of the deliveries illustrated in Figure 39, which one matches Bedser's famous ball? Since it turned from leg to off on pitching and, since Bedser tells us that it was a true fast leg-break, not cut but spun from his fingers, it must be b, perhaps with the axis of spin tipped further down at the back than is shown here, a ball with that inward swerve in the air from off to leg. If this analysis is correct, Bradman was beaten by inswerve and leg-spin. Bedser's own description of his ball as having 'swung' is merely the language common among cricketers.

Fred Trueman, with characteristic frankness and in perfect agreement with Bernard Hollowood, vividly underlines the uncertainty as to whether all, some or none of the potential deviating influences associated with the delivery illustrated in Figure 39c will actually take effect. This is not a twisted ball like Bedser's, but released with (off) cut at the accompanying seam angle for outswing, in the hope of deviation in the air and, maybe, back the other way off the pitch. In Trueman's words:

Time and again I have pitched what I believed to be the perfect out-swinger on the leg stump only to see it whisked away for four as the ball went straight through. At other times, with equal certainty, I have aimed that same outswinger at the off stump only to see it come nipping back off the pitch to hit the leg stump while the batsman shakes his head in astonishment and the fielders congratulate me on bowling the unplayable ball. And all the time I am wondering how it happened! That is how I have come to develop a fireproof philosophy about cricket. I take whatever comes my way as my due right, for I have discovered over the years that the unexpected is commonplace.[2]

In this chapter we have begun to reduce the level of ignorance about the way in which swing, spin-swerve and turn off the pitch, those wonderful servants of the skilful bowler, can act together. Both here and in the chapters to come I hope to convince bowlers that they can benefit from trying to be more specific rather than being content with vague words and phrases like 'movement', 'moving around', 'doing a bit', 'leaving the bat' and 'seaming'.

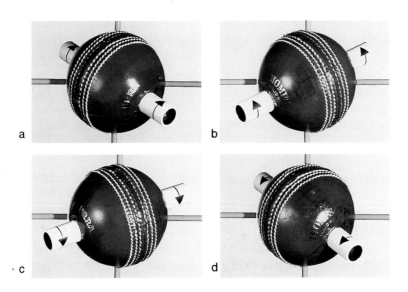

Fig. 39 Off-breaks and leg-breaks. Off-breaks; **a** with top-spin, **c** with back-spin, both with a certain amount of side-spin. Leg-breaks; **b** and **d** similarly carry top-spin (**b**) and back-spin (**d**), both with a little side-spin.

12
COMING TO TERMS WITH OVER-ARM

As a result of the legalisation of over-arm bowling in 1864, scoring runs generally became easier. A similar peak in run-scoring accompanied the change from under-arm to round-arm in the 1820s. Perhaps batsmen adjust more readily than bowlers.

An historian[1] of the period regards the low scoring in the later round-arm period as due to the high number of deliveries wide of the wicket which were difficult to score from, or at least difficult to score from with safety. The hand coming across the line of flight during delivery is a natural problem with round-arm bowling in any case, particularly since round-arm bowlers usually bowled around the wicket to avoid hitting the umpire. Over-arm, although it posed the additional problems of greater pace and bounce, at least involved an arm action which was more or less in line with the pitch.

If bowlers needed any stimulus to come to terms with their newly granted powers, a certain gentleman named W. G. Grace (1848–1915) was there in 1865 and still there in 1908, during which time he must have given those bowlers determined enough to fight back, plenty of reasons to look for better ways of plying their trade. W. G. himself played a not insignificant role in this development, by means of his own bowling, as we shall see later.

Effective spinning from above the head took some time to develop. Spin bowlers, fast and slow, commonly take years to learn to control a new delivery. They will understand the problems which faced bowlers of the 1860s and 1870s.

Nevertheless, some outstanding bowlers played during that period. Cambridgeshire was one of the strongest counties during the 1860s. Its greatest bowler and one of the best in the country, who played for them in the years 1857–61, was W.

(Billy) Buttress (1827–1866) who bowled vicious leg-breaks at medium pace, and has been called the father of leg-break bowling.[2] Since generations of under- and round-arm bowlers had already demonstrated great skill in turning the ball from the leg, it would be more correct to nominate Buttress as the father of *over-arm* leg-break bowling. Brown ale got the better of Buttress and death ended his career when he was only forty-one.

Tom Emmett (1841–1904) of Yorkshire, another bowler of the 1860s, who bowled a ball round-arm that whipped sharply from leg to off, was a left-hander, inaccurate at times, but often unplayable.

Over-arm bowling came of age at the hands of Frederick Spofforth (1853–1926). Spofforth, an Australian, was an under-arm bowler as a boy, but changed when he saw George Tarrant bowling for George Parr's visiting English team in 1863–64. He experimented with various types of spin in his twenties, and consulted a university professor about the reason for the ball 'curling' in the air; only to be told it was impossible!

As well as bowling off- and leg-spin at pace, he bowled what was described as 'vertical spin', which must have been the ball we describe today as a top-spinner. He also bowled a ball which dropped far shorter than the batsman expected. Although this is how a top-spinner would behave, it is described as an additional ball and therefore most likely the result of a clever change of pace.

Spofforth is generally credited with having introduced true, high, over-arm bowling into England in 1882. His pace was the subject of a good deal of argument. Some said he was medium or even slow-medium, but the truth was that although he was capable of real pace, he often modified it in order to get the best out of the prevailing conditions, and employ his other skills.

George Lohmann (1865–1901) was inspired by Spofforth. For eight years he was the most successful bowler in England, capturing over 200 wickets in each of the three seasons from 1888 to 1890. H. S. Altham describes him as follows:

We have the testimony of both W. G. and C. B. Fry that Lohmann was the best medium-paced bowler they had ever met, a combined verdict, it will be noticed, that embraces half a century. In an age still wedded to the formalism of length, he was the first English bowler really to master the revolutionary lessons of Spofforth, and to make length the handmaid of variety in pace and spin and flight. He was on the slow side of what we now call medium; he could break the ball back as he chose from the off, could bowl a leg-break at will, and always had in reserve the ball that looked like spinning but went straight on. But subtlety of flight was his greatest asset; with his very high delivery he was always dipping short of what the batsman expected; he could suck him out with his held-back slow ball, or get him driving at the half-volley which somehow 'swam' on into a yorker.[3]

In one respect however, Lohmann may not be the best model for a bowler aspiring to a long life at the crease. In Altham's words: *'His whole heart was in the game, which indeed, he loved not wisely but too well, crowding into thirteen years more work than even his magnificent physique could stand'*.[4]

Another medium-pacer who could spin the ball both ways was H. F. Boyle (1847–1907) who had good length and flight, and played in 10 Tests between England and Australia in the period 1878–85. On his first tour of England he took 250 wickets at very low cost. His figures for twelve Tests are 1732 balls and 82 wickets at an average of 20.05; first class by any standard.

Schoolboy leg-spinners, collecting a rich harvest from among their fellows, are not uncommon. A. G. Steel (1858–1914) was one of the few who carried on with spectacular success into first class cricket. In his first year out of school, 1878, he took 164 wickets at 9.60 apiece, and was described as:

... slow, yet fast enough to make jumping out to him a matter of great difficulty, he could alter it at will, and had quite a fast ball in reserve. He was a master of the short half-volley, the slow bowler's best length ball, and he could spin the ball either way, though favouring the leg-break.[5]

'Short half-volley' is a term not used these days, but one which aptly describes the ball carrying enough top-spin to make it drop a little shorter than expected.

Pitches were not as well prepared as today. As a truer measure of a bowler's ability it is preferable to use Test match performances, which generally take place on better surfaces. Steel played thirteen Tests, bowled 1404 balls and took 29 wickets at an average of 20.86; excellent figures. His effective career was no more than eight years and by 1885 he was a spent force. Whatever the reasons for his decline, we can be sure that batsmen were learning. The English batsmen certainly had no trouble with the Australian leg-spinner Harry Trott who in 24 Tests (1888–98) took only 29 wickets.

Two notable fast bowlers of the period were the Surrey pair, T. Richardson (1870–1912) and W. H. Lockwood (1868–1952). Richardson, with splendid physique, a high action, sheer pace, and an off-break produced by body turn with a cross sweep of the arm to the offside, showed a great sense of fair play in moderating his pace if the wicket was dangerous or when he had hit a batsman. The reader should be reminded that the 'sweep of the arm' referred to in the literature is not necessarily a guarantee of any particular result. As discussed earlier, it is the final release process that matters. Lockwood was less consistent, but an inspired bowler on his day, with a great break-back, bounce, and control of a well disguised slow ball. Arthur Mold was another fast man at that time with a devastating break-back, who after eleven years in Test and county cricket was banned as a thrower. Prominent slow bowlers were the left-handers Briggs, Peate, and Tyler, and Flowers who was an off-spinner.

In terms of the technical evolution of bowling, the latter years of the century were something of a mixture. Right-hand leg-spin had been on the scene since Buttress in the 1860s, and its left-handed mirror image, the chinaman, was first bowled by Edward Barratt (1844–1890) in the 1870s. But in spite of the success of Charles Townsend (1876–1958), leg-spin was almost a forgotten art. Leg-spin of the fast and medium variety had declined with the departure of Spofforth and Lohmann. The leading fast bowlers appear to have relied only on break-back from the off. However, some fine bowlers of non-chinaman left-hand leg-spin were on the scene, and some famous exponents were about to appear.

John Barton King (1873–1965) was perfecting the inswinger. King, whose career coincided with the prominence of Philadelphia in the cricket world, was better known by sight in England than any other American. He was fast and accurate, keeping his good form for twenty years from 1898 to 1912 against touring teams, including Australian national sides in the USA, and on three tours with Philadelphia in England.

If faster leg-spin had declined, a figure capable of filling a proud place in the lineage of this most effective bowling skill was about to emerge: he was Sidney Francis Barnes. Exploitation of the Robins Force, following experiment at the hands of George Hirst, a true over-arm successor to Noah Mann, was about to bring spin-swerve to the fore again. Barnes and Hirst were soon to display the fine fruits of their labours, and in a sense, the labours of all bowlers from the time the ball was 'pitched' rather than bowled along the ground.

13

HITTING THE PITCH

The pitch, good, bad or indifferent, makes cricket the game it is. Earth, whether bare or grassy, hard or soft, crumbling or sticky, rough or smooth, wet or dry, cracked or continuous, constant or changing, is something that plastic, the synthetic brew from the chemist's pot, will never be. A major part of cricket's fascination comes from the soil. On any other surface cricket acquires an element of predictability, ceasing to be the unique game it has been for more than two centuries.

Soils and grasses differ throughout the world. I would hope that there will be as many solutions to the problem of providing a good pitch as there are cricket grounds. In combination with the particular qualities of local climates, this will ensure a fine degree of individual flavour in keeping with the best traditions of the game. However, we must put the hard question to every pitch; does it serve the best interests of cricket?

By 1876 Lord's had ceased to be kept in order by weekly flocks of sheep, and the playing area was described as being 'in faultless condition'. W. G. Grace was by then well into his stride and the mainly single digit scores of the Hambledon men began to be replaced by large numbers all over the world. Australia made 551 against England in the Oval Test in 1884 and England replied with 346, no less than eighteen bowlers being used in these two innings. Was it a good pitch? What is 'good'? A lot of runs were scored. Maybe it depends on who one asks. Will batsmen and bowlers ever agree on the answer? At least they may agree that a level, but poorly rolled, 'dead' club pitch does *neither* of them any good.

One hears commentators expressing the wish that the pitch will 'help the faster bowlers for a day or two, then begin to take spin later in the game'. Many of today's pitches show up these words as nothing more than platitudes. Fortunately, either by accident or design, some groundsmen produce pitches that respond to spin from start to finish while good batsmen respond to the challenge. If fast bowlers do well at the beginning of a game it frequently has nothing whatsoever to do with the pitch; the new ball swings well and comes through more quickly, while moisture in a watered outfield may help swing by reducing microturbulence.

In what sense, if any, do groundsmen prepare pitches that are planned to deteriorate?; a risky business for someone engaged in an occupation where one's reputation is constantly on the line. I suggest that groundsmen might liken it to being asked to design a racing car for a five-lap race, but one that must begin to fall apart after the second lap. Most likely they ignore such dangerous advice. On a pitch completely covered with grass, however dry and well rolled it may be, the grass can only get drier and shinier and less able to grip the ball, and therefore more friendly to batsmen, as the game goes on.

But what about wear, won't that let the spinners and cutters in? What wear? Many groundsmen's sole intention is to get a good vigorous grass cover firmly matted over a hard base. When they chose that grass, were they required to demonstrate its ability to wear out at a certain rate? I doubt it. Modern sports grass is not easily worn away. But won't it wear under boots and spikes? It may do, but not under a modern *batsman's* friendly spikes. If it is a *bowler's* more aggressive spikes that we are relying on to produce the expected wear, then the umpires and/or the Laws have failed.

The Laws are intended to protect the pitch on

areas where 'normal' deliveries are expected to land. The ball alone, repeatedly landing on the pitch, will not wear the pitch by legal means; just go out and look at some modern Test and first class pitches at the end of the game.

Who do we listen to, the people congratulating the groundsman for a job well done, or the bowlers sitting in the dressing rooms, dismayed at not getting any worthwhile turn or cut throughout the whole game except when they pitched the ball wide of the stumps? As long as there was good air for swing and hardness for bounce, maybe half the bowlers were moderately satisfied. But groundsmen don't provide the good air. All that they may have provided is hardness; and hardness alone, when it comes to allowing bowlers to demonstrate the whole fascinating range of cricket skills, is not enough.

If the grass used on the pitch has the capacity to shrink cricket into some limited and ultimately boring form of ballistics, we must change our methods. Fortunately, an almost total cover of drying grass is not the norm. Pitches in various parts of the world tell us that the grass mat need not dominate the surface and that there are other ways; ways that make *all* the bowlers in a team feel as if they have something to offer: pitches where the groundsman's skill has allowed the hard, well consolidated and durable *ground under and around the grass* to play a part. When cricket escapes from the dominance of dry grass it will also escape from relying on that 'pie in the sky' called 'wear on the third day'.

The last thing that groundsmen would be likely to do these days is to take the advice of the great English captain and batsman A. C. MacLaren (1871–1944), interviewed in his later years:

> *I feel very much that the bowler has been badly treated ever since the groundsman has taken to doping the wicket. That robs the bowler of fifty per cent of his skill... I'd like to see a return to the natural wicket and shorter Test matches, where it forces the batsman to play a more lively game.*[1]

In fact many pitches get 'better' during a three, four, or five day match. 'Better' of course is better for batsmen. Groundsmen committed to particular types of grass cover may have only limited room for variation. But who decides whether, and to what extent, they should use the variations open to them? And on what basis are such decisions made? Would it be true to say that many pages of cricket history are being written, however unintentionally, in the groundsman's office; written, in a sense, by default? Do cricketers, and their representatives who organise the game, grasp the issues well enough to be able to 'order' pitches?

When will statistics tell us whether runs were made on surfaces which negated half the skills of bowling, or on surfaces which revealed the true batting heroes worthy of our admiration?

Then there is a possibility that certain techniques might bring closer the day when turf can be produced with the boring predictability of a synthetic pitch. In a technological age, uniformity and standardisation will always be a threat.

Doping once involved animal manure rolled out and allowed to dry as a shiny coating. We know that dead-looking grass still attached to its roots is equally fatal to balanced cricket. The most recent addition to the doper's formula book comes, not surprisingly, from the shelf of technology. Whether we regard the record New Zealand first class score of 777 runs made by Canterbury in March 1997 as admirable or not, the fact that it was made on a pitch at Lancaster Park that had been treated with plastic glue must enter our assessment. We may also consider whether the use of glue on a pitch is contrary to the spirit of cricket. Although the ground had been used for a rugby game a few weeks before this match, the use of glue on this ground, according to the local newspaper, is not uncommon. Otago, the visitors, needed to beat Canterbury outright to win the final of the Shell Trophy in a four day game. The glue coated every particle on the surface and dried out leaving a slippery finish that was described by on local journalist as bare, rock hard and providing no turn or seam. The coating prevented all grip and therefore must have prevented the abrasion that would normally be seen on the cover of a ball landing on a bare pitch.

The way a pitch plays is *capable* of being brought more or less under control, either in the long term by choice of soils, clays and grasses, or in the short term by final surface treatments. Whatever is chosen, I hope to show that it must to some extent be based on the *friction* by which the surface can grip the ball.

New information points to a central role for friction, not only in determining the *turn* available for spinners, fast and slow, but also in controlling the *pace* of all bowlers, and therefore accommodating the necessary balance between pace and spin.

The book *Great Bowlers and Fielders*[2] gives us a close look at the methods of the leading English, Australian, and South African bowlers almost a hundred years ago. Of the thirteen right-hand medium-pacers, ten broke the ball from the off, seven broke it from the leg and six of them broke it both ways. We must assume that all of these bowlers chose their particular style because it brought them success. The success that today's bowlers seek is partly redefined by limited-overs cricket as not necessarily requiring the bowler to take wickets, but if we agree that bowlers of all types, displaying the entire range of skills, will make cricket a better game, then we can learn from the past.

The misunderstanding of spin at pace is widespread. Derek Underwood saw fit to write in italics the statement *'I am not a cutter'*.[3] Alec Bedser likewise drew attention to the fact that the famous ball with which he bowled Don Bradman in 1947 was not cut but spun with his fingers.

We saw earlier that all deviation off the pitch, cut as well as slower spin, requires the pitch and the ball to grip each other to some extent. We are wrong therefore to lament the decline of slow bowling and ignore the decline of spinning skills in faster bowlers. The destinies of slow spin and fast spin are inextricably linked; where one has gone in the past fifty years, so has the other; conditions unfriendly to one are also unfriendly to the other; wickets unhelpful to slow spin bowling have profoundly affected a major proportion of the entire range of bowling arts.

And why have we meekly accepted the notion that wickets must not take spin early in a game? Do batsmen run the game, and if so, don't they want a contest? Chris Cowdrey, captain of Kent and England, discussing the possibility of increasing the power of umpires over the quality of pitches, chose as a hypothetical situation the following example: 'If the pitch is so obviously devoid of grass that the ball might turn excessively on the first day, they should authorise a new wicket to be prepared'.[4] Coming from a country where the skill of spin at all paces appears to be in decline, and where spin no longer appears to play an important part in the game at any stage, early or late, such remarks from one of England's leading cricketers may give a valuable insight into a particular way of thinking and one of the very reasons for that decline. The established practice today is probably better described by omitting the word 'excessively' from Cowdrey's description. Even the most cursory reading of cricket history tells us that spin has played a part right from the first hours of many memorable games.

Although spinners play a part in many one-day games, the basic conflict between the rules for such games and for mainstream cricket has done little to encourage the development of bowling arts.

When we read that pitches are 'doubtful', 'suspect', 'deteriorating', 'substandard' or 'minefields', it is worth reserving a little scepticism and allowing for the possibility that those writers are rather too well conditioned into accepting as normal the current anti-spin environment. A similar mind automatically takes the view that a country providing pitches that take spin indulges in somewhat unfair tactics to suit their own bowlers. Should not a well balanced team sent on tour possess bowlers able to exploit pitches of all sorts?

A bowler hoping to put 'real work' on the ball must, at least in the final moment before release, grip it firmly. Many bowlers grip a worn ball better during this action than they do a shiny ball. Balls wear less today both on pitches and on out-fields which are generally regarded as being less abrasive than in the early years of the century. However, for some, the stitching compensates and supplies an adequate grip, provided it is not flattened.

Unless the ball and pitch can lock together to some extent during their fleeting contact, much of the sweat and courage that goes into putting a spinning cricket ball into the air is wasted. Spin-swerve on its own may promise a little consolation, but because it usually sends the ball in the opposite direction, it will always work best in combination with turn off the pitch.

Friction, or more correctly kinetic friction, describes the grip of one surface for another moving relative to it. Just as the friction of tyres on the road allows us to turn without sliding off at corners, so does the friction between ball and pitch allow the ball to change direction off the pitch in response to the skill of the bowler.

'Friction', 'grip', 'bite', whichever word is chosen, is therefore basic in determining whether or not the bowler is adequately armed in his duel with the batsman.

Since all bowlers, strictly speaking, apply spin of one sort or another to the ball, we are closing in on a factor of profound significance for the entire game.

Common experience tell us that certain combinations of materials exhibit low friction, such as a shoe on a banana skin. But I am not so sure that bowlers are alert to those surfaces that bring them equally catastrophic results. New Zealand and Pakistan played a Test at the Basin Reserve in Wellington in 1989. The pitch was well rolled and quite hard; a normal pitch, except on one count, beside which all the others paled into insignificance: it was completely covered by a thin carpet-like layer of grass recently growing on the pitch, but now dead-looking and brown in colour, not thick enough to affect the feel of it as a hard pitch, but fatal to any hope that the ball might grip on that surface. The result was a boring draw, in which the bowlers on neither side were allowed to demonstrate their skills, a game which did no good for cricket in New Zealand.

Shortly after this match the teams played a one-day game on an adjacent strip which was covered with the same dead brown grass as in the Test. In the sense that the surface provided all the conditions that suit batsmen — it was flat and what little grass there was dead — the one-day pitch was ideal for the batsman's game. But sadly, by accident or design, this philosophy had spilled over and ruined a Test match.

During the tour of New Zealand by England in 1997 the Test pitch at Christchurch, which had been used for five days, was then used two days later for a one-day limited-over game between the two countries. Since this decision was announced at least two days before the end of the Test we must assume that the organisers knew, in advance, that it would remain a batsman's pitch right to the end of the Test! Indeed such was the case: cut was scarcely to be seen at any stage during five days and the one spinner for New Zealand, Daniel Vettori, a lefthander, was forced to make do by bowling wide into footmarks. The English spinner, Robert Croft, got his wickets not from turn but from changes of pace, and from arm balls that went straight through. The conflict of objectives and methods represented by this example must be resolved if cricket is to prosper.

When India toured New Zealand in 1990 this same type of brown grass surface mat was seen on most pitches. Fifteen hundred runs were made for the loss of only twenty-five wickets during the five days of the last Test at Auckland. Some spectacular batting was seen, but in the end it lacked the tension necessary to sustain interest. Spin, fast or slow, played no part. The admirable skills of the Indians in swinging the ball both ways and the hostility of New Zealander Danny Morrison were ultimately ineffective. The bowlers, who included Richard Hadlee and Hirwani, were unable to play a significant role. Media commentators, unaware of the real problem, criticised the New Zealand captain John Wright, already one up in the series, for not contriving a close finish. Given the conditions, there was no reason why runs could not have been churned out for another week.

A year later Sri Lanka played New Zealand on a similar pitch at the Basin Reserve. Apart from the first day, when grass stems and soil were a little damp, the bat dominated totally and run records galore were broken. Aravinda da Silva, John Wright, Andrew Jones and Martin Crowe batted admirably, but such a pitch requires that our praise for them be somewhat muted.

One way to create such a dismal surface is regular rolling without cutting the grass and without finally removing the thin carpet of dead-looking grass that remains. Congratulations to groundsmen for having produced, by this method, a hard pitch with good wearing properties, are misdirected. Only the removal of most of this gripless covering will help bring about at least the surface quality of a good pitch. The image of a billiard ball being bowled on to an oil slick suggests the reality underlying too much of today's cricket. There is more to cricket than pace, swing and bounce.

Drawn games may fascinate or bore. Mammoth scores need not be boring, but the dangers are obvious.

In spite of their best intentions, turf culturists working on cricket pitch research have recommended procedures not in the interests of good cricket. One such practitioner advises:

Living or dead leaves and grass clippings are good for the surface because they reduce evaporation. A good grass sward is necessary. On match day the grass cover should be incorporated into the pitch surface to produce a glazed shiny surface.[5]

No need to dope the pitch, as was done in 1938 at the Oval, to nullify Bill O'Reilly's spin; turf culturists may be on the way to making it official policy!

Friction great enough to satisfy the needs of good cricket will only exist when every particle of the top material is rigidly linked to the ground. Any *movable or slippery* material, stalks in dead-looking grass, dry grass mats, grass cuttings, sand, wet or not well consolidated soil, destroys grip. For that fraction of a second when the ball is in contact with the ground it merely slides over them or pushes them aside. Movable materials are unable to return the push and change the direction of the ball.

Friction also depends on the strength of the soil; there is no point in growing a network of roots and stems only to have them swept aside on impact. The soil therefore needs a good set of properties of its own. Poor consolidation is common in club pitches.

So-called seamers need not learn the real skills of medium and fast bowling if they rely, for deviation, on the ball striking tufts of coarse grass growing near small, frequently soft, bare patches. Hitting the front of a tuft facing the bowler, the ball lifts; worse if the soil in front of it is soft enough for it to dig in deeper. Hitting the back of it gives a shooter. Hitting the side produces a seam-for-no-effort. Such bowling requires less skill than anything else in the repertoire. But sooner or later, on better pitches, these bowlers will be exposed.

Surprising though it may seem, friction not only allows turn but reduces pace. If balanced cricket is the aim, and if batsmen are to face the full range of challenges that give cricket its fascination, we must sacrifice a certain amount of pace in order to provide grip.

Commentators often retreat from their predictions about how pitches will behave. However, although we might wish them to be a little less dogmatic at times, they need not feel ashamed. Even after the games had finished, reports on particular first class pitches in New Zealand, from three sources — one from each of the two captains and one from the umpires — were frequently found to be mutually contradictory.

To obtain reliable measurements of pitch quality, I invented a device for firing balls into pitches at proper bowling angles (16° or 20°), and measuring the speed before and after landing, and the angle of bounce. The prototype gave much new information, some of which forms the basis of this chapter. An advanced form of the device, incorporating new research by Dr Colin Cook and myself, is now being developed at Victoria University of Wellington. Unlike bowling machines, it has the ability to make the ball land quite precisely on any chosen part of the ball's surface, such as 'across the seam', or with the seam pointing along the pitch, or on the smooth leather face.

In Chapter 15 we will talk about the potential advantages to the bowler who exploits the 'cross-seam' delivery. Information obtained with the pitch machine provides a solid basis for that advice. Some of these results, along with others, are set out in Table E, which reveals how the speed of the ball from the pitch is very much at the mercy of the friction of the surface.

A number of interesting comparisons can be made using these results. The Test match figures are from the Basin Reserve pitch where New Zealand played the West Indies in 1994. It was not so completely covered by dry grass as was the case with the pitches described earlier in this chapter.

The easily obtained — and totally concealable — pace variations available to those who bowl for the 'cross seam' lottery are obvious and quite enough to upset the timing of a well-set batsman. The figures for the damp club pitch would certainly back up the old phrase 'it's not coming on to the bat today'!

The other surfaces were chosen to show the clear influence of friction on pace. Five of the situations, the three soft club pitches and especially the two soft wallboard surfaces, involved not only friction but major deformation of the surface as the ball pushed down to make a crater. Some of the ball's energy was lost into causing those deformations. But the lesser slowing from the greased wallboard shows that sliding up out of the crater restores most of the pace. This is what happens when a firm turf pitch which is greasy on top still shows plenty of pace.

English bowlers, playing on the highly abrasive pitches of South Africa early this century, found they needed to bowl a fuller length because the ball came off more slowly. The friction

Table E   What helps to make a slow pitch ?

Speed loss from cricket balls fired at 90 km/h (56 mph) on to various natural and artificial surfaces at a normal bowling angle (16°)

Balls worn (w) or new (n), four-piece (4) or two-piece (2)

Ball	Landing area on ball	Surface	% Loss of speed
W4	Leather face	Coarse sandpaper	34.0
W4	Leather face	Soft wallboard (25 mm)	27.7
N4	Seam across	Soft turf club pitch	25.9
N4	Seam in line	Soft turf club pitch	22.0
N2	Seam across	Test match turf pitch	18.7
N4	Leather face	Soft turf club pitch	17.3
N2	Seam in line	Test match turf pitch	14.4
W4	Leather face	Solid aluminium plate	13.0
W4	Leather face	Soft wall board (greased)	12.5
N2	Leather face	Test match turf pitch	12.2
W4	Leather face	Aluminium plate (greased)	3.5

(Pitch research, Wilkins 1994-97)

experiments underline this. Good bowlers know that for every different pitch there is a proper length that is best for their stock ball. If spinners are getting turn then faster bowlers should be aware of the judgements that they must make.

Does this mean that faster bowlers will be less effective on such pitches and that they should discard their shorter deliveries? No. There are good reasons why such surfaces can be exploited by fast bowlers. Firstly the grip of pitch and ball for each other challenges faster bowlers to demonstrate their skills in cutting and/or twisting. Without swing from the shiny or the deliberately mutilated ball these are the skills of the great bowlers. The second reason, and one which is supported by research, is that there is a tendency for balls that grip more to come off the pitch at a steeper angle.

But if 'slow and low' being common, are frequently associated with only moderate grip, what length should medium and fast bowlers bowl on these pitches? Batsmen tell us the answer: they can't afford to risk playing back and being caught in front, or bowled by a low ball; we therefore make their constant forward play a little more risky by shortening our length a little. Having done that, the onus is on the bowler to bowl straight or get punished.

'Slow turner' is a common phrase. What about 'fast turner'? One wonders whether such a thing as a perfectly level fast turner exists.

Lost speed means lost energy. Science tells us that energy must go somewhere. Where has it gone? Although they may not realise it, every TV cricket watcher knows part of the answer. While the ball in the air might be spinning in all sorts of directions and at different rates of spin, I have seldom seen a ball leaving the pitch without topspin, unless perhaps it has acquired a little side-spin by catching the edge of the bat as it goes past. Here is the answer; some of the ball's speed energy has gone into giving the ball rotation energy.

No matter how fast the ball might be spinning (spins of up to 15 revs/sec have been recorded for cricket), a little simple arithmetic tells us that the surface of the ball is always moving around the ball at no more than about 8 km/h (5 mph), which is a lot slower than the speed of the ball through the air. The greater the grip of the ball on the pitch the more it 'catches' on the bottom and gets turned over. We will return to some of the interesting consequences of this in Chapter 25.

About five per cent of the total energy of a ball that lands on a good turf pitch goes into spin. Energy is proportional to the square of the speed. But rotation is not the only 'energy thief'. A delivery losing, say, 15 per cent of its speed up on to the bat will have lost about 28 per cent of its energy. If any confirmation was needed, these figures show that a full toss, a 'beam ball', can do a lot more damage than a rising ball. Of the 28% energy loss about five will have gone into rotation, another five will be lost into the ball and into the pitch, while the major loss of about twenty goes into friction as the ball skids on the surface.

Our results show that the bottom of the ball is never slowed enough to actually stop, but always skids to some extent, making skid marks that are normally around 30–50 mm and sometimes, on wet pitches, as long as 90 mm. The energy goes into wearing both the pitch and the ball.

If cricket balls were like super bouncing balls the stumps might need to be at least ten feet high. A superball dropped on to a hard surface will bounce to about 90 per cent of its original height. The USA standard tennis ball must bounce to 53–58 per cent, whereas the British standard for cricket balls requires them to bounce between 28 and 38 per cent.

For the standard bounce test on cricket balls they are dropped on to concrete. All the bounce comes from the ball; virtually none from the concrete. Likewise on turf; not only does all the bounce come from the ball and none from the turf, but the turf *can only take away bounce* in varying degrees. How then do we explain why this leather-covered object, with quite modest bounce properties, can sometimes come up off a good length to hit a batsman's gloves or his head, very often from softish damp surfaces, from which the ball, if dropped vertically, would hardly bounce at all ?

We will rule out bumps and assume that the pitch is flat. The explanation lies in the small depressions that are commonly made by balls landing on softer pitches. The ball, being harder than the pitch, pushes down and forward producing a little elongated crater, and is simply deflected up off the sloping end face of the crater. In other words it is not really a bounce at all, in the sense that the ball has been compressed and springs out again, but merely a *deflection* from a surface which was not hard enough to compress the ball very much for a genuine rebound.

Leaving aside softer pitches, what a variety we see even in hard turf pitches around the world; fast, slow, turning, little turn. And then there are the changes that pitches undergo, or are said to undergo, during a game. The sages of the media make a good living from peering and poking into pitches, but such reported observation, even when it is based on years of play at the highest level, has its limits. Hard numerical information, such as that on frictional effects, when it becomes available, must be accommodated. It has a number of interesting consequences which we must look at.

Because friction on hard pitches is a surface property, our attention, for the moment, can focus on what we see, and on what the ball feels, on the surface. The surface is accessible and, as groundsmen know, it is a relatively simple matter to manipulate it. The task for cricket is to protect diversity, and the full range of skills, and this requires at least some control over decisions made in the groundsman's office.

If friction slows the ball a little, then it follows that the very fastest pitches won't turn as much as slower pitches. Turn and pace are to some extent incompatible. The frequently slowish and turning pitches on the Indian sub-continent seem to fit this scenario.

Where does bounce fit into all this? ' Pace and bounce' is a well-used phrase; can the two ever be separated? A number of common situations invite us to separate them, but we don't seem to do it. A spinner getting a good deal of turn can sometimes make the ball hold and lift from a hard pitch; bounce but not pace. Another situation; the batsman plays back to the opening bowler; the ball, even though pitched shortish, slams into his pads low down and he is lbw; pace but not bounce. Information we are collecting in our current research tells us these two examples are not unusual, but in fact tend to be the norm. The trend we are finding is for balls bowled on to lower friction surfaces to come off lower and faster, and for those from higher friction surfaces to come off steeper but slower. Pitches with the best bounce need not be the quickest but, if they are hard, they are likely to give some encouragement to spinners.

It would be naive to expect cricket to mirror exactly the experience of tennis where grass courts tend to be lower and faster, while clay courts are slower and very bouncy. In tennis, pace and bounce definitely do not go together, but in cricket, the bounce of a harder ball, which is so much at the mercy of the complex properties of soil and clay, is less predictable.

Another variable is the ball itself. Careful bouncing tests designed to land balls on particular points on their surface show surprising variations. Cricket balls are by no means perfectly uniform spheres; another endearing thing about the game.

However, if pace and bounce cannot be divorced, some degree of separation seems to be called for. A warmed-up pace man is in full cry with the new ball. Because the wicket-keeper is standing well back, the bowler is said to be getting plenty of pace and bounce, or, as is more likely, that description is being applied to the pitch. But are we sure about this? Is the wicket-keeper back because of the bounce, or is it because of the carry? Maybe the bounce is relatively low, but the good pace means plenty of carry. Alternatively, on another pitch, he is back, not because of good pace, but because the bounce is so good that he must be there for the higher ball, even though it comes to him slower on the higher trajectory. We know that lesser or greater friction could bring about either of these two situations for a fast bowler. When we start looking carefully at the path of the ball through the air, the link between pace and bounce might not seem so strong.

Although a pitch that is taking some turn will generally not be the quickest, fast and medium pacers will be expected to get both cut and lift from it.

The words 'juice' and 'drying out' frequently accompany the familiar opening lines, 'a bit of life early on but settling down later'. First class pitches, these days covered against rain, are most often hard and quite dry from the beginning of the game to the end, whether or not the surface is grippy. A little late and light watering, just before the game, may make the grass slightly moist and in a state where it can respond for a very short time to any 'work' on the ball. These days such a response period, depending on moisture, appears to be non-existent in most cases. But, in the view of some commentators, this body of quite dry-looking hard soil, which has most likely been exposed to the sun since the early daylight hours will 'settle down' from the time the first ball is bowled. And if for some reason the starting time was different, it would start 'settling down' at that new time!

We will assume that it is not just that the bowlers are tiring, or that the batsmen are getting set. Pitches *do* appear to 'settle down'; so what is my point? Again the pitch machine provides the answer. Starting with a new ball on a hard turf pitch, and firing the same ball repeatedly into nearby spots on the pitch, I found that the ball began to come off slower and slower as it became more worn. Since all this took place within a few minutes it could not have been caused by changes in the pitch. And vertical dropping tests on concrete showed that there was no change in the bounce of the ball. Repeated on other pitches, and with balls of various degrees of wear, the results showed that 'settling down' is *wholly or partly the result of wear on the ball rather than a change in the pitch*. Repeated measurements with both old

and new balls showed old balls, on average, to came off about five percent slower than new balls. Batsmen get just that bit of extra time. These results suggest that, when talking about changes during an innings, we must pay more attention to the ball.

There is always a tug-of-war taking place in the best cricket. Pulling in one direction is the steadily increasing wear on the ball which makes it come off slower and therefore makes batting a little easier. Pulling in the other direction is the increasing turn available to bowlers, both cutters and slower spinners, who have the ability to spin the wearing ball. The batsman will have a little more time to play shots, but also new problems to overcome within that time. If we interfere in any way with this subtle and essential source of tension within the contest between bat and ball we do so to the detriment of the game. Removing the ability of a pitch surface to wear and grip the ball is a gross interference.

'Speedy is about to take the second new ball. The better bounce will help him but, on the other hand, the ball will come faster off the bat.' Another subject for our little witch hunt!

We have broken the automatic link between pace and bounce.

The ball will be coming off faster because it is less worn, but the odds are that it is coming off *lower rather than higher*. We must question the assumption that older balls bounce less. Results we have obtained, both by the vertical bounce test, and from balls fired at cricket angles, show that *worn balls bounce just as much as new balls*. The balls were not soft and ragged, but moderately worn from games of 50 to 80 overs played on partially grassed pitches.

Therefore we have no reason to believe that a new ball comes higher off the pitch or faster off the bat. If the batsman feels that there is something better about stroking the new ball, then it can only be due to it coming *on to the bat* faster.

Cricketers must analyse their own experiences in the light of these findings. New Zealand opener, Bryan Young, nearing his century in 1995 at

Napier, played back to place the second new ball behind point, but was caught at third slip. He had played this shot safely all day throughout the life of the first new ball. It would be easy to say the ball bounced higher but this is not what TV viewers saw. Rather, it came on *faster* while he was still turning the bat over in the stroke: the bat had not reached the angle required to keep the ball down. If Young had seen the ball bouncing higher he would have been warned, but it didn't. This tells batsmen that they must be extra vigilant in picking up the less obvious danger from a new ball. Though he sees it approaching through the air *before landing* at the same speed as the old one, it will show its new pace only at the very last fraction of a second *after landing*, in the few feet between the pitch to the bat. The legions of batsmen going out to mistimed shots of all types, especially hooks and pulls, may wish to reassess phrases like 'climbed on to him' or 'got up' in terms of pace rather than bounce.

Against Sri Lanka in 1993, after New Zealand's opening bowlers wasted the new ball, slowish off-spinner Dipak Patel came on and surprised the batsmen who had been playing him comfortably during the earlier part of the innings. A commentator put this down to increased bounce, but the real reason was increased pace. Previously he had been bowling with the old worn ball; now, for some of the ways the new shiny ball would land, it would experience less friction and come off quicker. Patel was not the type of bowler who could add to his zip by means of the top-spin which is available to many other spinners, especially leg-spinners. In this case there was a gain to be made from sacrificing some turn for increased pace: a reminder that success in bowling depends ultimately on giving the batsman as little time as possible in which to adjust his stroke. If something needs to be sacrificed to that end, then so be it. In this case it would also help to have information about the degree to which the seam on the old ball had been flattened.

In the light of what we now know, what do we make of the phrase 'two-paced pitch'? No one would ever claim that a turf pitch is totally uniform like some giant strip of steel rolling off a production line; and, apart from anything the bowler might do, balls have their *own* variability. Even the best pitches can never be totally uniform. The area of pitch that any one delivery contacts might be as small as 20 mm wide and 30 mm long. We can never be sure that every little patch of that size has the same frictional effect on the ball as every other patch of the same size. Soil can never be guaranteed to dry out uniformly, or have uniform solidity or abrasiveness. Nor can grass cover ever be totally uniform. By its very nature, right down to the smallest blade of grass or tiny patch of exposed soil, cricket is a game of the variable and the unexpected; always a challenge, even for the greatest of batsmen.

But even if the pitch was perfectly uniform, we now have several reasons why a ball could come off at different heights and speeds, reasons which have nothing to do with pitch quality. We have seen how the ball is affected by how it lands, across the seam, along it, or off it. Experience tells us that balls cut or spun vigorously, provided they grip to some extent, tend to kick a bit. Balls themselves are not perfectly uniform. Both variable bounce and variable pace, or rather, variable loss of pace on pitching, could be the work of a resourceful bowler. In Chapter 15 we will look at how the bowler can add these valuable weapons to his armoury.

Research continues on all these factors. It would be rash to claim that we know it all. Cricketers pay large sums of money for the preparation of pitches. Without demanding uniformity, they are entitled to demand quality within flexible standards appropriate to the level at which they play.

14

CUTTING, ROLLING AND SPINNING

The sun shines, the wicket is friendly, the ball is showing a little wear, and the opening bowlers, hoping for swing, are merely bowling the batsmen into form. The great pioneer of inswing, J. B. King, helps us realise that the bowler relying solely on swing has not much of a future:

We must always remember that the ball that curves is just an adjunct to the stock in trade of a good bowler. It is a very valuable weapon; but first the bowler must be able to hit the wicket with a good length ball, to turn it from the pitch, and at times to send it down with a deceptive change of pace.... If he always curves, a good batsman will find him just as easy to play as the man who bowls perfectly straight.[1]

C. G. Macartney (1886–1958), the dominant Australian batsman of the early twentieth century, dismissed mere swingers:

Since its introduction, bowlers have sacrificed the natural spin for the swing, and nowadays we find ourselves possessing more of the straight up and down type of performer than the clever bowler of former days.[2]

All fast and medium-pace bowlers aiming to be something other than batsmen's fodder, unless they have exceptional pace, must enter the world of cut, change of pace, change of angle, change of grip, including cross-seam bowling, and, if possible, twist. There is no hiding place. A bowler with too narrow a range of skills will be exposed sooner or later, especially on better pitches.

The often-quoted comment that spinners take a long time to develop probably applies to all bowlers, fast and slow, who acquire these skills.

Alec Bedser was well established in his career before he achieved confidence with twist, his leg-spinner. How many fast or medium pace bowlers are complete with these skills today, if not in twisting, at least in cutting? But if bowlers do go to the trouble to learn, let's hope that groundsmen realise that if their pitches are frictionless it will all slip away.

A young bowler thrust into a high grade of cricket must attempt to reconcile two potentially incompatible lives: in one he seeks consistency, using a modest range of variations; in the other he experiments, practises, and unveils new variations in less important matches, until such time as these are fit to parade at large.

To read a respected spin bowler and author, Ian Peebles,[3] describing Bill O'Reilly's leg-break as having been 'rolled' may come as something of a surprise. Perhaps every bowler, written off as 'just a roller', will now emerge to stand proudly alongside 'The Tiger', especially as Peebles goes on to attach the label 'superlative quality' to those same leg-breaks.

We can look at some of the other terms used to describe various types of bowling. Does it matter if the language of cricket lacks precision? If Richie Benaud writes a chapter[4] on the 'over-the-wrist' bowler, comparing him with one who 'merely bowls with his fingers', we all think we know what he means.

Fast bowlers bowl cutters, so we are told; people who had been watching Derek Underwood bowl for twenty years said he bowled cutters too. But as we saw earlier, he himself said he did not bowl cutters. Besides, spinning over the wrist is anatomically impossible. Nearly all bowling is done from above the wrist; some spinners deliver a ball from below the wrist, while others deliver it from alongside the wrist. As for the so-called finger-spinners, are we to assume that off-spinners and 'orthodox' left-handers would bowl just as well with their wrists encased in plaster of Paris?

Finger movement combined with the forward hinging of the wrist would not be capable of generating the amount of spin obtained by the best bowlers, were it not for the extensive rotation provided by the forearm and upper arm. The hand, held out palm upwards in front of the body, should be capable of rotation through at least three-quarters of a circle (270°). The muscles and bones of the *forearm* give the hand most of the twist required for spin bowling. This is obvious when we try to twist the hand while resting the arm on a flat surface, and holding down the forearm near the wrist. In all bowling, spin and non-spin, the main function of the wrist is to provide a backward or a forward hinging movement, not a twist.

Bowling is difficult enough without it being confused by vague description. Why seal off various types of bowling into separate compartments, when it is infinitely more interesting and productive to regard all bowling as one basic technique, upon which numerous possible variations can be grafted. Obscure language makes it difficult to understand the methods used by bowlers of the past, the best of whom have often defied categorisation.

There are only two basically different methods for spinning a cricket ball. Either it is spun out of a grip involving two opposite sides of the ball, or it is pushed away, as the pressure of the fingers, biased a little to one side, moves down and/or around the ball against its own inertia. The two types of delivery are illustrated in many of the photographs in this book. Cricket has already realised the need to distinguish them by applying different names; Nyren's 'twist' for the former, and the more modern term 'cut' for the latter. They both involve 'spinning' but, for that very reason, 'spinning' does not allow us to distinguish between the two in the many situations where it is useful to make the distinction.

Of less importance for cricketers is our habit of saying that a bowler is 'getting spin' when we mean 'turning the ball off the pitch'.

Figure 40*a* illustrates the fast and medium-pace off-cutter, and Figure 40*b* the leg-cutter. In its 'pure' form, cutting involves finger movement against one side of the ball without any twist being applied from the other side. The bowler's task is to pull the fingers down off the back of the ball, to the right for an off-cutter, or to the left for a leg-cutter, while at the same time sending it straight off in the direction of the arrow. The position and spin of the ball in the air should be checked using a video or a marked ball. In Figure 40*a* the first finger along the stitching will apply most of the back-and-side-spin, while in Figure 40*b* it is the second finger. The angle of the seam to the flight may not appear to be very great in the photos, but it is about 30°.

Larger angles can be used, and a bigger angle will give more turn, but the larger they are the less is the control, since the fingers cutting down along the seam would be required to come down more to the side, while at the same time attempting to deliver the ball straight. These are also potential outswingers (*a*) and inswingers (*b*).

Because these are two of the most important types of delivery for faster bowlers, they demand great attention and plenty of experimentation to find the most effective combination of seam angle and finger action.

While these actions should pose no great difficulties for the serious bowler who is prepared to practice hard, he needs to see clearly what he is doing, and where it stands in relation to swing bowling, on one hand, and to fast and medium pace spinning (cut, not twist) on the other.

What exactly is the cutter doing? He is releasing the ball at a good angle for swing, and because his fingers come off the ball slightly to one side or the other, making the ball rotate not only backwards but a little to one side or the other, he is applying spin which has the potential to make the ball turn one way or the other off the pitch.

Put another way, the bottom of the ball is not

only rotating forward but, in the case of the leg cutter, somewhat from off to leg. Therefore the ball will, if it grips, turn from leg to off. For the off-cutter the bottom of the ball is moving forward but also from leg to off, therefore the turn will be from off to leg. We must admit that most of the spin on these balls is 'wasted' in back-spin and only a fraction of it is available to turn the ball sideways. Nevertheless it works, and it is worth looking at why this is so.

Since, from the earlier chapters, we are now clear about swing, we should be ready for the possible sparring match which takes place when the flight path of the swinging ball takes it on a curve, say, heading for fine leg, while, after pitching, the turn-from-cut attempts to take it back the other way, to the off.

It is not just a matter of which gets the upper hand. Some days one or the other, or even both, may not even show up! Maybe everything is right for swing, but there is no grip in the pitch: the batsman has only swing to worry about. But if swing has gone, because of bad air or a worn ball, and the pitch is gripping, then what remains is turn-from-cut. If on another day they both turn up, life for the batsman becomes more precarious.

To say that a cricket ball can only move under two possible influences, either the influence of the air, or the influence of the pitch, is boringly obvious. Why then are commentators on the game frequently so careless, or thoughtless, or perhaps so unobservant, that they don't tell us where the change of direction took place, and frequently don't appear to give it even a passing thought?

Let us assume that our commentator is up to the job and we hear 'Speedy is not getting much movement in the air today, but a certain amount off the pitch'. Assuming that Speedy has all the necessary skills and the ball is new, but the air is not right for swing, why does this relatively inefficient-looking method work, especially, as often happens, on a new grassy pitch?

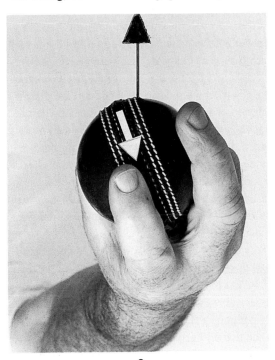 

a b

Fig. 40 Fast and medium pace off-cutter (*a*) and leg-cutter (*b*). The seam may be held at bigger angles than shown here, but control at speed will be more difficult the more the fingers move off the side of the ball during release, rather than coming down nearer the back of it.

89

Faster bowlers cut their fingers down off the back of the ball quite quickly and the potential exists for quite a high spin rate, probably higher than many spinners attain. The best bowlers will do everything they can to make this back-and-side rotation as great as possible. Both the stitching and the fingers need attention. The stitching should be cleaned regularly with the thumb nail running the full circumference on each side of each row. The well cleaned stitching has more chance of gripping the pitch. Nothing slippery or oily such as hair oil or sunscreen or excessive sweat should be on the fingers. However, a little moisture, to make the fingers just a little sticky, will help.

As for the green grassy pitch, it has more grip than many realise. A few years ago, during research on the friction of pitches, I measured the amount of pull needed to move a sledge across various pitches. The greener the grass the more the pull that was needed. I should have known this anyway from my boyhood days sledging down the grassy hills of the South Island; late summer dry brown grass meant real speed. Mike Atherton[5] tells of the mistake Mike Gatting made in 1992 in putting Middlesex in on a grassy pitch where they went on to make 456 for 3. The grass happened to be dead and gripless. But Atherton admits to his own mistake when, in 1994, he batted first on a pitch without much grass, not realising that the grass which was present was quite juicy. Will captains in the third millennium carry portable friction meters or will they just have to learn to read the signs a little better?

We return to the question of why faster bowlers can turn the ball by this apparently inefficient method at a time when slower spinners probably won't be asked to bowl. The implication that slower spinners would not be effective is, of course, not necessarily true. Plenty of spinners have been brought on early on all sorts of pitches and have done well; but swing and pace stand for onslaught, and that is normally where to start.

However, the faster cut-spin merchant does have an advantage over the slower spinner because he fires the ball down faster into the surface and makes the ball grip through sheer downward force. Grip which is improved slightly because the force may be enough to depress a little crater and thus increase the area of the contact between the ball and the pitch surface; a significant factor if the surface is slightly moist, and an advantage for the taller bowler. All this is related to the ability of a tall fast bowler to exploit any weakness in a pitch surface and get lift by 'going through the top'. Covering pitches cannot prevent the diffusion of moisture from the surrounding earth. Soils and clays will vary in the rate at which they allow this migration of water from outside the square. Even on a hard pitch, where there is not even the lightest mark betraying permanent deformation of the surface, the area of contact must be greater from a faster delivery because the ball itself will squash down a little flatter during impact.

On the day when swing takes a back seat, the bowler, not relying on sheer pace, hopes that his grip and his action will bring him some reward from cut.

But why, on another day, does the new ball bowler find that swing wins out and there is no turn from cut? Good swing air obviously. Maybe there is no grip for the ball on the pitch; maybe the bowler is not good at giving the ball a sufficient amount of back-and-side rotation, or maybe the swing is so dominant that it keeps the ball on its original curving parabola right through the bounce, at too big an angle for any turn to ever take it back in the opposite direction. A combination of any of these is possible; but the most common is the pairing of good swing and not much grip on the pitch.

One of the great sights in fast bowling is the ball that both swings *and* cuts: the off-cutter that starts as an outswinger, and the leg-cutter that starts as an inswinger; deadly deliveries that need smooth air, a shiny ball which will swing, and a pitch that will grip.

If the above description of cutting, and the relation between cutting and swing, seems to be excessively detailed, then I ask the reader to listen again to the words that one frequently hears from cricketers and media commentators. TV viewers see the ball swing to the off, pitch, and then carry on to be taken by the wicket-keeper in front of first slip.

'There is some dampness around this morning and Joe Speedy is getting the ball to move around in the air and off the pitch.' Or: 'The ball is moving a little bit off the seam. You would expect that from the overhead conditions.'

We should be grateful that they left out the humidity bit, but the remaining vagueness, the failure to put the dampness in the ground and/or the grass, *which is the only place where it can have any effect on a cricket ball,* except rain drops sitting on a ball and upsetting the air flow (an experiment I carried out in the wind tunnel), shows that the old bad habits die hard. Nothing that viewers saw in those deliveries indicated that anything noteworthy happened when the ball contacted the pitch. Why then mention 'movement off the pitch' at all? To do so devalues those balls that *do* change direction off the pitch. One wonders whether those who make these clearly untrue comments are looking for the true sign of deviation off the pitch, following swing, and that of course, is normally deviation back in the reverse direction, or at least a straightening up against the swing.

The prize must go to 'There's quite a bit of *late movement off the pitch'*, especially as it was used by one commentator to describe a ball that could be seen to swing all the way! Perhaps the only way to get that person to think about what he said would be to ask him what he would expect to see if there was *early* movement off the *pitch*! Even ex-Test players are sometimes careless about distinguishing between deviation in the air and off the pitch. Can we hope that media commentators do not feel obliged to make a definitive statement about every delivery?

'Whacker moved forward to that ball from Speedy which was well pitched up on his leg stump, but moved late off the pitch and left him groping.' Whacker was not the only one groping. Speedy had bowled nothing but outswingers and straight balls until then, and when this particular

ball was viewed in slow motion, it proved to be another outswinger, and one which swung so little, just enough to beat the bat, that it appeared to swing late. The ball did not deviate off the pitch. Because, at full speed, it is so often impossible to tell whether the deviation is in the air or off the pitch, I would like to think that TV viewers or radio listeners prefer honesty to guesswork. Whether or not a particular bowler can move (turn) the ball off the pitch is surely an important fact to report; important enough to warrant trying to get it right.

There are no limits to the lengths to which some will go in attempting the wholly wrong-headed linking of moisture with swing. One recent version involved 'moisture rising out of the pitch'; this from a hard dry Test match pitch! In Chapter 7 we saw that there is no way moisture can affect swing except through the cooling that takes place on a moist outfield, not on a dry pitch.

'Seaming' is another term for our witch hunt. What does it mean? Tags like 'seaming around' and 'seaming away', when tested against what we see on our TV screens, appear to allow for anything and everything in swing and cut. A little careful observation tells us that 'seaming', as used by many people, is more of a cop-out than an informed comment. Among its other deficiencies, the phrase 'the ball is seaming around today' appears to make many of the skills that we have been talking about in this book somewhat unnecessary, because it implies that the bowler does not *do* a great deal except stand back and watch!

Description based on careful observation can be improved, but what might be more difficult to get rid of is the notion that a ball will deviate sideways off the pitch just by landing more or less vertically on the stitching: landing 'seam up', 'hitting the seam'. If this was true every club bowler who can release the ball by bringing his fingers straight down the back of it with the seam vertical would be bowling 'seamers'. Yet how many times do we see, in all grades of cricket from club to Test match, the ball delivered and landing that way, and yet nothing untoward happens?

Some commentators go to great lengths to point out that the seam is vertical and that this is the secret of 'movement off the pitch'. But viewers listening to this frequently see nothing but swing in the air. Why therefore don't commentators inform us properly and say that it is best to have the seam vertical for swing? They can be excused for not telling us what angle the vertical seam is to the pitch, although this is frequently clear enough for all to see, because we know that even if the seam is pointing straight, the uncertainty of air flow or the wind can effectively do the job on its own. When we see *swing* from a well-delivered ball with the seam in the upright position, it is insulting not only to the viewers but to the bowler, to say that 'it moved away off the seam'.

The stitching protrudes probably no more than one millimetre from the surface of the ball, which,

at least in the case of good quality, undamaged and unsoaked balls, is close to spherical. In some eyes the claimed cause of the deviation is the box-falling-over-sideways-off-its-edge idea. But this is simply not possible. If it did happen that way it should be more pronounced on hard, perfectly flat pitches, and impossible on softer surfaces where the seam can penetrate. We know that the latter is simply not the case.

Do people who praise bowlers for 'hitting the seam' know that seaming (deviation off the pitch), comes either wittingly or unwittingly from *something that the bowler has done with his fingers to give the ball some sideways movement?* It may be time to ask them.

Cutting a new ball does require the seam, but it is for grip in the fingers and on the pitch. *On its own, the seam does not make the ball deviate off the pitch.* Cutting an older ball may involve the

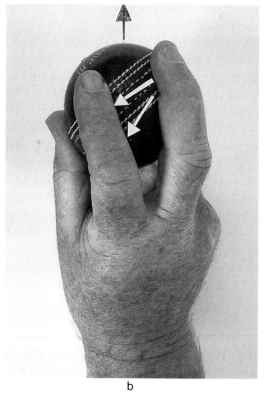

a   b

Fig. 41 Grips where cutting is giving way to twisting: *a* spinning in from the off through at least some twist between the first and second fingers: *b* spinning from the leg through some twist between the first and third fingers.

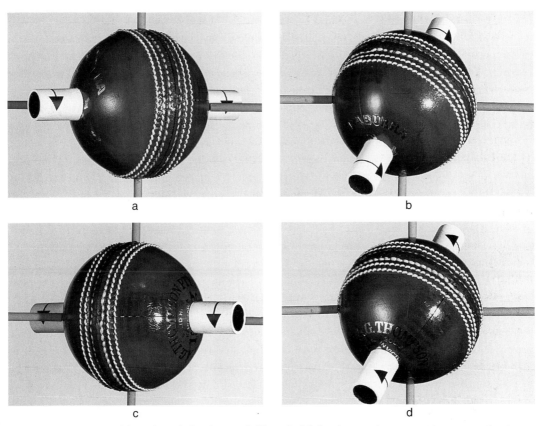

Fig. 42 Arm balls; *a* and *b* from the right-hander; *c* and *d* from the left-hander; *a* and *c* are 'pure' swingers with no spin-swerve; *b* and *d* will only spin-swerve.

grip, both in the fingers and on the pitch, of the larger worn leather surface of the ball.

What about the commonly heard description: 'There is seam movement today in the air and off the pitch'? Readers will know that the seam, in response to the skill of the bowler, affects the air flow around the ball, and that, on contact with the pitch, again in response to the skill of the bowler, the seam helps the ball to turn. Why not therefore just say 'Speedy is making the ball swing and cut today'? Give credit where credit is due.

'Twist', where spin is applied to both sides of the ball, and 'cut' to describe a push against one side, is a useful distinction, but by no means the whole story. What about the cutter who starts experimenting with his fingers further apart until he reaches a grip which is indistinguishable from that of a slow off- or leg-spin bowler? To some

degree or other he is now able to exert at least some *pressure across the ball, from one finger to the other, which is the essence of twist*. Even fast bowlers can, and do, employ the whole range of finger positions from cut to twist.

If young bowlers, looking to the great performers of the past for clear instructions about cutting, are confused, it is the existence of this continuum between cut and twist which is the most likely reason. As we have seen, the 'pure' ends of the spectrum are straightforward enough. But when famous bowlers talk about 'rolling the fingers over the ball' for cut, we need to ask a few questions. How far apart are their fingers? If they are far enough apart for twist, do they feel pressure between the two points? If they are not 'twisting' how far away from the back of the ball are their fingers when they come down? Whatever is the answer, we can rest assured that there is little future in merely adding 'rolling the fingers over the ball' to the normal techniques of swing and 'pure' down-the-back-and-side cut. If a bowler feels that good control is under threat he should be guided by his instinct and return to what he feels is sound technique.

Balls delivered from the grips shown in Figure 41 will have the seam fluttering around at various angles; an advantage when swing is not desired and an in-built source of variation on landing, depending on whether the contact is on the seam or on the smooth leather.

A warning: some coaches give the impression that off-cutting and leg-cutting is a matter of rolling one's fingers down over one side of the ball or the other. If this is what we assume to be cutting, and not twisting, it is in danger of giving the bowler an impossible task. How can one control pushing a ball straight down the pitch at high speed while sliding one's fingers off the side of it? I suggest that the chance of maintaining accuracy would be minimal unless most of the push is behind the ball, as for the type of cut deliveries we have discussed. Because this impossibly extravagant version of cut is basically a push from one side it has limited control. We looked at a perfectly feasible and controllable method for cut earlier in this chapter.

Only when it comes to twist, or some suitable intermediate between cut and twist, can the fingers begin to go off the side of the ball. Twist, with at least some two-point contact, offers the chance of much better control. If a cutter is to be any good it must be fairly quick, otherwise the spin on the ball is not good enough and the fairly moderate amount of turn that is achieved on most pitches happens too slowly to worry good batsmen.

Maybe, lurking in this spectrum between twist and cut, there are imposters, say slow off-spin or slow non-chinamen left hand bowlers, who we all see going through the motions, but not turning the ball very much. Are they really twisting, as they should be at that pace, or are they too far towards the cutting end of the action spectrum to have any chance of ever developing into attacking bowlers unless they change their spinning action?

We saw earlier that the principal movement of the hand at the wrist is not a twisting but a hinged movement in a forward or backward direction. What then should the bowler do with the wrist-hinge when preparing to deliver the ball; cock it forwards in a cripple-like inward curl, or bend it back with the palm of the hand facing the sky? Bowlers in fact do both. But whichever they employ, the hand always hinges forwards towards the batsman at the final flick, cunningly concealed slower balls excepted. This wrist snap is one of the movements that bowlers must not allow to slow down as they become tired.

The major differences which we have been describing are easily discernible when one watches a bowler in action. They form the basis for the common but erroneous classification of some bowlers as wrist spinners of the leg-break or chinaman type. But such a label is no better than many of the others, because among slow to medium pace spinners there is a whole spectrum of actions ranging from extreme wrist curling to no curling at all. The faster spinners don't need the inward-coiled hand to gain pace or spin, although some may use it.

Bending the hand back but with the palm now facing the batsman is of course mainly associated with fast bowlers or off-spinners, as an examination of action photographs will show. There is no reason why such a bent position should be adopted at the beginning of the swing as is done by some faster bowlers. More freedom may be experienced if the wrist is bent back nearer the end of the delivery. The inward hand curlers, however, find it easy and convenient to adopt such an attitude early in the swing.

C. S. Marriott recommends the inwardly-cocked wrist to fast bowlers as well as slow:

I strongly recommend crooking up the wrist as you run up. It hides the ball from the batsman, and it will increase the effect of any natural wrist flick you possess as your arm goes over, a most valuable gift because it makes pace off the pitch, not only for spin bowlers, but for fast bowlers as well. E. A. McDonald, who ran up to bowl with his wrist bent up, had the most gorgeous wrist flick at the top of his delivery. There lay the secret of his terrific pace off the wicket. Wrist flick has evidently worked in the same striking way for many of the greatest bowlers: in 1963 we saw a magnificent example of Charlie Griffith, the West Indian. Keith Miller, who himself bowls with a pronounced flick of the wrist, wrote admiringly of Griffith's tremendous pace and lift off the pitch, which he rightly ascribed to his bowling with a 'full flick of the hand', which is the same thing exactly.[6]

Marriott's advice, as applied to faster bowlers, is understandable only if we see three stages in the process; an inward curling, followed by an uncurling prior to, but part of, the wind-up for a vigorous final flick in which the palm faces the batsman.

Spofforth, speaking of the different grips for concealing change of pace, says:

It is not the slightest use unless you learn to hide it. The sole object of variation is to make the batsman think the ball is slower or faster than it really is. The way to do this is most difficult to put down in writing but very easy to show or acquire. I have always considered the best plan is to hold a small portion of the ball and get the impetus that sends the ball forwards from one side. By doing this your arm will go through the air just as swiftly for a slow ball as for a fast one, which is very apt to mislead the batsman, and it is another advantage that the ball is likely to break.

The 'small portion' grip employed by Spofforth and commonly used by modern bowlers (the 'half-ball' grip) is never likely to encase much less than half of the ball. Since the ball now lies closer to the wrist than in the normal grip and because there is no way that the fingers can flick down across the back of it at release, the escape route can only be by means of a relatively slow roll out from under the left side of the forefinger. Other grips for change of pace involve holding the ball in or near the palm or, in a version of the baseball pitcher's knuckle ball we discussed in Chapter 6, releasing it from a grip in which the finger-tips point down into the ball.

To remove doubt and vagueness we now deal with the 'arm-ball', the ball often described as 'going with the arm'.

Bowled by a right-hander, the arm-ball curves from leg to off, and from a left-hander, off to leg. Since the arm naturally swings across the body in each of these respective directions during delivery, we see where the phrase originates. But this sweep of the arm does not guarantee that the ball will curve in the same direction. The right-hand leg-spin bowler swings his hand across the body from right to left, but the ball, which is usually delivered with the axis of spin tilted down at the back to some extent, does not go with the arm, but swerves in the reverse direction (Fig. 42d).

The phrase 'going with the arm' therefore implies that one or both of the following conditions must be present. One of these for a right-hand bowler is the seam pointing towards the slips (Fig. 42a), or from a left-hand bowler, to fine-leg (Fig. 42c). In other words, nothing more than simple outswingers or in-swingers.

The other type of arm-ball is a backward-spinning ball with the axis of spin tilted down to the rear on one side, and therefore swerving to one side or the other (Figs 42b and d). Therefore one type of arm-ball is a swinger and the other a swerver.

Arm-balls are 'natural' deliveries only insofar as the hand has a tendency to slide down the right side of the ball, in the case of a right-hand bowler, and the left side in the case of the left-hander.

Bowlers employing arm-balls generally hope to minimise the turn in the reverse direction which may accompany such deliveries. The various degrees of backward rotation (some of which are shown in Figure 42) can be reduced by releasing the ball from fingers splayed out wide on either side of the seam. The technique is the same as that available to faster bowlers and was discussed earlier.

The interests of good bowling are best served if we resist the temptation to put labels on twisting. The so-called finger-spinners will also rotate the hand while they use their fingers, and the so-called wrist-spinners will use many of the same actions perhaps to a greater degree in most cases. Fast spinners are not generally described as wrist-spinners, simply because the action of bending and straightening, to the extreme degree shown by some slow bowlers, is simply too difficult to carry out quickly enough. In fact, *it is quite unnecessary for the faster spinners to indulge in such actions because, for them, the whole complex of finger and arm movements occurs at such a speed that they are able to generate excellent spin with little wrist-hinging.*

O'Reilly's action was quick enough to provide a more than adequate rotation rate without any other contortions. Peebles' own leg-break at a brisk pace is described as having involved very little bend at the wrist.

Another versatile performer, Tom Wass (1873–1953), a genuinely fast bowler who could bowl leg-spin, is described by C. B. Fry as follows:

He obviously uses his fingers to produce the spin. At present his fast leg-break must be regarded as a curiosity. He turns his hand over as he delivers the ball, somewhat as does the slow leg-break bowler. Bowling at full pace on a good wicket he is sometimes able to impart a genuine finger-spin to the ball, which makes it break from the leg, the width of the wicket: this ball is quite distinct from that which is described as going with the bowler's arm; it is a genuine leg-break.[7]

In spite of Fry's puzzled description of Wass' grip as natural for an off-break, the presence of the first finger on one side and the third finger on

the other side, as seen in a photograph of Wass, is none other than the most commonly used grip for leg-spin.

Derek Underwood's protestation 'I am not a cutter' has also been mentioned earlier. One would hope that his exposure of the profound and widespread misunderstanding of his bowling, which he suffered, will go some way towards promoting a more informed appreciation of the bowler's art in future. In his autobiography[8] Underwood says that after two seasons with Kent, in which he bagged a total of 202 wickets (the youngest player to take 100 wickets in a debut season), people began to complain that his bowling style and action were not right. Twelve years and 1300 wickets later they were still saying it. Such was the criticism, that he was persuaded to try many times to change his action to imitate a classic model.

Because he bowled faster than the classic model, Underwood had difficulty persuading people to regard him as a spinner. It would be difficult to find a more telling demonstration of how some members of the cricket fraternity can lose sight of the rich variety of skills provided by bowlers of the past. Because his attack was not based on flight to lure batsmen down the wicket, he did not regard himself as an 'orthodox' spinner, an opinion which prompts me, for this and other reasons, to suggest that the term 'orthodox spinner' is meaningless.

Underwood contrasts his freedom from sore and split spinning fingers with the trouble experienced by bowlers who use:

... violent finger action in order to make the ball turn ... I use the word 'violent' deliberately because I do give the ball a tweak with my fingers, which is why I say I am not a cutter. At the same time I do employ part of the technique of a cutter by adding to the tweak a dragging motion across the ball as my arm comes over prior to the moment of releasing the ball.

He goes on to describe his bowling as slow to

slow-medium left-arm spin. Underwood did not need 'violent' finger action; his hand twisted rapidly enough to set the ball rotating at a rate which was at least as great as that of slower action bowlers who were forced to compensate by using an apparently more rapid finger action.

The fairly narrow range of variations in pace that Underwood employed prompted Mike Brearley to suggest that in Pakistan he should bowl slower to get more turn. Underwood tried this with disappointing results, losing both his turn, his elusive flight and his accuracy. In his account of this, Brearley admitted bewilderment.

Curiously for so marvellous a spinner,

Underwood has always found that he tends to lose so much of his zip when he bowls appreciably slower than usual. His range of pace needs to be small to be most productive.[9]

There is really nothing curious about this. The amount of spin is frequently linked to the speed with which the arm comes over. Slow down one part, such as the arm coming over, and the whole sequence of spinning movements can also slow down, resulting in less spin. With practice, the spinning movements can be uncoupled from the pace-generating movements to some extent in order to be able to bowl a range of variations.

15
COMING TO GRIPS

Grip is less of a problem when the ball is worn. C. J. Kortright (1871–1952), one of the fastest bowlers in the history of the game, interviewed in 1948, said:

> *Perhaps one of the greatest differences between modern and old-time bowling lies in the attitude towards the new ball and the method of gripping it. Personally, I didn't worry a great deal about how I held the ball in relation to the seam as long as I got a firm grip on it, and I think most of my contemporaries felt the same. We wanted to be accurate, and to make the ball move a little off the pitch through finger action. For that reason, fast bowlers often roughened a new ball by rubbing it in the dirt, to obtain a good grip. Now bowlers dirty their clothes in efforts to keep the ball shiny, but I feel sure they do not control it so well.*[1]

It was not that bowlers were unable to swing the ball in those days, as J. B. King demonstrated with his fast inswingers. Whether the balls they used were made in such a way as to be capable of swinging as much as today's balls is a question answerable only by finding some century-old new balls and measuring their swing force in a wind tunnel. Kortright and his contemporaries devoted their energies to priming the more enduring weapon of spin at pace.

Why, when pitches these days are generally not very responsive to spin, have cricket administrators removed from bowlers the right to improve their grip by rubbing the ball on the ground? Dull leather is not only better gripped in the fingers, but would also be capable of a better grip on the pitch, a small but nevertheless welcome pay-back which bowlers could expect for having to put up with covered pitches. For umpires it would be a simple matter to ensure that the process went no further than removing shine, and that both sides of the ball were rubbed.

For swing, we noted earlier, the way the ball is gripped is not, on its own, sufficient to guarantee success. The classic coaching book photographs are merely starting points for careful trials to ensure that these angles are maintained in the air. Depending on the results, the grip is altered to compensate for the distortions introduced by the individual action.

Other skills worth developing in this early stage are the ability to produce a slow seam wobble for experiments with late swing, the whole area of cut and twist, and the skills of change of pace.

Tom Cartwright, a master swing bowler, said:

> *The key to all movement of the ball is what you do with your wrist. Above the shoulder it's the only thing I alter each ball. On a wicket which gives some help to bowlers of my type...*
>
> *I can usually do something with the ball either in the air or off the wicket in this country, but swing doesn't get many good players out, in spite of what happened in Massie's Test match at Lord's. That was a rarity.*[2]

What better tribute to the attention a bowler gave to that crucial stage in the delivery than R. S. Whitington describing the South African medium-pacer Joe Partridge:

> *Often when watching Joe through binoculars I was reminded of a champion rink bowler*

delivering upside down. Joe released the ball as tenderly and meticulously as any rink bowler, as any trout fisherman casting his fly.[3]

The description of Maurice Tate by John Arlott, also interpreted in the light of the principles we established earlier, shows how brilliantly Tate exploited all the possibilities available to the medium-pacer.

Bowling into the wind on a heavy seaside morning, he would make the ball dart and move in the air as if bewitched. The inswing and the outswing were there as a matter of course, but, as every man who batted against him at his best will testify, the ball would sometimes seem to begin to swerve and then straighten again before it struck the ground. Once it pitched, the bound was full of fire and, because Tate was a 'long-fingered' bowler, on a green-topped wicket the ball would sometimes strike back in the direction opposite to the swing. That is to say, an outswinger would become, in effect, an off-break off the pitch, or an inswinger a leg-break. Sometimes this happened to his 'cutter' because of the tendency of the cut break to swerve; but it could also happen to deliveries which were not 'cutters'. Tate, of course, like any other swing bowler, could only produce the swing deliberately, the subsequent tricks of the swung ball off the 'green 'un' happened, but not within the command of the bowler. When he bowled thus on a green wicket, no batsman in the world was too good to be his victim; the ball pitched and left an ominous black mark on the damp turf where it landed; that was the danger sign. Batsmen, when they saw Tate's mark in the pitch at Hove, resolved to play forward, hold their bats very straight and hope.[4]

The term 'long-fingered' fits well with Tate's deceptively fast pace off the pitch. This, and everything one reads about him, implies a wonderfully efficient 'long lever' between the ball and the wrist-hinge. It means heavy back-spin so that any fraction of the back-spin present as off- or leg-spin will be accentuated. Arlott, in this otherwise perceptive description, over-steps the bowling crease a little in asserting that swing bowlers only produce swing deliberately.

Does a fast bowler's thumb have any influence apart from supporting from below? It is usual to assume none, but it is possible that the effect of the ball sliding off the thumb, although it occurs before the longer fingers have their effect, does reduce the desired back- and side-spin slightly. Perhaps G. A. Wilson (1877–1962), a leading county fast bowler noted for his ability to curve the ball in the air, had discovered something valuable in his grip which involved the first and second fingers on or alongside the seam as normal, but the thumb well clear of the stitching at the bottom and on the smooth leather. Such a grip would minimise any effect of the thumb in counteracting the back-spin.

An interesting ploy for encouraging the seam to point the right way was that used by the England bowler Johnny Douglas. With the seam running more or less between his first and second fingers, he moistened his grip, on the second finger for the inswinger, and on the first finger for the outswinger. The moistening aided grip and retarded that side a little. It is worth trying, although it would not do away with the need to use a good, non-wobbling release technique.

Some grips for swing and cut, but emphasising cut, were illustrated in Chapter 14. The difference between grips designed to accentuate cut and those mainly for swing — which is probably quite slight in most cases — is that for cut, the grip, from the friction of the fingers as they come down off the back of the ball and slightly to the side, should be as good as can be obtained. Also for cut, the grip may trend towards the twisting type of grip as in Figure 41. But for swing, backward rotation is less important than the angle and the lack of wobble.

Various other grips are shown in Figure 43.

a

b

c

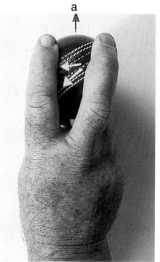

d

Fig. 43 Grips for swing and cut. In *a*, emphasising out-swing, the feeling is that the first finger is doing most of the guiding as it comes down in the direction of the arrow; in *b* it is the second finger that has the same role coming down to the left for inswing. In *c* with more emphasis on off-cut, the feeling is that the first finger is pushing a little to the right, and in *d* the second finger is pulling to the left for leg cut. Note that *a and b* have the fingers largely clear of the seam. If the pitch is responding to all four rotations, all four will turn the ball. The distinctions shown here are merely a slight emphasis one way one way or the other, towards swing or cut.

Numerous variations are both possible and useful, but they serve to illustrate the principles we have been discussing.

It is worth noting that if the fingers are to dominate, the more the hand points forwards at release, the earlier the thumb loses contact, and the less its effect in reducing back-spin. This may be another factor the 'long-fingered' fast bowler adds to the obvious advantages of long fingers in providing whip and good contact with the ball during the all-important release process.

J. B. King, as mentioned earlier, christened his pioneering inswinger 'the angler' after the curve or hook near the end of its path. He was careful to point out that it must be used only sparingly among other deliveries. The detailed account he gave of his methods is of great interest alongside our earlier discussion of swing and grip.

I found a new shiny cricket ball as favourable to a sharp hook but not necessary for it. I found I could hook or angle an old ball as effectively as a new one when conditions were right. My next problem was to examine these conditions, and by trial and error to identify those in my favour.

Some of them were beyond my control — for instance wind and weather. But I could study them and use those which helped most.

When I began bowling I liked best a following wind just strong enough to flutter the left corner of my shirt collar. Although later, when I felt completely co-ordinated and physically fit, I could swing the ball with a wind coming from any quarter. I preferred it coming from the batsman's off, and if I could make it to order, I would have a gusty wind sweeping up the gully to the right of second slip.

But still on some days I observed that the ball would swing more than on others; and, being by now convinced that I had in the angler a new and effective ball for occasional use, I began to make a careful study of what, in my bodily action, produced it.

The fundamental essential I found to be complete relaxation and co-ordination — an absence of any tension in arms, legs, or shoulders. This was necessary because my angler required a whole-souled follow-through of body and arm that would carry me well on down the wicket. When conditions were favourable I had the feeling that I was hurling myself after the ball towards the wicket.

In bowling the hooked or angled curve I found the second essential to be the height of the action and the grip used. I delivered the angler from full height straight above my head, indeed at times from slightly over the left shoulder. I held the ball consistently with the seam just between the first and second fingers, with the thumb opposed. The third finger was just in contact with the ball, and the fourth finger idle. It required only a very slight adjustment of this grip to make the ball go straight without any curve, or to give it enough spin for a slight off-break.

As to the control of the angler, I found it to lie in the wrist and the fingers. A strong yet flexible wrist, and long powerful fingers are desirable in every curve bowler; I found them quite essential for the control of the angler. Indeed the wrist and the first two fingers are the controlling factors in putting this ball where it should be. I felt the ball last, not with the side, but with the tips of the two fingers, and discovered that a delicate control of its flight depended on the final pressure. This finger pressure came at the end of a sharp downward flick of the wrist.[5]

We should be grateful to King for leaving us with such a precise description. It should be compulsory reading for all aspiring swing bowlers.

I am sure that King's advice is sound, but in case the reader should interpret this chapter as an infallible guide to bowling success, let him read of the many sad instances where coaches have interfered with naturally acquired actions. Bill O'Reilly's good judgement, or perhaps his stubbornness, saved him from one such interference. In his own words:

Arthur Mailey, then approaching the end of his career, was watching my first appearance at the SCG nets in 1926-27, where I bowled for the first time under the gaze of the New South Wales selectors. Himself a selector, Mailey drew me aside to show me the grip he used, fundamentally different from mine, with the ball held in the fingertips of his right hand. He suggested that I should imitate it if I ever hoped to be able to spin a leg-break noticeably. He went so far as to describe my own grip and to draw lines of similarity with the manner in which he himself held a golf club.

This advice appalled me. Here was a man trying to get me to dump all the lessons I had taught myself for nearly ten years: personal lessons which I had learned well enough to find myself in attendance at the nets that afternoon.

Not likely. I thanked Mr Mailey for the great interest he had taken in me but went on to say that I thought it was much too late to be fiddling about with an action which *even by that time had become second nature to me.*[6]

Among other things, Mailey obviously failed to appreciate that someone going through the complex action of bowling leg-spin at medium-pace, as did O'Reilly, does not need the finger action of a slower bowler in order to achieve the same spin rate.

Another argument against uniformity of grips, and a more fundamental one because it applies to all spinners, arises from the great variety of size and structure of the human hand.

In 1927, in one of the rare Law changes which assisted rather than hindered the bowler, the size of the Grade I ball was reduced from a circumference which had been between 22.9 cm (9 in) and 24 cm (9.5 in) maximum, to 22.4 cm (8.813 in) and a 22.9 cm (9 in) maximum.

The reduction of 4.8 mm (0.187 in) seems trivial, but the fact that the smaller ball does feel smaller and more compact in the hand, is a reminder that bowlers with larger hands must also feel the ball differently in their grasp. Arthur Mailey recognised the value of the smaller ball which was introduced during his active career: 'The ball was larger than it is now and consequently more difficult to grip unless you had a hand like a David Nourse or an Australian woodchopper.'[7]

Ray Illingworth is in no doubt:

All cricket balls are supposed to be the same size to a fraction of an ounce, but, believe me, they are not! I can tell certain makes with the ball in my hand and my eyes shut. That's how much difference there is in size. In fact, because of this variation in size, it does make my grip vary because I haven't got particularly long fingers.[8]

The 1980 code allows Grade 2-4 balls to be up to 23 cm (9.063 in) in circumference. Two top-grade balls I measured recently had circumferences of 22.5 cm (8.86 in). Surely manufacturers could do a somewhat better job for

bowlers than this, and make balls closer to the minimum allowable size.

The evidence available to us supports the view that the great majority of adult males possess hands capable of performing most of the required spinning actions. David Nourse, a South African all-rounder, was described as having hands bigger than anybody playing cricket, but S. F. Barnes, Mailey, Grimmett, O'Reilly and Laker are said to have had hands which were not abnormally large.[9] However, quite small differences in ball size can have very large effects on what spinning techniques are feasible for the great majority of bowlers.

Women's hands are smaller on average and do require a smaller ball. Young bowlers may pose a problem by adopting inefficient grips which suit smaller hands. An example of this would be a leg-break grip employing all four fingers and thumb in an equally dominant role. Most good leg-spinners find that a spinning couple dominated by the first and third fingers is more capable of imparting sharp spin, but such a grip appears to be beyond young hands.

No bowler should accept the additional burden of a ball swollen beyond normal size. Umpires are required to possess a pair of brass gauges: the ball should be able to pass through one but not the other.

The question of what size ball is best for cricket should not be regarded as settled. It is clear that a reduction in circumference of only 2.5 mm (0.1 in) would make spinning just that bit more accessible. In the period 1952-5 a trial was carried out in England, using a slightly smaller ball with a slightly thicker seam. The final trial took place in twenty-five non-competition matches in 1955. The players were almost totally unenthusiastic, and the idea was dropped.

Whatever the case for a smaller ball, the type of trial that lasts for a period of two or three years for a handful of cricketers is unlikely to be of any use. Unless players are told that the new smaller ball is to be adopted for a period comparable in length with a good proportion of their playing years, they cannot be expected to devote the time needed to become fully accustomed to it and exploit its full potential.

Similar considerations apply to other experimental law changes. No one, for example, would seriously expect a short period of trial for a new lbw rule, allowing a batsman to be given out to a ball pitching outside the leg stump, to lead suddenly to a resurgence in spin bowling, particularly leg-spinning. Nor could players, most of whom have no interest in the art, be expected to show any enthusiasm for the new rule. Yet such a trial was carried out for only one season in New Zealand and Australia in 1981. Some experiments in cricket require a long period in which to demonstrate their usefulness or otherwise. It is best that the changes be decided on the basis of sound principles and experience, and then given sufficient number of years in operation to allow both bowlers and batsmen to develop within the new conditions.

Finger length is not the only factor in grip; hand width and finger shape are also important. It is not uncommon for the index finger to be bent around slightly at the top joint in the direction of the second finger. Such a shape is of some value in both off- and leg-spinning, as the finger fits better over the ball. Individuals also vary in the size of the various knobs and bumps that are found on finger bones. Here is yet another reason why a particular grip should not be imposed on a bowler. The presence or absence of a particular structure or length of bone may make all the difference to the feel of a ball in the hands, without the reason being at all obvious to anyone else.

In addition to these individual characteristics, the ability of bone to respond to the stresses and pressures placed on it means that we influence the structure of our hands to some extent by what we habitually do with them. Frequent pressure on bone will cause thicker cartilage to develop which ultimately becomes bone: bunions on the feet are an example. Spin bowlers can expect this to some degree after years of practice and play. Jim Laker's spinning (index) finger was 'swollen and arthritic after years of service'[10], obviously a bunion-like condition rather than thickened skin, because it showed up alarmingly in an X-ray; only bone would do that. Not surprisingly, when Laker taught the young Tony Lock how to really spin the ball he warned him that it would hurt.

Capping the whole pile of difficulties that range against today's spinner is one which is especially tragic in its consequences, because it can strike bowlers at the peak of their powers. Finger wear is the problem and there is nothing subtle about it; bowlers may be injured so severely that for days or weeks on end they are simply unable to spin the ball. And it is those bowlers who try hardest to put work on the ball, the very people who would give the game more variety, who suffer most.

The list of bowlers removed from the crease as a result of finger wear during their prime years reads like a Who's Who of spin: Wilfred Rhodes (who by standing down because of a sore spinning finger allowed Colin Blythe to make his debut for England), McCool, Benaud, Laker, Gibbs, Pocock and others; a depressingly high toll, especially when most of them have lived in an era when quality spinners were not plentiful. Include all those spinners at club level and above who have suffered distressing problems with finger wear, and we have a factor of no small significance in today's cricket. We must ask the questions, why does the problem seem to be worse in recent times, and is it avoidable?

Skin is composed of two fundamental layers: an outer layer called the epidermis, and an inner dense connective tissue called the dermis. The epidermis contains layers of flattened dead cells derived from the living cells of the underlying layer which steadily move outwards as the epidermis sheds its outer cells. The outer, completely dead part of the epidermis, the horny layer, is normally replenished every two weeks in a mature adult. Its thickness varies in different parts of the body, depending on the amount of pressure applied to the skin. Thickened skin would take longer than two weeks to move through its shedding cycle.

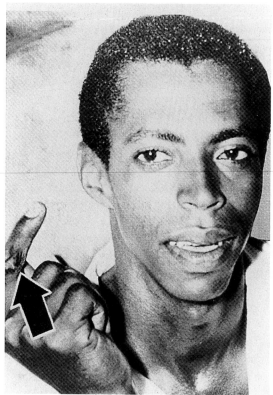

Fig. 44 Lance Gibbs' lacerated spinning finger. Gibbs was one of the best off-spin bowlers in the history of cricket. The best spinners pay too high a price for their efforts.

A bowler is subjecting the skin on his fingers both to abrasion, where the surface cells are worn away, and to a tearing action, where the skin is pulled to one side just before and during delivery. Repeated pressure, during weeks of practice, thickens the epidermis which is covered with an intersecting series of delicate grooves to allow stretching and provide friction with other surfaces.

So what goes wrong? In the first place the hand was not designed for bowling; the pressure points are in the wrong places. Not being on the pads of the muscular areas, but mainly on the sides of the fingertips or joints, the pressure is concentrated unnaturally at these points. Experience tells us that bowlers can build up thicker skin as a protection, but only to a certain extent.

Even when it is toughened by artificial means such as the calamine-boracic acid treatment found useful by Benaud, the skin still splits and tears.

Other treatment involving softening with oils or greases has not solved the problem either. Naturally, the *stratum corneum* has all the properties needed for normal use, and adheres well to the underlying tissue. Thickening can strengthen it, but in spite of all possible precautions, the violent and repeated stress involved in spin bowling can still tear it away from the living tissue below; a tragic outcome for spinners who put so much effort into perfecting their art.

The modern ball may well have exacerbated the problem. We appreciate its frequently quite hard and often rather sharp rows of stitching, as offering us the hope that as well as being the only thing to grip on an otherwise continually shiny ball, it may also slightly improve the grip on low friction pitches.

Whereas in the earlier years the ball more frequently wore rough enough to provide a grip over its entire surface, nowadays our grip is frequently confined to the relatively narrow band of stitches for the entire game. Such a concentration of pressure and stress must aggravate skin damage. This factor alone should be enough to encourage the development of a commonsense attitude to the use of skin protection by bowlers. We can and must improve pitches, but out-fields friendly to shiny leather are most likely here to stay. Can we hope for pitches in the future on which balls will wear a little more rapidly? Friction is not possible without wear. A naturally worn ball, not one that has been unnaturally mutilated on one side, brings spin to the fore.

Sharp spinning normally requires two points of intense contact with the ball. For the leg-spinner these are commonly the inside of the first finger joint or finger tip and the inside of the first joint of the third finger. Only one of these is usually subject to tearing. Over-thick skin or raised, jagged edges can be shaved carefully with a razor blade to reduce the chance of tearing at splits.

With the long hours of practice that spinners require, finger wear will always be a problem; under the present set-up it is far too frequently an insurmountable one. So what can be done? Grin and bear it? As Shakespeare put it:

*There be some sports are painful
and there labour
Delight in them sets off.*[11]

Not much delight if you can't bowl; the matter is too serious to be dismissed.

Back in the early days an enterprising wicket-keeper made a sort of tin thimble to protect two of his fingers. Once into their stride cricketers were not slow in adopting protective devices in the form of leg pads, gloves, thigh pads, shin pads, arm pads, body pads, boxes, and helmets when they needed them. When we consider that wicket-keeping gloves, and helmets, especially the latter when used by close-in fieldsmen, play a direct part in bringing about the demise of the batsman, we may take a different view regarding protection for a bowler's fingers. But suggest to fellow cricketers some form of protection for the bleeding finger of a spin bowler, and for many of them one may just as well have proposed that Lord's be given over to dog-racing, such is the infamy of the idea.

I was listening to a radio commentary on a Test match from Australia in the 1970s when Dennis Lillee had gone off for treatment to an injury and come back onto the field with sticking plaster on his hand. It must have been his bowling hand because one of the commentators said that there was nothing wrong with Lillee using sticking plaster, but if Ashley Mallett, an off-spinner, had used it, the commentator went on to say, he would have been able to generate 'fantastic spin'. Someone interested in the history of cricket may wish to trace the development of this idea into one of the more powerful myths associated with the game.

I invite the reader to carry out a few simple experiments. Take two cricket balls, one new, the other worn, and using the seam and the smoother portion in turn, rub these surfaces firmly over the skin of one of your fingers. The skin can be moistened slightly if you wish, as you may do to improve the grip when actually bowling. Note the amount of friction. Obtain some sticking plaster; if possible some of each of what are probably three principal types — one with a shiny plastic surface, another with a tightly woven fabric surface, and another with a slightly textured plastic surface. Another type with stretchable rubberised fabric moves too much under pressure and is useless for the experiment. Place an inch or two on your finger and rub the ball over it as before. If one of the fallacies of modern cricket has not taken a body blow in these few minutes I will have been very much mistaken. If there are any significant differences between the grip of a ball on skin covered with sticking plaster as compared with uncovered skin, it is more likely that the result, over the whole range of plasters, is *less* friction rather than *more*.

But what if the edge of the plaster is rolled up to expose the sticky part? 'You can't expect umpires to go around peering into bowlers' finger joints all day'. At this point the diehards do us all a service by inviting a more complete exposure of the fallacy underlying the whole idea that sticky fingers help a spin bowler.

Another experiment will readily provide the answer. Put something really sticky, as sticky as sticking plaster, on your bowling fingers. This can be a rubberised glue or some other adhesive. Now attempt to bowl. If you retain any touch and timing at all during the sensitive and intricately programmed operation of releasing the ball, you are better than I am, and I have tried this with a number of different glues. Add to this the problem imposed by the *changing* stickiness of the grip and the whole idea collapses.

In 1927-8 when J. Newman of Hampshire was coaching in New Zealand, he wore a finger stall in a minor match and was no-balled by the umpire on the grounds that he was employing a means of unfair advantage.[12] The opposing captain should have begged him to keep it on, such is the effect of any covering like that on one's control. Ian Peebles tells us that Walter Robins, a ferocious spinner of the ball, suffered from a raw third finger and used sticking plaster, but, in confirmation of my own finding, adds that it is likely to interfere with a bowler's touch. However, this interference is lessened with practice.

Law 8, Part 7 of the 1980 Code states that 'the umpires shall be the sole judges of fair and unfair play'. Since the matter presently being discussed is not mentioned directly or indirectly anywhere else in the Code, the question must be open to interpretation by umpires. If a close-in fieldsman, because he is wearing a helmet, can safely creep in an extra two yards to bring about the dismissal of a batsman, that may be classed as an unfair advantage, but I suggest that cricketers think again on the matter of finger protection before automatically accepting misconceived ideas from the past. An informed interpretation on the part of umpires is all that the spinner asks for. Since the matter has acquired, in the minds of some cricketers, a significance of unjustifiable proportions, umpires could rightly expect some support for a change of attitude on the part of respected leaders among players and administrators. It is too important to be left to the haphazard solution of mutual agreement between opposing captains.

One suggested law change that would do nothing to help spinners is the lengthening of the pitch by a yard or so, to take some of the menace out of intimidatory bowling. Getting the ball up to the other end, while spinning it at the same time, places enough stress on the fingers now without adding more. Quoting extensive figures from English county cricket for the period 1955-84, Robert Letham in an article in *The Cricketer*, entitled 'Cricket — more than ever a batsman's game', besides giving weight to many of the points raised in this chapter, dismisses the idea of a longer pitch on the grounds that it would merely aggravate the dominance of the bat.[13]

Bowlers are familiar with the loss of fine touch in their fingers after stopping a hard-hit shot. How many realise that by fielding at positions where the ball is constantly being relayed back through them to the other bowlers, their hands are subjected to a repeated impact which makes the fingers and

palms swell to the detriment of their efficiency as bowlers? For this reason, returns to bowlers should, where possible, be a gentle lob from close at hand.

Our discussion of the limitations of human skin under the stress of spin bowling inevitably veers towards artificially-aided adhesion. Although the two subjects strictly speaking are unrelated, they appear to be associated strongly in the minds of many cricketers. The use of resin and other substances has come to be regarded by some, along with finger protection, as unfair play. Again the 1980 Code makes no specific mention of the subject, the sole appearance of chemistry being a ban on the application of artificial substances to the ball; a slight move in favour of the spin bowler, but outweighed by the disadvantage, compared to what was permitted earlier this century, of not being allowed to rub the ball in the dirt to improve grip.

Bowlers who have slipped into their pockets a little of the pale golden powder, the same one that puts music in the violinist's bow and allows the gymnast to grip the bar, are in good company. Arthur Mailey would have no truck with fiddlers of a different sort; rule fiddlers:

I accepted these standardised rules [referring to various other laws of cricket] because I had come into cricket with them, but when the crazy idea of disallowing the bowler to use resin to allow a better grip of the ball — and a law forbidding the lifting of the seam blew in, I bade good-bye to this form of freedom and became a rebel. Although it was against the law, I must break down and confess that I always carried powdered resin in my pocket and when the umpire wasn't looking, lifted the seam for Jack Gregory and Ted McDonald. And I am as unashamed as a Yorkshireman who appeals for lbw off a ball which pitched two feet outside the leg stump.[14]

Ian Peebles comes down more gently, but still firmly on the side of bowlers:

There have been innumerable instances of sharp practice in the history of cricket, mostly trivial and usually laughable, to be grouped under the tolerant heading of 'gamesmanship'. When these have been mechanical rather than psychological, one regrets to say that the bowler has been the more frequent culprit, for, as the prime mover, his opportunities have been the greater. Resin or eucalyptus on a handkerchief, to give more grip, raising the seam, polishing the ball and suchlike, have been hunted down over the years, but the writer has an unconcealed sympathy for such gentle aids, for no petty restrictions are put upon the batsman in the maintenance of his implements.[15]

Resin is not a sticky substance but it improves grip under pressure. Base-ball pitchers are highly skilled in exploiting spin-swerve by means of a great variety of spins, and, as we saw earlier, also employ a version of swing, the knuckle ball. The rules of baseball recognise the need for a good grip on the ball, with the help of resin if necessary, so that players can get on with the business of exploiting their skills. In fact, unfair play in baseball includes having so much resin on the pitch that the batter can't see properly through the cloud of powder! The following comments of a leading American baseball coach are highly relevant to cricket:

If a new ball is too slick, it should be rubbed until the sheen is removed. This duty is assigned to the umpire as a pre-game task, but if it has been neglected it can be done by the pitcher or one of his team-mates as long as no foreign substance is applied. A resin bag should always be on hand for the pitcher's use. At any time that his hand becomes slippery or does not supply the desired resistance in releasing the ball, the pitcher should dust his hands by gripping the resin bag and squeezing it several times. Two words of precaution should be added:

resin may not be applied directly to the ball, because the rules consider it a foreign substance; and the application of resin should be done judiciously, because an excess of it can cause the fingers to adhere to the ball sufficiently to impair one's control.[16]

A spin bowler reacts to a poor hold on the ball by placing it nearer the palm of his hand, the very position that destroys spin. I wonder if the law-makers of the 1920s would have interfered had they known that the ball-polishing out-field era was looming. Spin bowlers have had to accept covered pitches; they have a right to expect that inadequately-based restrictions, such as those we have been discussing here, should be removed. The time for a return to sanity with regard to resin is long overdue.

Bowlers' tricks can be divided into two categories; those that do away with the need for real skill, such as obtaining assisted or reverse swing by damaging one side of the ball, and those that allow the application of real skill. When the need for a better grip is recognised as encouraging real skill, they will no longer be seen as tricks.

Well-worn balls are likely to grip the pitch better, but umpires have been known to change these balls and thus penalise spinners yet again. But we shouldn't blame the umpires for underpinning the sanitised cricket ethos of today which sends them scampering when a ball gets a little soft or a little out of shape (preventing swing) and which allows them to ban play when the run-ups are a little wet. The cricket world long ago stopped telling them that bowlers of skill can do plenty with a soft, worn or distorted ball, or that they can cut down their run-ups on a wet surface. Not quite all of the cricket world, however; the money-paying public, frequently forced to put up with annoying breaks in play and the most scandalous delays to the start of play, are brought face to face with this modern mollycoddling.

Bowlers should take careful note of the quite wide variation in matters of considerable

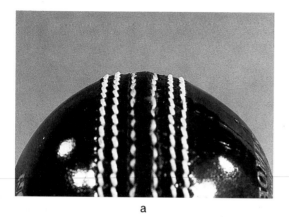

a

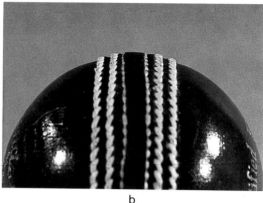

b

c

Fig. 45 Seam and stitching; *a*, *b*, and *c* are high quality balls. The true seam, which bulges only slightly, is seen to run down the dark area in the middle of each photograph. The four rows of stitching vary in thickness among the different balls. Ball *a* is a Kookaburra Turf ball; *b* and *c* are from Alfred Reader. Ball *b* was a make that was used for seven years before the thickness of the stitching was called into question and it was replaced by *c*. Ball *c* would appear to be less helpful to cutters and spinners than *a* and *b*.

importance to them. They should seek out balls with the most stitches, the widest area of stitching, the thickest thread, the best bounce, and the smallest diameter. These qualities don't always bring greater cost. Clubs and purchasing organisations can therefore give significant help to bowlers by asking suppliers to provide detailed specifications, checking measurements, and purchasing balls with the required qualities. Stitches must rise abruptly from the surface if they are to serve the bowler: gentle undulations which may or may not be submerged in a sea of lacquer are not good enough.

Cricketers throughout the world, hoping for a significant action on the part of ruling bodies to advance the cause of spin, must wonder about the wisdom of banning a Reader ball (Fig. 45*b*) with slightly enlarged stitching, a ball which incidentally had been manufactured for seven years. Although it was said to have helped faster bowlers, why was its long-term potential benefit

to spinners not recognised? I am not aware of anyone telling batsmen to go back to using lighter, more manoeuvrable bats.

While possible changes in the size of the ball and the thickness of the stitching are important issues for the art of bowling, the bowler anxious for immediate rewards need not wait for them. Without years of training he can immediately set about tormenting the batsman with the cross-seam delivery which I will explain.

First he looks at the ball. The external stitching on a good quality ball covers about 30 per cent of its area, so that if he bowls a ball at random into the pitch, using no particular grip in relation to the seam, it will land on the seam on average one-third of the time. Not exactly, though. The mark on a ball where it lands may be about 20 mm in diameter, depending on the deformation of the ball and pitch on contact. We may therefore enlarge our figure for the chance that there will be some contact of the stitching with the ground.

We know from the previous two chapters that both pace off the pitch and bounce are, to a great extent, at the mercy of the friction on contact, and that friction depends to some extent on how the ball lands with respect to the seam. Therefore any grip that introduces uncertainty as to whether or not the ball will land on the seam is an attacking delivery of the highest order.

Because the task is simply to bring the fingers more or less straight down off the back of the ball, this delivery could be called the legitimate member of the 'straight-out-from-the- fingers' family that also numbers 'tampered swing' among its members. Grips with the seam in various positions are possible, the most obvious being the 'fully-cross seam' delivery shown in Figure 46a. Any grip with the seam in a less 'cross' position is not worth bothering about because it will merely reduce the difference between the 'cross' landing and the 'smooth leather' landing.

Delivered as in Figure 46 with the seam lying across the grip, the ball rotates backwards in flight; the *seam flutters round and round, and may or may not be in the right place to contact the pitch on landing.* The chance of a full seam landing is about 20 per cent, and of at least some seam contact on landing, about 30 per cent. Therefore about 70 to 80 per cent of those deliveries are likely to skid through more quickly and lower off the smooth leather. And because the across-the-seam contact provides the greatest friction of all, the rest are likely to come off slower and kick a little. *Neither the bowler nor the batsman has any chance whatsoever of knowing the outcome of those deliveries.* Even if the bowler does not conceal his grip, the batsman is compelled to wait until the ball pitches to see what will happen. While commentators may resort to bland explanations like 'the pitch is a bit up and down today', the truth may be something quite different.

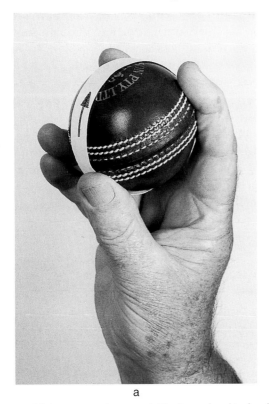
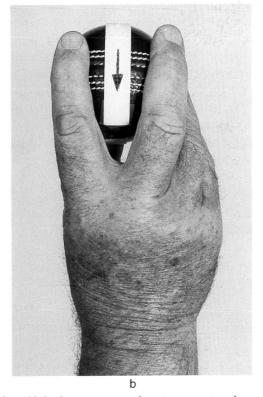

a

b

Fig. 46 Cross-seam grip, top and side views ; the white band of possible landing areas crosses the main seam in two places. The cross-seam landing lottery offers no prizes to batsmen but plenty to bowlers.

West Indian bowlers overwhelmed the Australians at Melbourne in 1996 to win the third Test in three days. The TV side-on view showed some deliveries lifting, but no more than would be expected, considering the height of the bowlers. But other deliveries, and these were frequently those that caused most trouble to the Australians, came through with great pace and rather low; lower than the batsmen might have expected from the length.

What happened at Melbourne appeared to be consistent with what has been written in these chapters, and it would have been intriguing to know whether the West Indies bowlers employed the cross-seam technique. Whether or not they did do so, it would be equally interesting to know whether that Melbourne pitch was patchy with respect to surface friction. Curtly Ambrose and Courtenay Walsh gave a magnificent display of fast bowling. We can improve our understanding if we realise that, as grass dries out, it becomes more slippery to the ball, and that dry patches are more likely to be develop after the first day or two, depending on the drying conditions. We may then view the comment 'the pitch is starting to play a bit low' in a new light: it was low and *fast, in patches*. However we must always allow for the presence of less consolidated areas, not on Test pitches but on less well prepared pitches; 'dead' patches where the ball would simply 'die', coming off low and not necessarily more quickly. A pitch covered with slippery, dead-looking grass may suit real pace but not the full range of spinning and cutting skills.

My experiments with the new laser-timed bowling machine mentioned earlier, show that the ball landing cross-seam comes off the pitch significantly slower. Tests with the machine on the first day of the Test between New Zealand and the West Indies at the Basin Reserve Wellington in 1995 showed that those landing cross-seam came off, on average, 6.5 per cent slower than when they landed on the smooth leather. Balls landing with the seam along the line of travel lost only about a quarter of this amount. This across-the-seam result also applies to spinners. Spun balls that land with the seam more or less across the pitch on landing may therefore 'kick' a little, although the accompanying loss of forward pace may not be desirable.

Although the cross-seam delivery is well known, and used by many bowlers, some of them believe that because the seam is across the air stream rather than being more or less in line with it, as in the case of most other deliveries, this must slow the ball. They need have no fear. The cross-seam delivery has no more drag than a normal delivery.

The standard for cricket balls says nothing about swing or swerve. Most of my work, and the work of Barton, who published the first results on the swing force, has been done on Australian Kookaburra balls. Some new English balls are quite rough on the leather faces, the leather appearing to be squashed down rather than spread out smoothly. This reduces new ball swing. Kookaburra balls appear to meet the needs of cricketers better, although the thread in the external stitching is unnecessarily thin.

16

S.F.BARNES: LEG-SPIN, OFF-SPIN, SWERVE AND PACE

The name Sydney Francis Barnes no longer appears in the coaching books. Coaches could be forgiven if, like the worshippers of old, they were in dread of even uttering the name of the awesome deity. Is a bowler who could curve the ball both ways in the air and break it both ways off the pitch, all at more than medium pace, too remote a model for mere mortals? His 189 wickets in 27 Tests at an average of 16.48 certainly inspire awe.

Why do so few of today's bowlers try to imitate him? I suggest that our thinking today takes us past him, leaving him mounted as some sort of museum piece. Explain this attitude and you explain a good deal of twentieth century cricket, preoccupied as it is with swing and cut. Barnes didn't swing and cut, he swerved and spun. He upsets our preconceptions of what fast bowlers do and what slow bowlers do. Standing astride the boundary between the two, he tells us that there is no boundary.

Barnes lived a long and active life, during which he wrote a little and talked freely about his bowling. As a result we are able to piece together a picture of his development and methods. There will only be one S. F. Barnes, but why should bowlers born a century after him not aim to use those same methods, adapted to their own powers?

Fry's description, although vague in parts and written during the middle years of Barnes' Test career, paints a picture of a great bowler:

In the matter of pace he may be regarded either as a fast or a fast-medium bowler. He certainly bowled faster some days than others; and on his fastest day was certainly distinctly fast.

He obtained his pace from a peculiarly loose, long, circular swing; he did not put much body weight behind the ball and, unlike most bowlers of his pace, he obtained very little power from the bend of his back. The life of his bowling came from the liveliness of his swing. At the same time he had a remarkable power of hand, and worked the ball with his fingers at the moment of delivery in a way which is very uncommon with bowlers of more than medium pace. He is usually regarded as being able to break from leg as well as from the off, his leg-break being similar to that of a slow bowler. But his leg-break was not really quite of this kind. He had a natural power of bowling a ball which swung from leg to the off after pitching, and he increased this cross swing by finger work so that it became something more than merely 'going with the arm' and yet was not genuine break. In any case it was a very difficult ball to play.

When he was bowling well he kept a very accurate length on the off stump, and made the ball go first one way and then the other without betraying any difference in his delivery. As his bowling came very quickly from the pitch he was troublesome to the very best batsmen. To get his best results he required a wicket with a bit of life in it.[1]

Modern coaches intent on getting young fast and medium-pace bowlers to bend their backs, perhaps excessively, could learn something from the above account: unlike many of today's bowlers, Barnes remained untroubled by spinal injuries throughout his long career.

He began as a fast bowler, playing an occasional

county game without much success. In later years he commented that fast-medium is the ideal pace on which to build a range of variations of spin and pace, adding that: 'it is much easier for a fast bowler to become a slow or medium-paced bowler than for a slow bowler to become a fast bowler'.[2] He might also have said that since faster bowlers vary in their actions, not all are necessarily destined to make the transition with equal ease. Barnes himself, relying more than many on arm action, is a case in point. Tall at 185 cm (6ft 1in), but by today's standards not unusually so, he was noted for his high, smooth, flowing action. Building on this foundation, he turned to spin. In three hours of coaching he learned how to bowl an off-break, but having decided that it was the ball going away off the pitch that would cause batsmen most trouble, he set out to teach himself the leg-break.

His grip for the leg-break (Figures 49c and 49e) was identical with that of most slower bowlers. The first and third fingers did the work, with the ball held out on the first joint of these, along with the second finger and thumb for support. But there was no slowing down; his leg-break was perhaps at least as fast as anything seen before, and his accuracy unrelenting. With his new-found skill, he took more than a hundred wickets in his first season for Lancashire in 1902, at a tidy average. He didn't feel the need to use his off-break, since Wisden that year said that he needed to cultivate one. Nor did it hold back his rocketing career. A. C. MacLaren, the previous year, invited him straight from the Lancashire League to join the English team to Australia for the 1901-2 tour. When the off-break became an integral part of his attack it was, like Barnes himself, something out of the ordinary.

Before that comment appeared in Wisden, Barnes had encountered M. A. Noble in Australia, and learned from him about the ball which swerved from leg to off, then broke back into the wicket. We have previously discussed Noble, right-hand medium pace, and George Hirst, a left-hander faster than Noble who pioneered the curved ball

derived from baseball, that strikes back in the reverse direction off the pitch. In acquiring this knowledge, Noble and Hirst demonstrated the principle that for every ball bowled by a left- or right-handed bowler there is a mirror image available to the bowler of opposite hand. Hirst bowled the ball that swerved in to the right-hander before turning away off the pitch; Noble bowled the ball that swerved away to the off before turning back off the pitch. As we would expect, Hirst was most effective when bowling into a head wind. But all the exponents of swerve have experienced its unreliability, and Barnes was no exception. 'It would simply drift in late, driving all the way' he said, dismissing such an innocuous parabola. 'When you were bowling it well, it would go (straight) and then dip in.'[3]

How did Barnes and Noble bowl this ball, and why was Barnes' leg-break famous, particularly for curving to leg before effecting its more obvious destructive purpose? A bowler who in eleven overs can take five wickets for six runs to remove the cream of Australia's batting, as Barnes did in Melbourne in 1911, must have something special that we could learn about.

Accurate fast-medium to medium-pace leg-breaks were special enough on their own, but when we look at Barnes' hand, high above his head at the point of delivery, we can't help noticing how different it is from the numerous leg-spin bowlers photographed since then. Many writers have attested to this individuality. As if in royal command the wrist, seen clearly in Figure 48, is straight or, as in some photographs of Barnes, bent back, and the palm faces the batsman or a point above the batsman. No horizontal crooking or inward curling of the wrist here, but a rapid rotation of the forward-facing hand as if unscrewing something anti-clockwise from an imaginary ceiling above him, while at the same time imparting a violent leg-break flick with powerful fingers. Now we see that there was more to Barnes' high action than achieving height and bounce, important though these are.

The action described here is potentially capable

a

b

c

d

Fig. 48 S. F. Barnes: four views of the great bowler; the hand bent back at the wrist to produce the spin-swerve that accompanied his medium to fast leg-breaks and off-breaks. The grips pictured here all appear to be for the leg-break. Figure 49 shows modern reconstructions of these deliveries.

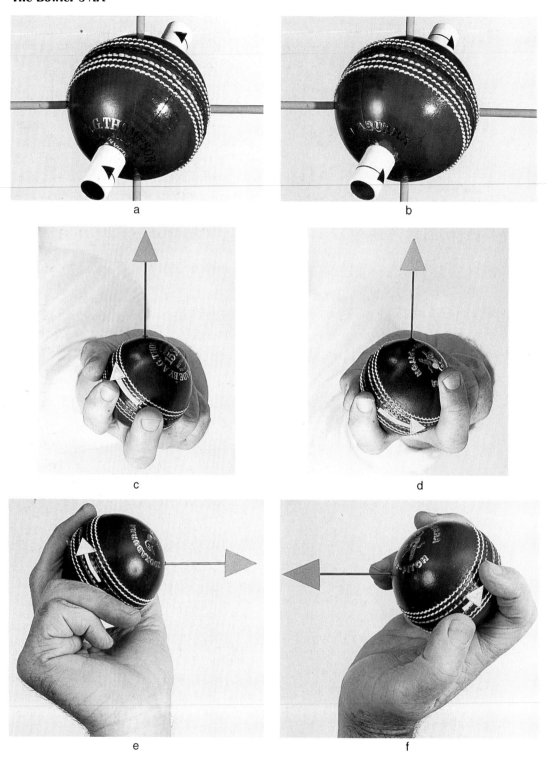

Fig. 49 The two principal Barnes balls: *a*, *c*, and *e* are for the in-swerving leg-break; *b*, *d* and *f* are for the out-swerving off-break. *c* and *d* are top views, and *e* and *f* from the side. In *c* and *e* the third finger generates most of the spin, while in *d* and *f* it is the first finger. Note the hand bent back at the wrist; this is the essential feature of the Barnes deliveries.

of imparting 'pure' side-spin which would give, by means of the Robins Force, nothing more than swerve from off to leg as well as being likely to land on the smooth part of the ball most of the time. But, like most of the situations in bowling, Barnes' ball was a mixture of spins, in this case mainly side-spin and leg-spin. Improving on the analogy, we now say that he wasn't unscrewing something from the ceiling immediately above, but from a surface above, yet somewhat in front of him. For the out-curving off-break we may repeat the analogy exactly, except that in this case the hand is screwing clockwise rather than unscrewing. His grip for this ball differed from the leg-break grip in the position of the index finger which now lay more along the seam than across it. As with all off-spinners, the index finger generated most of the spin.

Another notable characteristic of Barnes was his ability to conceal his intentions from the batsman. Without needing to resort to the googly, he solved the problem of making the leg-break and off-break indistinguishable in a number of ways. 'I want to drive home that the whole run-up action and follow through should be the same', he said. 'The arm should stay at the same height and come over in the same way.'[4] The hand action described earlier maintains the deception by avoiding the typical leg-spinner's coil and uncoil which, when seen in good lighting and against a good background, is frequently not difficult to distinguish from the usual high, forward-facing hand of the off-spinner. Barnes therefore, like all leg-spin bowlers who might be described under that inaccurate tag as finger spinners, managed to make his leg-break look more like an off-break. And what little indication the batsmen might have had of the direction of spin, took place at such a rapid rate as to increase their difficulties even further. Because of the high proportion of side-spin generated by his action, the amount of top-spin would be less, in proportion to the leg-spin, than that bowled by other bowlers. However, some top-spin must have been present, since P. F. Warner wrote of the deceptive dip of the leg-break:

On first going in to bat one is apt to think, judging by the flight of the ball, that this leg-break will pitch off the leg stump, while, as a matter of fact, eight times out of ten, it will pitch on the wicket. This is probably due to his bowling from the end of the crease[5]

In later years, Barnes said that he did not use the width of the crease, but simply concentrated on a good foothold. Barnes said he attacked the stroke rather than the stumps: 'At the start of an innings, when the wicket was absolutely true, I always used to bowl outside the off stick so that when the ball did dip there was a chance of hitting the wickets. It was also a good ball against left-handers'.[6]

His field for the famous performance in Melbourne in 1911 had only three men on the leg side: short square-leg, mid-on and fine-leg. He was meticulous in setting his field. Captains found him difficult to handle and openly critical of their methods.

For C. S. Marriott, as a boy in 1912, the sight was overwhelming:

Never again have I seen such bowling: I sat there deaf and blind to everything except the miracle unfolding before my eyes, memorising every move, my fingers itching for the feel of the seam. Without the slightest change of action he bowled every conceivable variation of pace from fast-medium to slow, making the ball hang in the air, and dip and leap like a devil from the pitch.[7]

Marriott, spurred by this experience, later became a star leg-spinner himself and he too, at a slower pace than Barnes, based his attack on the leg-break and the off-break, having abandoned the googly, but nevertheless very satisfactorily solving the problem of concealing his intentions from the batsman.

We give The Master the last word, taken from a letter he wrote to Jack Fingleton. Not attempting to distinguish between swing and swerve, and comparing himself with swing bowlers he said:

> I thought I was at a disadvantage in having to spin the ball when I could see bowlers doing the same by simply placing the ball in their hand and letting go; but I soon learned that the advantage was with me, because, by spinning the ball, if the wicket would take spin, the ball would come back against the swing... I may say I did not bowl a ball but that I had to spin, and that is, to my way of thinking, the reason for what success I attained.[8]

17
CHOOSING WEAPONS

Do coaches follow trends or lead them? Following may not lead to anything out of the ordinary, and leading may stifle the extraordinary. Top players may inspire, but, as coaches, be limited by being able to pass on only what they themselves do. Whether or not coaches give their pupils the knowledge, drill and inspiration to move out freely beyond coaching, they are all swimming in a sea of widely held and agreed ideas and assumptions that make up the cricket culture of their age. The bowling paradigm, like a giant ocean tanker that takes miles to turn around, has an overwhelming momentum. Years of experimentation and development must precede the flowering of a good bowler, even at club level. If changes are to come about, it is up to players to think as individuals and, if necessary, break out of the conformist mould.

No one would question the idea that spinning the ball in two directions is better than spinning it in one. This concept, a cornerstone of cricket thinking, is proving, in the way we have used it, to be somewhat less solid than is good for us because it leaves out five vital words, 'all other things being equal'.

To begin with, a discussion of two-way spin would be more enlightening if greater attention was paid to spin-swerve, which usually acts in a direction opposite to that which the ball turns off the pitch. On a pitch not offering much grip, an off-break carrying a sufficient amount of side-spin will swerve away to the off, and carry on in that direction after landing. Similarly a leg-break may swerve in and carry on inwards. From one type of delivery the off-break bowler may achieve an off-spinner if it grips, or a ball that goes the other way with the out-swerve if it doesn't; and possibly both,

if there is swerve as well as some degree of grip. In the same way, the leg-spin bowler can achieve through in-swerve what is effectively an off-break on such an unresponsive pitch.

Where friction on the pitch is variable, or where the amount of spin is varied deliberately, a bowler who is capable of using the wind and a certain amount of minor variation including top-spin can be very effective, without having mastered the art of spinning the ball both ways. Dick Tyldesley (1898–1943) needed only the leg-break and top-spinner. He played seven Tests for England and helped Lancashire dominate county cricket in the late 1920s. He gained many lbw decisions with his top-spinner.

We like to talk about beating the bat on one side or the other, but we can inject more subtlety into the business of misleading on length: the business of using spin to change length, not to beat the middle of the bat.

Whatever stock delivery justifies one's presence at the bowling crease, it will have its own characteristic flight. However brilliant it might be, an attacking delivery of the highest quality, batsmen will become accustomed to it. You may have spent years perfecting something that has taken you far beyond the capabilities of the average cricketer. You may be the only bowler in your province or country who can send down such a venomous delivery or range of closely related deliveries. On most days this is enough, but the higher the level at which you play, the more you face better batsmen, and the more often you find yourself up against the same batsmen.

If I am telling experienced cricketers nothing, I apologise; but that is what I am leading up to; nothing. The major problem for our brilliant bowler is the problem of doing nothing; the problem of bowling, as a variation of the highest rank, a nothing ball. This is a ball which will take wickets in Test matches by capitalising on its association with good quality swerve and spin, but which, if bowled in a lower grade suburban cricket match, would not have the benefit of this association and would be seen merely to do nothing.

Consider Mushtaq Ahmed as an example of the leg-break bowler who also bowls the googly; one of the very few who have mastered this mainly ruinous delivery. No matter how brilliantly he mixes the spin, the trajectories, and the angles, every ball he bowls is channelled along a flight path more or less dominated by the top-spin which is an essential component not only of the top-spinner but also of the leg-break and the googly. For the leg-spin bowler without the googly and without other types of spin, the problem is even more serious; not only is the flight stereotyped, but (ignoring the inward spin swerve) he is unable to bring the ball back the other way off the pitch.

What therefore does our star bowler require from the nothing ball? Very little: straightness, maybe a faster pace, and the ability to choose to pitch it either on a shortish or a fullish length. That is why it can be frustrating and annoying to find that the different bowling action required for the nothing ball may make it difficult to bowl, while maintaining the good control which characterises the other, more complex deliveries on which he has based his whole career. The sheer simplicity of bowling a ball that escapes from the sameness of the flight trap by carrying no top-spin, creates its own problems for fingers and muscles attuned to bowling something much more demanding.

In Chapters 18-21 we look at ways for making trajectory variations (among other things) a lot less comfortable for batsmen; but there is no chapter for the nothing ball.

If the previous paragraphs have not convinced readers that the matter is worth our attention, I invite them to look closely at TV film of three Test bowlers: Pakistanis Mushtaq Ahmed and

Afridi, and Australian Shane Warne. Analysing present-day bowlers who, for obvious reasons, have not yet written detailed accounts of their methods is almost certainly bound to be inadequate, but modern TV technology frequently shows the rotation of the ball in the air very clearly.

Warne's heavily spun and well-controlled leg-breaks and his variations of pace have been a joy to cricket lovers. No doubt his methods have evolved and will continue to evolve, but what we see tells us that he wishes to escape from the top-spin-dominated dipping flight trap, and that he uses a nothing ball spinning exactly as the leg-cutter pictured in Figure 42c.

But this is not to say that Warne delivers it that way. Following the generations of good spinners who have learned concealment, he appears to have his hand, at least for part of the delivery action, side-on to the line of the pitch. This action alone, with a bent wrist, at a reasonable pace, is enough to create some resemblance to the leg-break action and fool a batsman twenty yards away.

There appears to be no reason to imbue the rest of his action in bowling that ball with any unusual qualities. The fact that the ball carries back-spin and leg cut shows that during the final contact between Warne's fingers and the ball, his fingers came down across the back of it, exactly as would the fingers of any club bowler. That the ball came out from under his hand is not unusual. Every bowler, and this includes all fast and medium pace bowlers, who produces backwards rotation must release the ball from under the front of the hand. The rotation, in Warne's case, is nothing special; merely the result of getting the hand into that side-on bent position required to confuse the batsman. We must conclude that he had more on his mind than *turning the ball* by this method which, according to his standards, is second rate.

Although Warne's ball, at least on a good Test pitch, does not actually turn (cut) from the leg; by reversing the spin from top-spin to back-spin, he has flattened the trajectory. This is achieved not by change of pace, but by change of spin: something of far greater importance for disturbing the batsman who is getting complacent on judgement of length.

Because flipper-type deliveries are distinguished by a degree of off-spin to accompany the back-spin, Warne's variation is not a flipper. Nevertheless it is a real achievement in overcoming the problems faced by a bowler who needs to insert the ordinary among the special. He has bowled a ball which, through spin-reversal, 'carries' further up the pitch than the previous deliveries, and when he bowls it more quickly it is well set up to get through a batsman's defence or catch him lbw.

Afridi, new on the scene, includes among his brisk top-spinning leg-breaks a ball that rotates as an off-cutter (Fig. 42a), the fingers coming down off the back of the ball a little to the right. Again there is no sign of this delivery turning, but the spin-reversed variation in flight and therefore in length has all the advantages described for Warne's ball. One would need to ask batsmen whether or not they detect Afridi's less disguised release of this delivery. As part of such a fast action it is unlikely to be picked up easily.

Mushtaq must also have arrived at the same conclusion and his nothing ball can be seen occasionally in the slow replays.

While this is all very interesting, there is a lot more to it than the strategies of three particular spinners. We have merely begun to look inside a large box labelled 'Spin-controlled Length Variation'. The possible combinations for unsettling batsmen go beyond the leg-break-plus-nothing-ball pair just described. In later chapters, we will look at the ways that cricketers for more than a century have manipulated flight changes through spin, while relegating turn the other way off the pitch to an insignificant role. The 'pure' 'square' leg-break is one such variation and the group of thumb-generated back-spun balls, one of which is the flipper, is another.

Although relatively few bowlers might be willing to attempt to master the flipper Chapter 20 should be compulsory reading for all cricketers because spin-controlled length variation is of widespread importance.

Young bowlers, at least in the early school years, will normally bowl at a gentle, uncomplicated medium pace, learning the rudiments of run-up, delivery and length. We will assume also that they possess the spark to go on and explore the limits of their ability. What then are the influences that govern the scope of their exploration?

There is no evidence, as far as I am aware, that being trained first to swing only in one direction offers any advantage. I suggest that bowlers should start to learn to swing both ways as early as possible. Spin at pace is usually described as 'cut', whereas we know that twist is also available at pace. Spin by faster bowlers, using finger and hand movements resembling those of slow bowlers, seems to be largely ignored, such as the genuine spinner's grip for a fast leg-break as used by Wass, Barnes and Bedser. As for advice on the mechanics of obtaining spin-swerve, cricketers are usually not well served.

Why do coaching books not suggest that a bowler could or should learn to bowl both off-breaks and leg-breaks? Before Mount Everest was climbed there was another barrier ranging behind the gaping crevasses, the unstable ice, the inhuman severities of wind, cold and lack of oxygen; this was the psychological barrier. No one had done it; could it really be done? Hundreds have now climbed Everest; the dangers remain, quite a number die in the attempt, but the psychological barrier has been removed and they go on, confident of success.

But although the off-break/leg-break twin peak, the Everest of spin bowling, was well trodden by the first years of this century, the reluctance of the cricket world to repeat the climb in the late twentieth century seems to mean that the removal of the psychological barrier means nothing. Barnes was by no means the only fast or medium-pacer of that type in those years. At least half-a-dozen others were in the highest class, including Hugh Trumble (1867–1988), one of Australia's great medium-pacers. One is tempted to describe A. G.

Steel (1858–1914) as the Sir Edmund Hillary of slow off- and leg-break bowling, and in a sense he was; but when he took his 788 first class wickets at 14.80, and his 29 Test wickets at 20.86, he may not have had to overcome the psychological barrier of modern discouragement against such an undertaking.

Some not so modern discouragement came from W. G. Grace who, in 1907, warned against the dangers to accuracy of bowling both off-breaks and leg-breaks, and the physical dangers of bowling leg-breaks and googlies. We can be thankful that all who came after him did not regard the off-break/leg-break pair as off limits, otherwise we would not have had the likes of C. L. Townsend, C. S. Marriott, T. B. Mitchell, S. Ramadhin and K. J. O'Keeffe.

From the time B. J. T. Bosanquet bowled a ball that bounced four times at Lord's in 1900, and had an unfortunate named Coe stumped from it, we have had available to us three methods of bringing the ball back off the pitch from the off: the off-break, the flipper and the googly.

Derek Underwood based his brilliant career on spinning in one direction, from the leg, but he offers an incentive to bowlers to learn to spin both ways:

> *My line has always been to push the ball in the direction of the leg stump against the right-handed batsmen, tucking them up and forcing them to play on the leg side. But today more and more batsmen are standing outside their leg stump and are still able to hit through the off side.*[1]

A young bowler developing both types of spin may not use both in serious games for many years. Nevertheless, the sooner he embarks on the long process of perfecting both, the better. Assuming that our bowler decides to spin both ways, he must decide which of the four off-break techniques — the above three and the off-cutter — to adopt as an accompaniment to the leg-break. A bowler cannot avoid a certain amount of trial and error but, in the initial stages at least, it would waste time and effort not to draw on the experience of other cricketers, provided that this experience is reported objectively. Scientists are not condemned to repeat all the experiments of their predecessors before they attempt to launch out from existing boundaries.

'Orthodox' is not much of an adjective to apply to a bowler who puts every fibre of his being into each delivery; the term tends to drain its subject of individuality. It implies a rather mean little package, lacking flair and imagination. We could well do without the word in the language of cricket. Off-spinners and left-handers probably suffer most from it.

Is off-spin really as easy to bowl as many imagine? The fact that the fingers of a right-hand bowler tend naturally to come down slightly on the right-hand side of the ball at the moment of release might give this impression, but has it got much to do with sharp attacking spin? I would call the natural delivery a slow cutter because the fingers do nothing more than that. Such is the reason why off-spinners are regarded as steady and accurate; many, maybe the imposters we discussed in Chapter 14, don't do anything much with the ball, good or bad. As for good, sharp off-spin, with real twist, it is not 'natural' at all and, as far as I am aware, not in the slightest degree more or less difficult to bowl than the leg-break. Lance Gibbs didn't rip the skin from the inside of the second joint of his right index finger by bowling 'naturally'.

On the evidence presented in Chapter 20, candidate number two, the flipper, also has a claim to be the accompaniment to the leg-break. As for the googly, Bosanquet shook them all right; the cricket world still vibrates. Purple prose flows freely at its mention. Media commentators see googlies where there are none. The magic word cascades forth every time a top-spinner or a leg-break that fails to grip (or one that swerves or angles inwards) hits the pads. Yet the construction of a profit and loss account for the googly is not too difficult; plenty of information is available.

C. S. Marriott, one of the leading spinners in England between the wars, who like many others suffered from 'googly disease' (in his case a torn muscle in the elbow), found the off-break to be a very adequate choice to go with his leg-break and top-spinner. He writes:

Which of these forms of off-break the bowler uses is immaterial provided it is absolutely first-rate of its kind. This includes the skill to conceal it from the batsman and in the case of the googly, the physical ability to bowl it without strain. It is true that the googly has some advantage on a fast wicket because of its extra pace and lift from the pitch, but a bowler using the off-break, who possesses a top-spinner as well, need not worry as I proved for myself by experience. For me the top-spinner and the off-break did everything that the googly could have done.[2]

Marriott didn't know about the flipper, but when shoulder problems associated with the googly threatened to end his cricket career, Benaud turned to the flipper, although he has stated recently that he never fully mastered it.

We now begin to see that when it comes to choosing which technique to use in making the ball go the other way off the pitch, 'other things' are by no means equal. Yet writers of coaching books, following a well-worn path, usually offer the off-break (possibly with a few variations) as one set of possibilities, and the leg-break, top-spinner and googly as another, not forgetting to include the old nonsense about leg-breaks being difficult, inaccurate and likely to be expensive.

Depending on one's point of view, such advice is either highly complimentary to leg-spinners or quite irresponsible. Highly complimentary in the sense that whereas the off-spin bowler is entrusted with the relatively modest task of mastering spin in only one direction, along with a few associated tricks which don't cause exceptional difficulties, the leg-spinner is assumed to be capable of producing spin in two directions. Irresponsible because one of these deliveries, the googly, has caused many, including some of its best practitioners, to question its worth and abandon it in favour of an alternative.

18

OFF-SPIN

Off-spin bowling of slow to slow-medium pace can look vulnerable under pressure; more so than leg-spin. A murderous batting onslaught is one of the highlights of the game, so they say; clapping by bowlers is optional. The ball coming in to the bat often seems to be helping itself on its way to the boundary from the time it lands. R. C. Robertson-Glasgow puts it bluntly:

> Now the off-spinner is a good prop, but a remarkably poor stick: a sudden off-spinner inserted in a series of swinging deliveries will sometimes find the batsman unready, but the habit of bowling off-spinners regularly, on all types of wicket, as practised and advised by so many school professionals of the recent past, is a drudgery that neither 'makes the action fine' nor leads to success. It may worry an average amateur player; but, to a first class professional or amateur, it is a prolific source of run-getting, even of amusement. Correct back-players have little or no difficulty with it: after a few such balls the amount of the spin on a good-length ball is easily gauged; and if over-pitched ever so little the off-spinner is the heaven-sent ball for a big hit, a four or a six over mid-on or mid-wicket's head.[1]

The modern off-spin bowler is frequently aided by a helmeted close-in fieldsman crouching at the bat-edge. The stalemated long series of low-scoring and wicketless overs that frequently accompany such tactics demonstrate that even some of the best off-spinners are achieving little in the way of effective variation.

The choice of weapons for effective variation lies generally between two groups: firstly, off-spin, out-swerve and/or outswing and top-spin; secondly, off-spin and leg-spin, with swerve or swing. It is assumed that the basic ball is the off-break in both cases, and that this ball can be spun sharply and bowled accurately over a range of paces. It is not necessary that this range be very great: subtle variations are the stock-in-trade. Out-swerve resulting from spin, or the outswinger resulting from seam angle, are, for the off-spin bowler, probably easier to master than the top-spinner.

Members of the family of off-spins obtainable from both cut and twist are shown in Figure 50. Group a-c spins on a level axis while group d-f has this axis tilted back, in this case 30 degrees towards the bowler. The latter group represents the more common type of delivery, carrying side-spin as well as off-spin, and will swerve out before turning in. More tilt gives more swerve. A pronounced tilt will prevent the seam from being under the ball to grip when it lands, resulting in less turn, a deadly variation to land on the smooth leather and carry on quickly to get the edge of the bat, hopefully held waiting for the inward turn. It is also a good ball for a stumping. It is worth examining the mark on the ball after a delivery to check the contact. The technique for increasing the amount of tilt has been introduced when discussing S. F. Barnes and is also discussed in the section on leg-spin.

It is characteristic of the normal off-spinner's action that at least a small degree of back-spin is common unlike a twisted leg-spinner where it is entirely absent. The off-cutter, pure or with some twist, will always carries some back-spin.

Most off-spin involving twist has the first and second fingers splayed out for the twisting action.

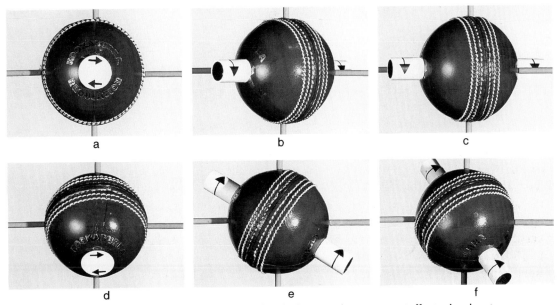

Fig. 50 Family of deliveries for the off-spinner, derived from both twist and cut; *a* is 'pure' off-spin; *b* and *c* spin on horizontal axes at various angles to the line of flight; *d, e* and *f* all have axes tilted backwards; *b* and *c* will swing away before turning back; *d, e* and *f* will swerve away before turning back.

A common grip (Fig. 51*b*) for the off-spinner has the seam pointing behind square-leg at about 45 degrees to the line of the pitch. But this is not to say that the normal off-break delivery in the air has this degree of forward-spin. The first finger, which does most of the work, lies across the seam, and, depending on the length of the fingers, may be hooked around so that the first joint lies partly along the seam. The second finger is also on the seam but spread out wide, away from the first and, for real spin, a certain amount of compression is felt between the two. The third finger is tucked away under the ball more or less opposing the pressure of the first finger. The thumb steadies the grip and the little finger plays no part.

A variation (Fig. 51*a*) of this grip uses finger separations identical to the above, but has the seam pointing more or less towards slip and the first finger running along its left-hand edge. Bowlers of off-spin show a great deal of variety in the placing of their fingers in relation to the seam, such as having the seam parallel to the first finger as in Figure 51*a*.

A rare but effective grip was that used by the Australian Bruce Yardley, who spun the ball with his second finger instead of the index finger. Such a grip requires that the major splitting of the fingers is between the second and the third. Whatever the grip, a good, sharp clockwise twist of the hand must be made during release.

As bowled by the off-spin bowler, the top-spinner requires that the palm of the hand be turned more to face the off during the twist. If the axis is tilted back as in Figure 50*f* this delivery will swerve away to the off. Like all top-spun balls it will dip in flight. To prevent it from dropping short, it must therefore be flighted a little higher, even more so against the wind.

Good present-day models for a top-spinning off-spin bowler are the Sri Lankan, Murilitheran, and Saqlain from Pakistan. With an action so flexible that it has led to accusations of throwing, Murilitheran succeeds in tossing his hand forward during the twisting action with a flexibility one would previously have thought possible only for right hand leg-spin bowlers. It is bowlers like these who expose the fallacy of trying to distinguish between 'finger spinners' and 'wrist spinners'.

The out-swerve is delivered by keeping the palm up and bringing the hand around the

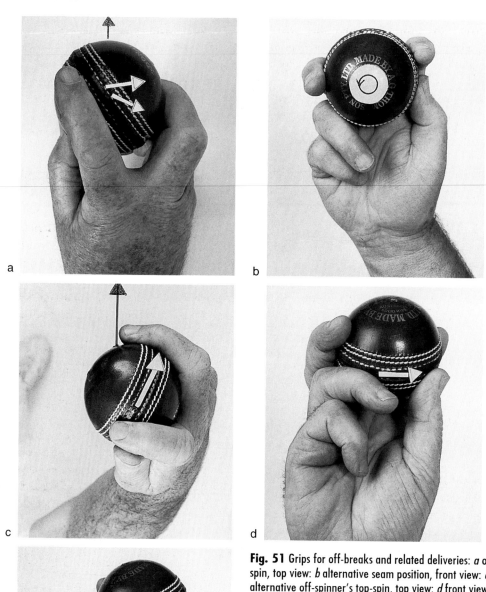

Fig. 51 Grips for off-breaks and related deliveries: *a* off-spin, top view: *b* alternative seam position, front view: *c* alternative off-spinner's top-spin, top view: *d* front view of off-spinner's side-spun out-swerver : *e* side view of out-swerver .

'equator' of the ball on the right during delivery. A degree of round-arm action is found helpful by some bowlers wishing to accentuate the out-swerve. The feeling here, and it is nothing more than a feeling, is that the hand is sliding underneath the ball. If swing is chosen, the normal outswing bowler's action is used with the seam pointing somewhat wide of the slips. Obviously, swing is only possible if the condition of the ball and the air allows it.

The demands faced by a good off-spinner are evident in the following remarks about Fred Titmus by his wicket-keeper John Murray:

Even when Fred was an established Test player, I'd get him in the nets and tell him what he was doing wrong. If he was bowling badly, he was being cut to the boundary; his arm would get a little lower and I'd do my sergeant-major bit and remind him of the basics. For a slow bowler, it's important to realise that the margin of error is just a few inches. To bowl at middle-and-off from 22 yards takes hard work and great skill and I'd point out to Fred that off-breaks on leg stump was a case of bad bowling. [2]

The second group — off-spin and leg-spin — is, as we saw earlier, a proven winner. Adding the off-spinner's top-spinner to this combination would not seem to be worth it. Even if the leg-spinner's attempted top-spinner often turns out to be a slight leg-break, there are plenty of balls that simply fail to bite and end up effectively as top-spinners.

Disguising the difference between the off- and leg-break is the secret of success here. Ignore the fact that one's teammates can spot it at practice but try to make it as difficult as possible for them. The hand, usually bent inwards towards the forearm as the arm swings up, signals the leg-break loud and clear. C. S. Marriott, who solved the problem, has this to say:

The leg-break bowler must conceal his off-break until his arm is coming over at the top of the delivery, when his hand is moving at its fastest. This is done by still crooking up his wrist as he runs up, to make it look like the leg-break, and only allowing it to straighten as his arm swings over. If he finds this a little awkward at first, he will soon get used to it. The gain is more than worth the trouble. [3]

Sonny Ramadhin shone brightly among the stars of the twin skills of off- and leg-break bowling. His 158 Test wickets at 28.98 runs apiece attest to superb 'concealment. When English batsmen finally began to interpret the signs, one of which was the higher flight of his leg-break, it is said that he was poorly handled by his captain and over-bowled: a warning that batsmen do learn, and that for a bowler there is no such thing as invincibility.

On which line should the off-spinner bowl? The answer must depend very much on whether or not a leg-break is likely to arrive at any time. If it is, bowl nothing outside off; then there is no let-up for the batsmen.

There has probably never been a bowler who at some time in his career has not been worked out by a batsman. Even S. F. Barnes was worked out, by the South African batsman Herbert Taylor who said he looked at a spot a yard above the bowler's head as his arm came over. Such a diagnosis can be based on the whole range of signs from bells ringing and lights flashing to differences so subtle as to produce nothing more than a vague feeling of 'something different'. No matter at what part of this range of uncertainty the batsman is operating, the necessity for constant vigilance puts the bowler at an advantage. At the very least it upsets the routine, in the same way that a change of bowler may break a partnership. At best the bowler will dominate completely. Even if a few batsmen in a team work a bowler out, there will always be some who don't. Other factors, which may change by the minute, the hour, or the match, can affect the degree of doubt: whether or not the batsman has previously faced that bowler, and if so how often; the light and background as it affects the view of the bowler's hand; whether or not players have been briefed about the opposing bowlers. Even clothing may have an influence: Ramadhin bowling with his shirt sleeve buttoned up to the wrist must have made it just that bit more difficult for the batsman to see which way the forearm was turning to generate spin. Tom Graveney tells of having difficulty with Ramadhin only when the background was bad or the sun directly behind the bowler;[4] dark skin may have added to the difficulty.

I wonder how many bowlers have been discouraged from using a particular variation, say, off-breaks or nothing balls, in among stock leg-breaks, or vice versa, because their teammates batting in the nets spotted it straightaway. While it is obviously important to adopt measures for concealment, such as those recommended by Marriot and earlier, by S. F. Barnes, the bowler should realise that what happens in the more relaxed and familiar environment of a practice net is not necessarily what will happen out in the middle, with more tension, and possibly different light and background. The presence of two or more bowlers queuing to bowl to the same batsman in practice nets sensitises the batsman to change at every delivery; so much that those introduced by one bowler are probably more likely to be noticed. The chance for leading a batsman astray by stages is diminished.

Whatever means of disguise are adopted, the universal rule is that the quicker the movements, the more difficult it is for the batsman to read them. However this should not be taken as a con-demnation of the much slower ball. The slow ball, even a very much slower ball, provided it is used sparingly, has an important place among the many problems that a bowler can set for a batsman. And, as we saw in Chapter 17, turn as a variation can quite happily take a back seat to spin-induced flight variation.

Without the leg-spinner, there is still plenty to try: different batsmen, different lines, consistency, variations used sparingly. A batsman eager to sweep from the leg stump may fall lbw to the out-swerve which unexpectedly lands on middle. If the swerve is good and the break not so good, attack through the off side can be accented by posting a gully and short-cover. Conversely, if the break is good the leg-side field can be strengthened.

Where the bowler obtains sharp turn through his own ability, alone or with the help of the pitch, there is less demand for subtlety; the ball is pushed through accurately and the rewards will come. Where, through lack of real ability or because of a frictionless pitch, little deviation is obtained, we arrive at the classical dilemma which all bowlers will have faced: bowl faster and flatter, and in doing so reduce even further the chance of deception; or keep flighting the ball and 'buy' a wicket. The choice depends on whether the state of the game allows buying or demands stealing. Putting on one's sweater is an option.

Body action for spinners gets a good deal of attention from coaches. Since many of the best bowlers in the history of cricket have had unusual actions and have resisted attempts to change them, caution is called for. When M. A. Noble delivered his famous out-swerving off-break, C. B. Fry noted that he released the ball from a bent-back hand, which is essential for the side-spin, and went down 'rather low' over a partially-collapsed left leg. Coaches, requiring the high, straight-braced left side as the essential basis of right-hand bowling, would have soon nipped that one in the bud! It has been suggested that the highest position of the bowling arm at delivery is not necessarily the best: the principle behind the suggestion being that a little lowering allows the body turn to increase the hand speed through a longer lever starting at the spine and out through the shoulder and arm.

Mass-produced bowling actions always risk stifling unorthodox talent. Careful experim-entation, where the bowler is alert to every result of his actions, is essential to a bowler's development.

19

LEG-SPIN

Like the giant pandas carted around the world's zoos and stared at by millions, leg-spin bowlers — also an endangered species — attract attention which is inversely proportional to their numbers. Selectors, normally hard-headed members of the cricket establishment, can become irresponsible gamblers at the sight of a right-hand bowler turning the ball from the leg. Inexperienced leg-spin bowlers *(from their mother's womb untimely ripp'd)* have been sent on major tours, with less than notable results. New Zealanders Bill Bell (South Africa, 1952-3) and Graham Vivian (India, Pakistan and England, 1965), and the Australian, John Watkins (West Indies, 1973) are examples. We applaud the tacit recognition of an effective bowling skill, but just as the pandas need a friendly natural environment in which to thrive, so do leg-spinners need a cricket world where they are no longer oddities, but a natural part of the game.

The original method of spinning the ball, as described in the earliest recorded accounts of the under-arm game, was from the leg to the off, the finger and hand movements being no different from those required for the over-arm leg-break bowled today. The rotation is anti-clockwise whether it is below the shoulder, level with it, or above it. Off-spin came later. Neither history nor the structure and function of the arm and hand support the contention that leg-spin is less natural than off-spin.

There were a few good leg-spinners bowling in the late nineteenth century and plenty in the first half of the twentieth. We know that conditions such as covered pitches are now less favourable to spin than they once were, but where did we get the idea that leg-spin poses difficulties for bowlers which are found nowhere else in the game?

If leg-spin was inherently more difficult than other types of spin we would not have seen it proliferate everywhere cricket has been played. Australia, on the basis of its population, must have been the greatest producer. In the first half of the twentieth century nearly every leading cricket team throughout the world contained a right-hand leg-spinner; two in a team was not uncommon. Even these days, a considerable number of club cricketers can bowl leg-spin in the nets; but why not in games as well? What do we do to them?

When we stop regarding them as curiosities we can then go quietly about the tasks of encouraging them, restoring friction and bounce to pitches, and allowing bowlers to regain the right to take measures to prevent crippling skin injury and keep an adequate grip on the ball. Leg-spin bowling usually means attacking bowling. By limiting the amount of limited over cricket that is played we tell bowlers that, to win, they must take wickets.

As discussed earlier, another unnecessary difficulty placed in the path of leg-spinners is the almost automatic assumption, on the part of the cricket world, that they should choose the googly as their main variation. The number taking this path who have maintained consistency and a freedom from injury is disappointingly small; the number who have failed to master the combination is by no means small.

Why do writers of coaching books, after discussing off-spin and topping it off by indicating the valuable accompaniment available in the form of the arm-ball, then ignore the corresponding ball when discussing leg-spin, and move straight on to the googly? I refer to the ball delivered with some degree of side-spin to make it swerve in to the bat.

Of all the barriers placed in the way of the leg-spinner there is one which will be more difficult to remove than any of the others. I refer to the spendthrift label, the conviction that the leg-spinner is expensive by nature. Repeating a familiar phrase, Richie Benaud writes: 'The over-the-wrist spinner distributes his gifts like a millionaire'.[1]

Benaud was obviously too modest to admit his own miserliness. Come to think of it, who exactly were these generous bowlers? Are we expected to believe that selectors have been including leg-spinners in teams for the last hundred years knowing full well that they were almost certain to be expensive to the embarrassing degree suggested by much modern comment? The bowling analyses we read in the history books don't support the notion. Even Arthur Mailey, the archetypal millionaire, who on occasion could be expensive compared to other top bowlers, took his Test wickets at 33.9 apiece, only 7.7 runs more than Maurice Tate, 7 more than Wilfred Rhodes and 5.5 runs more than Harold Larwood, all of whom bowled under more or less the same conditions. More than this, like many leg-spinners, he took his wickets quickly enough to give his teams the priceless gift of time, without which victory is impossible in true cricket. I don't think he was chosen from among the bountiful crop of good leg-spinners in Australia at the time so that Neville Cardus could wax lyrical on the delights of the summer game.

C. S. Marriott spoke from personal experience:

The truth is, that if a leg-break bowler has learned his art in the right way and, by hard practice, has achieved real control of length, there is no reason whatever why he should be any less accurate or any more of a gamble than say a Titmus, an Illingworth, an Allen, a Cartwright or a Shackleton. What is more, he should be able to maintain that accuracy for fifty overs in a day's cricket, or right through an innings, in any conditions or situations.[2]

Fig. 52 Family of deliveries for the leg-spinner derived from both twist and cut; *a* is 'pure' leg-spin; *b* and *c* both leg- and top-spin; *c* will have some outswing; *d* has almost 'pure' top-spin along with outswing and a little leg-spin; *e* leg-spin on a backward tilted axis, giving in-swerve; *f* and *g* leg-spin with a little top-spin, and inswerve from the tilted axis; *h* leg-spin (from cut) with inswing and upward Robins force.

The leg-break bowler must earn his place like every other bowler. There may be periods in a game when tactics demand that runs be given away for some reason or other, but unless he has complete control over his stock ball, he has no claim to a place at the bowling crease. Many leg-spinners have achieved this goal; they could defend or attack and they were neither odd nor extravagant.

The family of leg-spinning balls (Fig. 52) can be looked at in the same way as for off-spin. Any ball landing with the contact point moving more or less from left to right is a leg-spinner. The possibilities range from a nearly pure top-spinner (*d*) to a nearly pure back-spinner (*h*), both with level axes of spin. Tilt this axis back and we get another series (*e, f, g*). Tilt it much more than that and there is less chance of the ball landing on the stitching to obtain a grip on the pitch, although the in-swerve is increased. In this case it will carry on in to the batsman instead of turning back to the off. As for the off-spinner, it is worth checking the landing mark on the ball. Balls carrying top-spin are the typical products of finger movement and hand rotation; those carrying back-spin are the typical products of the fingers being dragged down the back of the ball and slightly to the left side of it. We saw earlier that it is often incorrect to place fast leg-spinners in the back-spinning (cutting) group. Any bowler who does not apply a twisting force to both sides of the ball is a pure cutter, and that means some degree of back-spin.

Tilting back the axis of spin to increase the amount of swerve either way as developed by S. F. Barnes, G. H. Hirst and others was discussed earlier. The analogy of screwing or unscrewing something on the ceiling above and somewhat ahead of the high delivery arm was used. For both the out-curving modified off-break and the in-curving modified leg-break, the palm of the hand must be more or less facing the batsman during the finger-spinning and hand-rotating delivery. This is awkward to achieve merely by bending the hand back at the wrist, but if the ball is released slightly earlier than normal there is more chance of the hand being at the right angle. However, unless some adjustment is made, this will always be a slower and flightier delivery which may not be intended. One experiment on this would be to try to get the body ahead of the arm and release the ball slightly behind the body without too much loss of pace.

When the in-swerving leg-break fails to grip and carries on inwards, a not uncommon situation against the wind, the line of attack must be moved from middle-and-leg to the off stump or just outside off. Most deliveries will be played solely as inswervers, but one may grip occasionally and take the outside edge of the bat.

The pure top-spinner is a most useful ball, and methods of accentuating the top-spin component of the leg-break demand experimentation. The top-spinner is a different ball in a number of ways. The less the arm swings across the line and the more it swings up over and straight down the line, the better; easier with a side-on action than front-on. The hand should be bent down at the wrist more than for the leg-spinner. It is better for some bowlers that the ball be held out in the finger-tips, although with most hand sizes this is not possible. Needless to say, it must be thrown a little higher to allow for the downward force of the top-spin, especially against the wind. It is worth trying a more square-chested action for the top-spinner. The idea here is to imitate the action of some inswing bowlers who, by not rotating their bodies around to the offside, ensure that their arms can swing through straighter.

A useful set of variations for leg-spinners involves bringing the arm over at different heights. With practice it is not difficult to bowl anywhere in the arc, from near round-arm to high over the head, and perhaps bending the body back left. Whilst the high delivery is obviously the best for generating bounce, and whilst the ball coming steeply down on the pitch will generally grip more, a surprising result from the round-arm leg-break, especially where the fingers are pointed somewhat towards the batsman, is that the ball will generally turn more. This is because the direction of the spin

Fig. 53 Delivering the leg-break and top-spinner: *a* and *c* are the leg-break as seen from the top and side respectively; *b* and *d* are the top-spinner viewed from the top and side. The thumb is merely helping to support the ball, while the principal spinning force is felt between the first and third fingers, the latter also being placed on the stitching. The different angles of the hand to the line of flight can be seen in *a* and *b* . For the leg-break carrying a 'purer' leg-spin approaching that in Figure *52a*, the fingers are pointed more in a direction straight down the pitch than shown in *a* and *c*. For the topspinner the hand follows more over the top of the ball in the direction of the arrow than it does for the leg-break, where it moves out to the left.

on the ball, as described above, is 'purer' leg-spin, i.e. more like the ball illustrated in Figure *52a* than in *52b*. Furthermore, a ball coming from a different angle upsets the batsman's rhythm a little as he prepares for the stroke.

However the 'purer' 'squarer' leg-spin delivery, spinning as in Figure *52a* from fingers pointing down the pitch, need not be confined to round-arm variations; it is a useful variation in its own

right. Delivered from anywhere, since it carries little or no top-spin, it will have a flatter trajectory; this in itself being a useful variation. Although it will approach the pitch at a lower angle and for that reason might not be expected to bounce as high, the fact that the spin is so much *across* the line of flight might make it kick a little on landing. It is an interesting delivery, worth trying on pitches not giving much turn. Because it lacks the topspin that makes a ball dip in the air, it will not need to be tossed quite so high in the air and it will tend to land closer to the batsman than does the normal top-spinning leg-break.

Hold a cricket ball with the tips of the fingers and thumb arranged more or less equally spaced around it and facing away from you. Now try a few combinations for turning it anti-clockwise. We would be unwise to condemn any particular grip, otherwise we fall into the trap that Bill O'Reilly escaped. If sharp spin is generated, what more is required? (Remember that an apparent lack of sharpness, when demonstrated with the stationary arm, for example an action that some may class as a roll, may in fact produce a perfectly adequate rate of spin as long as the delivery action is quick.) We all have our views on grips however, and there is plenty to be thought about when we look at what bowlers have been up to.

The little finger can probably be dismissed, even from a supportive role; not so the thumb. The thumb is one of a notable spinning pair in what has been named the 'Iverson grip', after Jack Iverson (1915–1973). It has also been called the 'Iverson-Gleeson grip'[3] (since that used by Johnny Gleeson is virtually identical), but could properly be renamed the 'Armstrong grip'. Warwick Armstrong (1879–1947), Australian captain and all-rounder, used the three-point grip of thumb, first and second fingers, fifty years before Jack Iverson. Photographed by Beldam (Fig. 54a), the second finger is bent under the ball, although not quite as tightly into the palm as with Iverson or Gleeson. Fry's comment appears to give Armstrong clear priority in this particular invention: 'An uncommon grip for a leg-break bowler. Apparently the second finger, curled under the ball against the seam, is the one that takes the purchase when the hand is turned'.[4] Armstrong's bowling was noted more for its accuracy than sharp spin. He didn't bowl the googly but got many of his wickets lbw with top-spinners, or leg-breaks which failed to grip.

Where Armstrong, Iverson and Gleeson differ, however, is in the variations they used to accompany the leg-break. Armstrong didn't bring the ball back from the off, but Iverson did, by letting the ball go when the back of his hand was facing the batsman. By this means he converted anti-clockwise spin to clockwise. Gleeson also bowled this ball, but added a normal off-break to his repertoire, thus having two types of off-break to add to his leg-break.

Related to the Armstrong grip, but placing more work on the first finger, was the grip used by 'Tich' Freeman (1888–1965) who had comparatively small hands. He bunched his second, third and little fingers under the ball and gripped it between his first and second fingers and thumb. He took 2776 first class wickets at 18.42 runs each.

We now leave the thumb in a minor supportive role and focus on the first three fingers. Photographs showing the ball resting within these three and the thumb fail to convey their relative importance. Whilst many leg-spinners appear to use all four, it is the first and third which possess the length, leverage and strength for explosive compression and release. The third finger is under the ball and bent in towards the palm as far as is comfortable, with the first finger opposite and stretched out across the seam. The second will also be across the seam, helping to steady the whole grip. Abdul Qadir used a version of this grip, unusual in that the first finger is not straight across the seam on top of the ball but hooked a little towards the thumb.

Without wishing to discourage experimentation, I conclude this account of grips by pointing out that the majority of top-class bowlers, fast, medium and slow, who used the leg-break as their stock ball or as a variation, employed the first-and-third-finger grip (Fig. 53). The pressure points for this grip, the inside of the end section of the first finger and the inside of the first knuckle of the third, vary in the relative amount of wear and tear they suffer. Sometimes, for no apparent reason, one appears to take over some of the punishment being inflicted on the other. But wherever it is felt, this damage is a sign that the bowler is well on the way towards real spin.

The first-and-third-finger grip, with the thumb and second finger in support, is also likely to be the best bet for fast and medium-pace bowlers. A quicker bowler beginning to practise this leg-break need only roll the fingers and hand around a little on release, maintaining control, and gradually building up a tighter spinning action. Few batsmen will find a ball turning at this pace easy to score from.

We encountered the fast and medium-pace leg-break earlier, in connection with swerve and swing. Less well-known than Barnes and Bedser is a bowler who greatly impressed the Australian batsman C. G. Macartney in 1921, who wrote:

South Africa that season had in J. M. Blanckenburg a bowler who should have been a world's champion. He was a medium-paced right-hand bowler, who spun the ball both ways, but was not a googly bowler. His deception in delivery was perfect, and all he had to do was to bowl to hit the wicket during the first few minutes. This, he did not do for some unknown reason, and therefore lost his opportunity.

I have never batted against a bowler who was so difficult to 'find' for the first few overs as Blanckenburg, and I know of no more peculiar feeling than to be opposed to such

Fig. 54a to d Warwick Armstrong and Jack Iverson, pioneers of the thumb-and-second-finger spinning couple. Photo *a* shows Armstrong's grip which allows the second finger to snap up and the thumb to snap down, producing leg-spin.

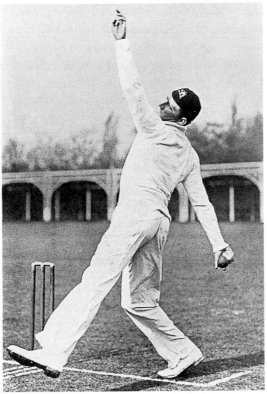

Fig. 54b Armstrong's delivery stride for the leg-spinner.

Fig. 54c Iverson's grip with the second finger closer to the palm than in Armstrong's.

Fig. 54d Iverson's release; his best ball was an off-spinner which he is seen delivering here, with the grip as in *c* and with the back of the hand facing the batsman.

deliveries. I can only compare it to a soldier out in the open when an aeroplane was dropping bombs at night, wondering where the next one is going to land.[5]

Like the great batsman he was, Macartney was being perfectly honest in admitting to no more than a temporary embarrassment, but Blanckenburg's figures of 60 wickets in 18 Tests at 30.28 runs each proves that for many of his opponents, the embarrassment was more than temporary.

Both the development and the maintenance of leg-spinning skills, and in fact all bowling skills, depend to a large extent on solitary practice with a box of balls and the willingness to think hard about every delivery. An unexpected bonus from such dedication, even for experienced bowlers, is the way it can allow them to forget that the batsman is there at all. Such was the advice given by Richie Benaud to help leg-spinner Bob Holland cope with bowling to Ian Botham: 'Imagine that there is no batsman at the other end — pick out your spot and bowl line and length'.[6]

Solitary practice of another sort is required to develop the ability to rehearse in the mind. Just as a top athlete prepares for a big race by mentally working through every detail, so must a bowler be able to bowl an entire over in the same way. The feel of the ball in his hand; the run-in; the delivery; the range of variations all can — and must — be felt in the mind.

Many a page has been written arguing the matter of whether a bowler should learn spin first, or line and length. Why should we focus on this particular division of skills when every single delivery requires the co-ordination of dozens of muscles from the toes to the finger-tips? Every time we bowl we should hope for a satisfactory outcome in all respects. If we accept that one or more of these is less worthy of our attention at any particular time, we are not only wasting time but in danger of wrongly grooving certain movements because they are in isolation and not related to the whole.

A leg-spin bowler should experiment with spin

over a range of different speeds. The limits will become apparent soon enough. No bowler will persist with hopeless inaccuracy for very long. He will reduce the amount of spin action or pace or both, in order to arrive at a combination offering at least a glimmer of consistency, even though acceptable results may be some years away. At the beginning of the process it may involve nothing more than spinning a tennis ball against a wall.

Assuming that the bowler has a range of speeds to choose from in deciding on his particular path to stardom, we can advise him to look in two directions: firstly, back through a century of spin; secondly, at the realities of cricket as played today. The answer from both is the same: bowl leg-spin as fast as possible, or, if adopting a relatively slow pace, opt for a low trajectory. Most of the reasoning for this verdict will already be obvious to the reader. Few of the successful leg-spinners of the past have bowled high and slow. From the time of Barnes and the pacey flattish leg-spinners of the early years of the century, through Grimmett, O'Reilly, Wright, Ramadhin, S. P. Gupte, Dooland, Benaud, Chandrasekhar, Qadir, Warne, and Mushtaq Ahmed, the most successful have made it extremely difficult, even for the most agile batsmen, to move out safely to the pitch of the ball.

Grimmett and O'Reilly paraded their contrasting methods throughout the most successful spinning partnership in the history of cricket. Grimmett: short in stature, delivering from no more than about head height, not quick, upwind, with a low, constantly modulated flight, probing with leg-breaks, seeking to drive the batsman back to be trapped in front by what may have been the flipper or sometimes the top-spinner. O'Reilly: tall enough to bounce a near medium-pace leg-break, downwind, drawing the batsman forwards to what was sometimes a googly, a little slower than expected, aimed, like the leg-break, at the middle and leg stump, and giving the close-in leg-side catch.

Today's leg-spinners, seeking to follow the example of some famous bowler, must be selective in what they adopt. The first lesson to be learned is that although famous bowlers themselves were influenced and inspired by seeing or reading about other great figures, they were, in the end, unique. Spin in particular helps make a bowler unique; too many medium-pace bowlers look as if they came off a production line.

Coaching books usually advise slow leg-break bowlers to bowl into the wind; such advice is questionable. Earlier we discussed how any ball carrying top-spin, including the leg-spinner, the top-spinner or the googly, will dip so sharply against a wind as to suffer a loss of forward momentum which is exacerbated by landing on a pitch lacking pace and bounce. A ball slowing and landing at that steep angle, and even slightly short of a length, is simply waiting to be hit. Even moderate breezes can bring about this undesirable state of affairs. Slow bowlers would like to have the wind as their ally, utilising all the extra subtlety that it can offer, including a magnification of the spin-swerve, provided that it does not nullify the turn the other way. Unfortunately, this assistance must be forgone on many occasions. On faster pitches they can bowl more effectively against the wind. A gentle breeze can be helpful but a strong wind, as well as causing the problem of loss of pace, can also cause loss of turn by accentuating the in-swerve. This may happen with the wind direction anywhere from the wicket-keeper to cover-point. A wind from the leg side will oppose the in-swerve, but *any* wind that aids pace is usually helpful to the leg-spinner on a slow wicket.

An attractive combination is the variation of the influence of wind, pitch and leg-spin from ball to ball. One ball may swerve in and not grip sufficiently to turn away (the commentator's googly), another may not swerve but turn away, and another may swerve in *and* turn away.

One of the most adventurous directions that a leg-spin bowler can take is to bowl around the wicket. Risks and rewards are its hallmark: batsmen and bowler can find themselves fighting on a cliff-edge, disaster beckoning either

protagonist. For the bowler the task is to land a full length leg-break on a line just outside the batsman's legs, preferably in foot marks. A short ball outside the leg stump will usually be expensive. For the batsman the task is to avoid being bowled behind his legs, getting a top edge from an attempted sweep shot, or an off-side edge from any other forcing shot on the leg side. On a wicket with some bounce there is also a chance of the forward defensive stroke popping up a catch to slip or gully.

Richie Benaud bowled leg-spin around the wicket to snatch victory for Australia at Old Trafford in 1963 against an England side needing 254 and coasting to victory at 150 for 2. He took 6 for 70 and England were all out for 201.

But it is not all easy pickings, as Abdul Qadir discovered at Hyderabad during the 1977-8 season. Boycott (100) and Brearley (74), who took England to a draw at 186 for 1, had worked hard on the problem during the rest day of the Test, using Ken Barrington to bowl his leg-breaks to them in the nets from around the wicket.

Leg-spinners may be a little amused to read that wide leg-side bowling of leg-breaks was employed by Armstrong in some of his Tests for Australia against England in 1905 and also in 1921, as a purely defensive measure. In one of these Tests his analysis read 52-24-67-1 and merited the comment that it 'shows what dull stalemate play such tactics can produce'.[7] Armstrong could bowl accurately at a fairly brisk pace and must have been difficult to get away without risk.

Before Armstrong, another Australian, W. H. Cooper (1849–1939), instituted leg-break leg theory on the 1884 Australian tour of England. He was said to be able to subdue even the best batsman with only two fieldsmen on the offside. W. G. Grace and L. C. Braund (1875–1955) also used leg-spin outside leg successfully. We are inclined to forget that the famous googly with which Hollies ended Bradman's last innings was delivered around the wicket. Its effectiveness may well have derived as much from its unusual angle as from any other factor. Even with modern field restriction, the challenging technique of bowling around the wicket is well worth the attention of leg-spin bowlers today.

Bowling leg-spin to left-handed batsmen often elicits the comment that it is not very effective. The basic ball is now a top-spinning off-break. Accurately pitched by a right-hand off-break bowler bowling to a right-handed batsman, it would most likely attract admiration. From the leg-spin bowler to the left-handed batsman it is no less a delivery. Bowled over the wicket and pitched on or just outside the off stump, it comes off hard pitches quickly and causes a hurried shot.

Another generally unrecognised, but most effective, variant for a leg-break bowler bowling to a left-hander is the ball pushed through a little more quickly, delivered over the wicket from wide on the crease, with the arm as high up over the head as possible to accentuate the angle across the batsman. Unlike leg-spin, it carries as much top-spin as possible, and is pitched well up towards the bat and a little wider to the left-hander's off than normal. All of these features, particularly the angle of delivery across the pitch and the possibility of the *outward* spin swerve, give this ball a good chance of beating the bat, not on the inside as might be expected, but on the outside. But bowling around the wicket to a left-hander shuts out this form of attack and can make life difficult for the bowler unless there is some compensation available from foot marks.

Pitching on the leg stump to a left-hander won't help the cause at all. Delivery towards the off can be aided by a more angled run-up and by more body twist around to the right as the bowling arm goes back before coming over.

'Spin and spin hard' should be the motto; even on unresponsive pitches, spin is always likely to do something in the air and may do the unexpected off the ground.

20

THE FLIPPER FAMILY

Good spin bowling, like all bowling, is many things; problem-setting, attacking, surprising, bluffing, training the batsman to oblivion, being patient, and, on occasion, retreating to a defensive position. The batsmen's network, their experience against a bowler and, at the higher levels, the prying TV camera all go towards laying bare the bowler's secrets. But knowing does not necessarily mean doing. The batsman may know that when a certain leg-spin bowler pitches on a certain length he can get out and drive him, but without some training in the process he knows it is risky. The longer time available in a Test match compared to a one-day game makes this training possible; batsmen can take their time and a bowler's inadequacies are more likely to be exposed.

Norman O'Neill tells the story[1] that when preparing for a Test in Brisbane in 1958, Peter May described Richie Benaud as a good steady bowler not likely to present any particular difficulties. After allowing two leg-breaks to pass harmlessly on the off, May, sincerely believing his own advice, padded up to the third and was out lbw for four. Writing twenty-seven years later May described this delivery as a googly.[2] Benaud's intensive two-year course in learning and developing what was for him an entirely new type of delivery, had obviously been kept discreetly 'within the family'. His delivery was apparently not a googly but a flipper. May apparently lacked not only training but knowledge.

This delivery may be better understood now. If so, I suggest that it is more likely to be in spite of, rather than as a result of, the many thousands of words that have been written about it during the last forty years.

My own contact with the flipper dates from the time I began to look around for a more reliable accompaniment to the leg-break than the too often wayward and muscle-tearing googly. What I found was vagueness and a great deal of confusion, a situation that Clarrie Grimmett would have regarded as highly satisfactory as he turned to walk back to his mark.

Grimmett himself was most likely the principal instigator of this confusion, in spite of giving an account of the delivery and its variations, when he wrote one of his books[3] in 1948, twelve years after his last Test. In an earlier book published in 1932[4], he outlined a number of spinning techniques employing the thumb, but did not propose them all as serious contenders for a place in the bowling repertoire. Although its emphasis is puzzling in parts, and the aftermath even more puzzling, one cannot accuse Grimmett of withholding the directions needed by those seeking to imitate him. I had read the 1948 book many years earlier, but because I did not get out and try every delivery that he described, I failed to distinguish the useful from the merely possible.

Grimmett was telling us that in the transition from under-arm to over-arm bowling, we had unnecessarily discarded a valuable means of spinning the ball using the thumb. In his own words:

In most of my experiments I bowled under-arm with a tennis ball and afterward adapted the principle to over-arm.

I was impressed about this time by a very fine under-arm bowler named Simpson-Hayward, who toured New Zealand with an English team. He could spin a ball more than any bowler I had seen at the time (see Fig. 3c). How could such vicious spin be applied under-arm, I wondered. Surely some different principle of spinning must be involved.

If I had asked Mr Hayward, perhaps I would have evolved my Mystery Ball sooner. But as it was, I went on experimenting and eventually realised that much more spin could be applied by holding the ball between the thumb and the second finger. The

problem was, however, to adapt this to over-arm bowling.

I put in hours of practice and experiment at this, and it was only after much hard work that I was satisfied and decided to use it in matches. The reason why I waited so long before trying it in a match, was that pride in my bowling wouldn't let me bowl a ball that didn't fit into the main scheme of my

a

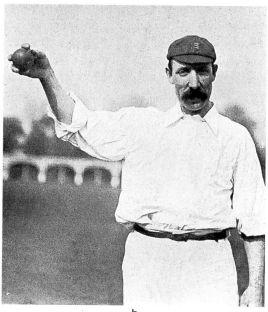

b

Fig. 55 Pioneering spinning grips employing the thumb. Photo a; Walter Mead, medium pace off- and leg-break bowler, with the grip for his back-spinning off-break. The ball sits in a cup made by the thumb and second finger, while the first finger is curled around the top of the ball. During release, as, seen in this view, his first finger would move to the left, while his thumb would straighten out to the right to deliver an off-break. (Photo from Beldam and Fry) Photo b; Mead's grip for the leg-break. The thumb is now away from the palm. The first finger is ready to flick to the right, in this view, and the third finger, ready to straighten out to the left, as normal for most leg-spin. (Photo from Beldam and Fry) Photo c. Grimmett's grip for the flipper, similar to Mead's but with the ball resting on the third finger and thumb. The photo (from *Grimmett on Cricket*) is the batsman's view just before the thumb snaps out to the right to impart off-spin. Although it appears here as 'pure', square, off-spin this is not the way it would travel in the air: the flipper carries a major amount of back-spin.

c

methods. This conception of bowling, too, caused me to use the pruning knife from time to time; so that when I had perfected this new kind of spin, I practically discarded the old googly. I used it only on very rare occasions, usually when I was opposed by a left-handed batsman. I realised that the new delivery had great possibilities. And it was sound in principle to concentrate on my leg-break and straight ball, since the fewer other balls I bowled the less risk I ran of losing control. [5]

Grimmett was fifteen years old when he saw Simpson-Hayward in Wellington in 1907, old enough to have gone to the Public Library in the city and read that remarkable book *Great Bowlers and Fielders* by Beldam and Fry, published in 1906, and discussed in earlier chapters. In this fascinating collection of photographs and detailed analysis of the methods of the bowlers of that time, one stands out (Figs 55*a* and *b*). Walter Mead (1868–1954), 'A medium-pace bowler of the highest class, full of life, very accurate in length, rather deceptive in flight and able to break the ball both from leg and from off' is shown holding the ball in:

> *... a very curious grip for his off-break; the ball sits in a kind of cup made with the thumb and second finger [both under the ball] and the first finger is hooped around over the top of the ball; the first finger aided by a quick twist of the wrist, manages to put a great amount of spin on the ball.* [6]

Although it is highly probable that the young Grimmett, intensely interested in bowling, would have read Beldam and Fry (the same copy in fact that eighty years later the Wellington Public Library staff retrieved for me from their basement), it is unlikely that the technique of one medium-pace bowler out of the sixty-seven bowlers of all types depicted would have stood out. The spotlight was on the googly artists, Bosanquet and Schwarz, who occupy forty pages of the four hundred devoted to bowlers.

Mead was not only one of the best slow-medium bowlers of his day, but, from the clear evidence in that book, should now be regarded as a fine exponent of thumb-spin, a missing link between under-armers like Simpson-Hayward and the Australian flipper merchants. He is described in a recent biographical work as 'generally off-breaking but sometimes sending down a leg-break or googly to good effect'. [7] H. S. Altham also credits Mead with having bowled the googly inadvertently, before Bosanquet. [8] This must now be reinterpreted, and the evidence from photographs and comments is that he bowled the delivery which the Australians, half a century later, named the flipper: Altham was by no means the only one who was confused by it.

W. G. Grace, as if his monumental batting was not enough, enters the picture as yet another missing link, with his slightly above the shoulder round-arm delivery. Not only has he a claim to being a pioneer of the top-spun leg-break with his hand turning anti-clockwise, but with Fry's description that he 'could put drag spin on it by turning his hand the reverse way and cutting under the ball' [9] enters the lineage of the exponents of the modern flipper (Fig. 55*d*). Fry admired W. G.'s bowling greatly: '[It] looks a great deal simpler than it is. A spectator watching from the side of the ground can easily see the length of the ball, but the batsman is often deceived by the flight'. [10] In Chapter 17 we looked at the importance of the 'nothing ball' for certain bowlers. This description of Grace places him firmly among the pioneers of that strategy. The inability of the batsman to judge the length accurately arises from the subtle difference in the influence of back-spin as opposed to top-spin.

The solid evidence supporting the English origins of the thumb-generated back-spin-with-a-little-off-spin delivery does not require us to assume that its only exponents were Mead and Grace. I would expect cricket historians to come up with plenty of others turning the hand clockwise and bringing the thumb around from underneath the ball. Monty Noble, at least, as described earlier,

Fig. 55d W. G. Grace kept them guessing. Is the hand rotating clockwise or anticlockwise? Here it looks like a top-spun legbreak but he could also turn the hand under the ball and bowl a flipper-type delivery. (Photo from Beldam and Fry)

based his devastating side spin on a thumb and first finger grip.

The grip Grimmett refers to, and which is shown in a photograph (Fig. 55c) in his book, is identical with Mead's except that his first and second fingers are much closer together than Mead's. The thumb is bent under the ball which rests on the upper edge of the thumb along the area between the joint and the thumb-nail. The other half of the grip involves the end joints of the first three fingers. Precisely which of these fingers, if any, dominates is a matter for personal experimentation. The second may dominate to some extent, but all three may well be important in working together. However I get the impression from my own experiments that the more fingers there are engaged in significant ways in the grip, the less the grip allows fine control of the release. Now with a flick resembling the action used in playing marbles, or flicking a ball of paper from the hand, quite good spin is obtainable.

Grimmett published descriptions of six deliveries based on this grip, but for the reader who sees them as opening up a new era in spin, a word of caution. Nowhere does Grimmett say he regarded all as worthy of development. We must see at least some of them as nothing more than the academic hypotheses of Clarrie wearing his gown as 'Professor of All Possible Spins'.

Anybody who has experimented in this way knows that, while there are numerous ways of releasing a ball carrying various rotations, they have no future at all unless they have zip, which means plenty of spin and a brisk pace. This means that unless they are capable of giving the ball a good sharp push or pull at the instant of release they are doomed to failure.

Two of Grimmett's six balls are worth some attention (Figs 56a and b).

Grimmett describes one ball as delivered with the thumb underneath and the hand pointing out to the right, and the back of the hand facing the batsman. He also said that this ball (Fig. 56a) has back-spin and slows up when it hits the pitch.

In another part of the book he reveals his Mystery Ball (Figs 56b and 57), again employing the same grip but, according to his description, applying more spin than when bowling his ordinary leg-break. I find this hard to believe. He states that he was only interested in balls that 'made pace off the pitch' except as an occasional variation. For twelve years he practised it, summer and winter, gradually increasing his length. As he spun it:

> ... the hand had to be pointed across to the left towards cover, the wrist had to be bent and the ball allowed to leave over the top of the hand, the back of which was facing the batsman. However, the real problem was to propel the ball and at the same time to synchronise the spinning of it with the moment of release. The hand had to be in exactly the right position, because even the slightest variation caused the ball to leave the pitch slowly ... This proved to be a very successful ball, being much harder to detect than the ordinary googly because I did not have to drop my left shoulder to bowl it. Its plain merit however was its pace off the pitch.
>
> By varying the hand position slightly at the moment of release I could bowl several different balls but they were slow off the pitch and I hardly ever used them.[11]

The Mystery Ball, as Grimmett describes it, is a top-spinner with possible off-break. I wonder very much about this ball. No one, as far as I am aware, bowls it. If they do, then it must resemble the weapon of science fiction, that having destroyed its victim, self-destructs to obliterate all trace of itself. I invite readers to try it with a cricket ball after having examined the photograph (Fig. 57) reproduced from Grimmett's 1948 book.

The arm is stretched out in front of the body, the hand no higher than his cap, the first and second fingers around the front of the ball with the thumb out of sight, presumably cocked behind it. I am reminded of nothing so much as the story of J. M. Barrie, of whom it was said that he bowled

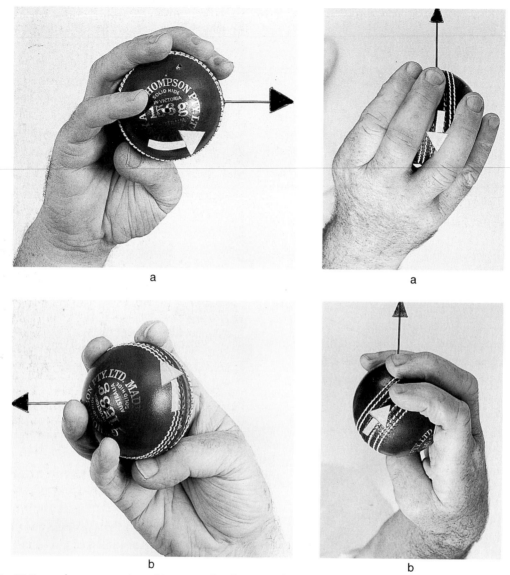

Fig. 56 Two modern reconstructions of Grimmett's thumb-generated spins, each seen from the top and the side; *a* with added off-break is the modern flipper; *b* is Grimmett's Mystery Ball.

so slowly that if the delivery was not to his satisfaction he had the time to reach out and snatch it back.

I have tried the Mystery Ball for a few hours, an insultingly short time I suppose in view of the years he worked on it. My efforts might have been inept, but my results showed none of the top-spin which Grimmett states is the essence of the ball.

The main problem is that the motivating forward force appears to depend heavily on the thumb during the final part of the delivery, and that the thumb is incapable of supplying the pace or zip at the angle required. Grimmett states that the 'wrist had to be bent' but in the photograph the wrist is perfectly straight. Perhaps it was bent in some direction (down?) before the final instant. If you hear a clicking noise sometimes, it is probably Clarrie making doubly sure we remain confused down here. I think I now understand why one writer wrote of him:

He produced a book on how to take wickets, but only told us how he took them himself... Besides, you might as well have read Dan Leno on the art of making faces, or the wind on the art of blowing.[12]

The other delivery Grimmett describes (Fig. 56a) is in a different class. It resembles Mead's ball, and is Grimmett's most significant discovery, or rather rediscovery. The use of the thumb in over-arm spin, as Mead found, is not necessarily restricted to slow bowling.

I had floundered around the literature on the flipper for a few years, finding it incoherent, and Grimmett's book, read thirty years previously, meant nothing to me in this vital area. As a last resort, in 1982, I wrote to Richie Benaud who obliged with a clear and simple reply as follows:

The 'flipper' was a ball that came out from underneath the hand. If you hold your arm erect with the back of the hand pointing towards the sky and turn your hand anti-clockwise, that would be a leg-break; but if you think in terms of the ball being held in the fingers and then 'flipped' out upwards and, in effect, clockwise, that is the 'flipper'. It actually comes from underneath the hand rather than from over the top of it. The result for the batsman is something like a skidding off-cutter and the palm of the hand will end up facing the batsman.[13]

Figure 59 illustrates this delivery, with two possible grips, one of which is an imitation of Mead's (Figs 55a and b).

We now have practical descriptions of two deliveries, one from Grimmett, a top-spinning off-break delivered over the top of the hand; the other a back-spinning off-break delivered from under the hand, drawn from century-old English descriptions of Mead and Grace, and modern accounts from Benaud, Dooland and others.

The first, meeting Grimmett's requirement (so he thought) of pace off the pitch, was the product of twelve years' work and was described by him

Fig. 57 The following description accompanied the above photograph in *Grimmett on Cricket:* 'The Mystery Ball is about to be released. The spin is applied at that moment. Note the position of the hand, with the thumb on the opposite side moved upwards to give forward spin.'

as 'a very successful ball'. It appears to have been universally rejected by bowlers. The second, apparently rejected by Grimmett because he (wrongly) regarded it as being slowed when it hit the pitch, but nonetheless linked to Grimmett in many people's minds, has been embraced by some of the best leg-spinners of the second half of the twentieth century.

Since many writers regard these two deliveries as identical, it is not surprising that, unaware of Mead's priority, they seem at a loss to convey their meaning precisely when discussing the Grimmett-Pepper-Dooland-Benaud genealogy. The examples that follow are not quoted in order to ridicule the authors of some interesting and instructive books, but to illustrate the problem the flipper has caused. Discussion on the matter should also prove useful in helping to clarify the more general topic of the relation between spin, flight, bounce and pace off the pitch.

Bruce Dooland, who with Ces Pepper first brought the flipper into post- Second World War cricket and used it with notable success, gives an interesting account of it, but in using the term 'top-spinner' in a way that is the opposite to the normally accepted usage, he has lent his considerable authority to a widespread misconception of its real nature. His account, which includes the role of the thumb — an omission from Benaud's reply to my enquiry — is as follows:

> *There is another type of delivery at the call of a wrist-spinner, one that should only be tried and persevered with after control has been learned and you have mastered the stock deliveries.*
>
> *This ball took me at least five years of constant practice before I attempted to use it in a match. It is very effective when bowled properly, combining the bosie and skidding top-spinner, together with a rather flat trajectory, floating it further up to the batsman than any other delivery.*
>
> *It has been called the 'flipper' as the ball is flipped by the thumb and second finger, much the same as clicking these fingers together, imparting an off-spin, which turns backwards to the line of flight. The great advantage of this delivery is that although acting like a bosie-top-spinner, unlike the bosie the ball comes from the front of the hand like a leg-break, and is harder to detect than a googly.*[14]

Dooland, who by emphasising the role of the second finger seems to show that he was not aware of Mead's grip, passed the knowledge of the flipper on to Benaud at Nottingham during the 1956 Australian tour of England, but C. S. Marriott in his book *The Complete Leg-Break Bowler* wrongly understood it to be the googly.[15]

No one would be much the wiser after reading Jack Fingleton's account of Grimmett's ball '...

known as the flipper because of the click of the fingers as he released the ball. He bowled it with a leg-break action and the ball making pace from the pitch would come in from the off'.[16]

Ray Robinson is equally vague in describing Benaud as: Commanding respect with length leg-breaks, he set batsmen up for his top-spinner.[17]

An early revision of *The Dictionary of Cricket* by Michael Rundell must be in order:

> *flipper, a relatively slow ball that behaves somewhat like a top-spinner and is produced by a particularly convoluted variety of wrist-spin. It is typically produced by gripping the ball mainly with the tips of the first and third fingers and squeezing or flipping it out so that it emerges from the back or the side of the hand with an extra helping of top-spin on it. If successfully executed it will hurry through without deviation, gaining pace as it pitches and keeping low. The flipper has been described as 'the most arcane and esoteric ball in cricket' (Scyld Berry, Observer 11 March 1984) and its invention is usually attributed to Clarrie Grimmett; more recent exponents include Richie Benaud and Abdul Qadir.*[18]

At least Scyld Berry found a couple of good adjectives to describe the confusion. Bruce Dooland, who could bowl the flipper at 'a Bedser-like pace' might not be too happy with the 'relatively slow' label.

In a description where exhilaration compensates in some degree for scarcity of solid information, Patrick Murphy, writing of Dooland in *The Spinner's Turn*, says:

> *In addition to the traditional leg-spinner's gifts, Dooland had another deadly delivery under his command: the flipper. He spun that from out of the tips of his fingers and it zipped through from off to leg at speed. It is quicker than the googly and Dooland caught out countless batsmen with it: they would shape up for the pull, only to see it hustle through,*

bowl them off the inside edge or trap them
lbw.[19]

Batsmen would find Tom Graveney's stark
description of Benaud's flipper upsetting: 'It
skidded on to you. If it caught you on the back
foot it nailed you before you could do anything
else.'[20]

Ian Peebles' description in the entry on
Grimmett in a recent reference work is unclear:

*His googly was a more modest affair, clearly
discernible and used mostly for tactical
purposes. His top-spinner was, on the other
hand, a wicket-taking weapon, delivered
rather faster and tending to dip late in its
flight.*[21]

Grimmett says that to all intents and purposes
he had discarded the orthodox googly for the most
successful years of his career.

An old mate of Benaud's, Norman O'Neill,
gave an account stronger on adulation than
information:

*Most people have heard of Richie's 'flipper'.
This ball is extremely difficult to bowl. It is
released with a quicker trajectory from the
tips of the fingers and hurries straight on.*[22]

Brian Close describes the results accurately
without detailing methods:

*Richie Benaud and Ces Pepper were great
exponents of the flipper. It is bowled with a
slightly lower arm action and quicker on a
lower trajectory, making the batsman expect
a long hop.*[23]

The word 'top-spin' as used unambiguously for
many years in sports such as golf, tennis, table
tennis and cricket, means the reverse of back-spin.
Eighty years ago, C. B. Fry left the reader in no
doubt with 'over-spin' and 'check-spin'.

The term 'googly' means an off-break with a
particular origin, but 'wrong 'un' in the hands of
some cricket writers can apparently mean anything
different from normal, whatever that might be.

Used this way, 'wrong 'un' declares an ignorance
which bowlers encourage.

The question now arises as to whether, in spite
of his own writings, Grimmett's flipper was not
the Mystery Ball at all, but was in fact Mead's
ball, arrived at independently or not and passed
on to Pepper, Dooland, Benaud and the others.

Benaud, writing about the flipper, was a true
son of the cagey Grimmett in this aspect of the art
as well. When he wrote *Richie Benaud's Way of
Cricket*[24] in 1961 his harvest, long in the ripening,
was beginning to come in. More awaited the
gathering during the next two years. Here was a
ball unknown to most modern readers and players,
and the story of its first apparent use in Test cricket
after the Second World War.

The journalist in him would not allow a good
story to go begging, but it was not the time to write
a coaching manual for the batsman facing up at
the other end. The result is two pages bearing the
threat of trouble in store for batsmen, and quite
unencumbered by useful details such as the grip,
the under-hand delivery and the type of spin given
to the ball. 'I recall adding to my variety after a
chat with Bruce Dooland during the 1956 tour'.
Benaud continues:

*There was a lot of talk in 1956 of how
Bruce took wickets with his 'flipper'. This
was a delivery that was spun out of the
tips of the fingers and hustled in off the
pitch from off to leg at great pace. He
explained the grip and then I went through
the motions. The first few I tried either
slipped straight through as full tosses, or
dropped half-way down the pitch. I kept
at it however and when I eventually landed
one or two I was delighted to see how they
fizzed through.*[25]

Then follows an account of the airing of the
flipper on the South African tour of 1957-8:

*The pitch was slow and my normal leg-break
and wrong 'un lacked penetration. Clive Van
Ryneveld was batting against me and I*

thought: 'I'll try the flipper' It dropped short, Clive stepped back to square-cut and the ball nipped back off the pitch and bowled him. It had worked like a charm. That success has encouraged me to use the flipper ever since, but not too liberally. It does not always take a wicket, of course: in fact it often gets hit for four. But I'm glad to have it as a trump card to be used in times of trouble.

The flipper also brought Benaud success on the Pakistan tour of 1959. Later, writing in 1984, he was more forthcoming about vital details.

The relation between spin, flight, bounce and pace off the wicket is commonly misunderstood. The basic rule is the simple one, probably learned at school, describing the reflection of a ray of light from a mirror: the ray reflects off the mirror at the same angle as it arrives. Grimmett illustrates this by describing throwing a flat stone onto water; a low skimming flight when it will bounce low off the surface. In general terms, that is how a cricket ball behaves. Figure 58*a* can therefore be regarded as illustrating the path of a simple delivery carrying no spin.

Consider a ball carrying at least a major proportion of top-spin. The Robins Force arising from that spin will push the ball downwards in flight, and the bowler compensates for this by tossing it higher. The top-spun ball, whether bowled into the wind or not, lands at a steeper angle (Fig. 58*b*) and therefore has less forward momentum than the back-spun ball in Figure 59*c*.

Bill O'Reilly, writing Grimmett's obituary, said of him: 'He seldom bowled the 'wrong 'un' because he preferred not to toss the ball high'.[26] Grimmett liked the ball to come off the wicket quickly, and since the 'wrong 'un' (googly) carries a fair amount of top-spin, it suffers from the loss of forward momentum described above, an effect accentuated by the fact that he generally bowled upwind.

Although a spinning ball coming down steeply on to the wicket will grip more than a ball coming through at a lower angle, the pitch may not give the bowler a return for his efforts because too much of the energy of the dipping ball may have been dissipated in the turf. The steeply dipping ball is quite innocuous therefore if it is not followed by good upward movement off the pitch. Bounce may force the batsman into error. Good bounce is critical to any form of upwind bowling involving an element of top-spin, whether it arises from the top-spinning leg-spinner, 'pure' top-spin or the top-spinning googly.

Grimmett (possibly) and some notable leg-spinners who came after him faced this problem and adopted novel solutions, including the old thumb-generated back-spin which has been called the flipper by the Australians, and the nothing ball we discussed in Chapter 17.

As in all deliveries carrying back-spin, the Robins Force acts upwards against the force of gravity, thus flattening to some extent the normal downward-curving trajectory. The contrast in flight resulting from the difference between upward and downward Robins Force is one of the surprises of the flipper when bowled after a series of balls carrying top-spin of one sort or another. This feature, frequently commented on by batsmen, recalls Fry's description of Mead's deliveries as, among other things, 'rather deceptive in flight'. Arriving at a flatter angle it therefore comes off the wicket at a flatter angle (Fig. 58*c*). This means good forward momentum with little bounce; just the ball to scuttle through and cause havoc.

A more subtle aspect of this flight is that because the approach is flatter through the air, the batsman is more likely to misjudge the length by thinking that it must drop down and land shorter like a normal topspun delivery. He will therefore go back to wait for it only to find it further up than expected and possibly coming in with a certain amount of off-break.

The 'possibly' in the previous sentence sends out a clear message that breaking in from the off is such a minor part of the flipper's value that it is irrelevant. As with the nothing ball discussed in Chapter 17, it is far more important that it allows an escape from the sameness of a repeated diet of topspin. If it did carry more off-spin it would have less back-spin and would therefore lose some of its contrast in flight compared with top-spin. It would therefore be less effective. However this should not be taken as a devaluation of those bowlers who choose real off-spin, not flipper off-spin, as the accompaniment to their leg-breaks.

Why did Grimmett think that all backspun deliveries come off slowly, and how does the idea of pace off the pitch fit in with all this? The two questions can be answered together.

In the present discussion, pace off the pitch is of most significance when the bowler can make it change from one delivery to another.

Although Grimmett used the analogy of the stone skimming through the bounce when thrown flat across water, he does not seem to have connected this with the type of flight shown by a ball carrying back-spin. This flight almost invariably overrides any slight slowing down caused by the bite and kick that sometimes result when a backspun ball lands, particularly on gripless pitches. Grimmett was right insofar as a ball landing with top-spin will come off the wicket faster than a ball coming in at the same angle with back-spin, but the essential point is that *top-spun and back-spun deliveries seldom do land at the same angle,* because the Robins Force gives them a different flight, especially against the wind.

Pace off the pitch, in this discussion, depends on how much of the total energy given to the ball by the bowler goes into forward movement on landing, and how much goes into upward movement. The flipper has pace off the pitch because a high proportion of its energy ends up as forward momentum. It is worth noting that the kick occasionally expected from the flipper has been reported as 'variable bounce'. Such a kick, and in fact the grip the flipper must get on the ground to show any off-break, will depend on how much friction is felt on impact, a matter which will depend on the pitch.

Since the whole essence of the flipper is concerned with variation, contrast and surprise, one would normally advocate its use as an accompaniment for the leg-break. However, a lateral-thinking medium-pacer, following Mead, may think it worth a trial as a new type of off-break to accompany other deliveries such as swing, or a ball that turns from leg to off. With obvious modifications to the action, it is possible to accentuate the off-spin a little, but it must be kept in mind that the more this is done, the less will be the back-spin and therefore the less will be the alteration in flight. My own trials give reason to believe that Mead's grip (Fig. 59a) offers more control than the alternative (Fig. 59b).

It is not difficult to deliver the flipper with the seam pointing towards the slips, and remaining in

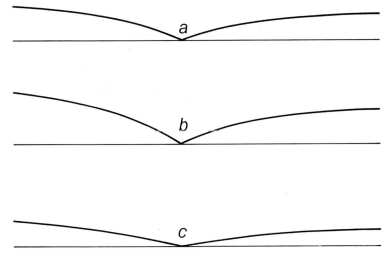

Fig. 58 Angle of arrival of ball on to pitch as it affects bounce (ignoring losses of bounce on turf): *a* normal delivery; *b* delivery arriving more steeply due to top-spin and therefore bouncing off more steeply; *c* low angle arrival and bounce caused by back-spin during flight, assuming that there is no kick or grip during landing.

that position during flight, such as in Figure 50*b* for the outswinging off-break. Bowled after a series of in-swerving leg-breaks, this ball, not exactly the most menacing in the repertoire, may surprise batsmen, even if it doesn't turn back. But a slowish outswinger is probably not the intended result and the bowler may choose to nullify the swing which tends to counteract the slight off-break. If unwanted swing does occur the ball must be delivered with enough quick wobble in the seam to negate it.

Fry describes Mead in action:

The batsman cannot easily get to the pitch

a

d

of the ball to drive and yet has very little time to watch the ball from the pitch if he plays back. Some bowlers who command a good off-break on sticky wickets are fairly easy to hit with a certain amount of pull in the stroke, but Mead's bowling comes off the pitch in a way that baulks the success of the pulled drive.[27]

Used in conjunction with the leg-break, both at medium pace, Mead was a most effective bowler. Compare this account with Alan Border's description of Trevor Hohns' delivery in the fourth Test of the 1989 Australian tour of England. Hohns had bowled a long-hop in the previous over:

Next over 'Cracker' produced the 'flipper'. This pitches half-way down too but it doesn't sit up and say 'Hit me!' It just looks like a long-hop. In fact what it does is skid through fast and lowish. Gower went back to belt it over mid-wicket but his bat was hardly even

b

c

Fig. 59 Two types of grip for a thumb-generated combination of back-spin and off-spin, each shown in front and top view: *a* and *b* are based on the original (English) Mead grip; *c* and *d* are based on one of the later (Australian) flipper versions. During delivery the natural action takes the hand into a position producing a large degree of backspin which is not apparent from these photos. Other finger positions are possible for this type of action but the thumb underneath is the essence of them all.

into the downswing when the ball rapped him on the pads. Out leg before...[28]

The photographs (Fig. 59) show the essential features of the flipper delivery.

Bill O'Reilly overcame the problem posed by the higher flight path demanded by the googly by using his height to deliver the googly in a more downward direction than that available to bowlers of lesser height, and also by bowling downwind. Bosanquet's legacy (Chapter 21) is something of a mixed blessing, to say the least.

Grimmett's twelve years learning what may have been the flipper are probably more interesting now as myth than as a practical guide to learning time. O'Reilly says that Grimmett used the flipper to good effect in his record-breaking last season before the Second World War.[29] Fry does not single out Mead's ball as being particularly difficult. Dooland's own apprenticeship was at least five years of constant practice.

Benaud tells us that Ken Barrington picked up the flipper quite quickly, and was bowling it well after a couple of years.[30] Trevor Hohns said that he had worked on it for six years. Until one hears of failures more serious and widespread than the disasters frequently associated with the googly, there is no reason to believe that bowlers will experience any unusual problems with the flipper. The advantages of a ball which comes through quicker and lower, especially on a slow pitch, are obvious. The future of this rivalry of the 'wrong 'uns' should be full of interest, and as long as cricket writers keep using the term 'wrong 'un', and misunderstanding the flipper, the confusion that bowlers thrive on will continue.

Benaud mentions shoulder trouble which forced him to give up bowling the flipper on the 1961 Australian tour of England, but none of the other exponents appear to have reported such problems. One suspects that Benaud's problem arose not from the flipper but from the more general effects of years of intense practice and play. Leg-break bowling alone can cause problems, but he also bowled the googly, which is notorious in this regard. My own experience is that the flipper causes less strain on the bowling muscles than does the leg-break.

Benaud's comments on disguising the grip contain valuable advice:

Bruce Dooland ... concentrated on disguising his hand before he released the ball so that the batsman couldn't see what was happening, whether the ball was coming out of the top of the hand or the bottom. The batsman could see that something was going on but couldn't pick it out clearly.[31]

These bowlers appear to have improved on Mead in this respect since Fry observes:

It is easy to detect whether he is bowling the off- or the leg-break because when he is going to use the latter he changes the ball in his hand at the last moment and arranges his grip with very obvious care. Needless to say, the batsman, although he knows what is coming, is not thereby relieved of all difficulty.

The deliveries we have been examining are at least a hundred years old, but through neglect and misunderstanding their true value may not have been fully appreciated.

As discussed in Chapter 17 spinners, during a sequence of deliveries, need to escape every now and then, from the continual domination of top spin on the flight. They can enter the realm of spin-induced flight and length variation in the flipper, but I suspect that most will find either the nothing ball or the off-break more easily attainable, and just as effective alternatives.

21

VARIATIONS: DECISIONS

Novelty brings rewards to bowlers, but batsmen, like a virulent infection, can develop resistance and thrive again. Bowlers recognise the value of depriving batsmen of the opportunity of learning to cope with their tricks. John Emburey played with Graham Gooch in the same team in South Africa and bowled to him a good deal to help him sort out his problems; later, to protect himself, Emburey refused to bowl to Gooch in the nets. Grimmett, likewise, refused to bowl to Australia's best batsmen in the nets. The batsman who most relished facing Gleeson was his wicket-keeper for Australia, Rod Marsh. On a personal note, I suspect that the main reason I was once selected in an elite squad was that the selector wished to get some practice against me before he faced me in an important club game.

S. F. Barnes had only two full seasons of county cricket, playing the rest of his career in the northern leagues. As well as avoiding the danger of burn-out from too much cricket, he certainly ensured that the top cricketers of the day did not become familiar with his bowling.

Novelty wreaked havoc when the tall and powerful Bosanquet wheeled over his contorted arm to deliver what looked like a leg-break, but was really an off-break. Bosanquet (1877–1936) recalls the first time it was ever bowled against the Australians: '... at Lord's, late one evening in 1902, when I had two overs and saw two very puzzled Australians return to the pavilion. It rained all next day and not one of them tumbled to the fact that it was not an accident'[1]

Arthur Shrewsbury, one of England's best batsmen, complained about Bosanquet's bowling saying that 'it wasn't fair'. The great A. C. MacLaren exclaimed in 1907: 'If this sort of bowling becomes general, I'm packing my bag for good and aye, and what's more, goodbye to all style and attractiveness in batting'.[2]

R. E. Foster, England's captain, bludgeoned by the onslaught of the South Africans who boasted no fewer than four googly bowlers in their 1907 team, wrote:

Personally, I think it will deteriorate batting. For this new kind of bowling is a very great invention, and it is possible it may completely alter cricket, and no one who has not played against it can realise the difference it makes to a batsman and his shots. It must again be reiterated that this type of bowling is practically in its infancy, and if persevered with, as it surely will be, must improve and become more difficult to deal with. Now a batsman, when he goes in, may receive a ball which either breaks from the off, perhaps from the leg, or again may come straight through very quickly. If he survives half-a-dozen overs he ought to be getting set, but such bowling never allows the batsman to get really set, because he can never make or go for his accustomed shots.[3]

— a batsman's point of view. But the learning was already under way and Foster's team in fact won the series of three three-day Tests with one win and two draws. What a sight it must have been to see that quartet operating on the bouncy South African pitches the previous year, when South Africa beat England 4-1. The subsequent history of the googly, while not bearing out Foster's fears, has nevertheless been fascinating.

Fingers wrapped around a ball smaller than a cricket ball are free to spin it in any direction. Jack

Iverson, in Port Moresby during the Second World War, discovered his unusual method with a table tennis ball. Bosanquet says he discovered the googly while playing a game where two people sat in chairs on opposite sides of a table and bounced a tennis ball across it, each trying to deceive the other with spin. This was 'somewhere about 1897' he wrote,[4] but his brother, in a letter to *The Times* in 1956, talks about flicking a tennis ball across the uncovered slate of a billiard table about 1892.[5] Years of practice with a solid rubber ball followed, involving his cousin Louise retrieving balls in the garden for hours on end.

Spinning was only an amusing sideline when Bosanquet played for Oxford University from 1898 to 1900. Although he was a useful medium to fast bowler and a good bat, his 'star turn', as he called it, was to bowl to famous batsmen who were enticed to the nets at Oxford during the lunch intervals:

> I was brought up to bowl him two or three leg-breaks. These were followed by an 'off-break' with more or less the same action. If this pitched in the right place it probably hit him on the knee, everyone shrieked with laughter, and I was led away.[6]

Progress was slow as Bosanquet gradually dropped his fast bowling. He accumulated a good deal of experience in captaining private teams to America in 1901 and to the West Indies in 1901-2. In 1902–3 he toured Australia and New Zealand with Lord Hawke's team with no great success but one delivery worth remembering.

The mystique surrounding the googly, enriched by journalists, victims, bowlers themselves, and nurtured on frequently erroneous observation, may have reached unjustifiable proportions. But there are two well-authenticated deliveries, at least, which deserve a place in the history books, and which in fact may have contributed substantially to that image. One of these is the ball with which Hollies dismissed Bradman in his last Test innings, at the Oval in 1948, for a duck. The other was forty-six years earlier when Bosanquet delivered the first googly to be seen on the Sydney Cricket Ground, and kept an appointment in history with Victor Trumper, cleaned bowled, third ball.

At home in 1903, still with more promise than achievement, Bosanquet took 63 wickets for 21 runs apiece, using leg-breaks and the occasional googly. This gained him a place in the MCC team to Australia where, with novelty at its maximum, and on fast bouncy pitches, he played a major part in England's win in the series.

Bosanquet took pains to conceal his methods and always tried to convey the impression that the dismissal was caused by something other than his trickery. In a county game in 1904 he is reported in Wisden as bowling a 'wretched length' to collect 10 Yorkshire wickets for 248. In another report Wisden claimed 'The home side indeed were quite demoralised by Bosanquet who, although making the ball turn, bowled in the first innings in very erratic fashion'; he took 14 wickets for 190 in that game. Surveying the season at its end, Wisden saw Bosanquet in a different light: 'The best man in the event ... a match-winner... unequalled in any county'.[7] Wisden can be forgiven for having difficulty understanding the new species; such a hot-and-cold attitude has been characteristic of the way cricket has treated googly bowlers ever since.

During his active cricketing days Bosanquet seems to have confided in only one person, his close friend, the South African R. O. Schwarz[8] (1875–1918). As if to emphasise the stature of his coaching, Bosanquet took 9 for 107 in one innings for MCC against the touring South African team in 1904, of which Schwarz was a member. The game, the first of the tour, was washed out, but two games later Schwarz showed what a good student he was by taking 5 wickets for 27 runs and ended the tour with 68 wickets at 18.26 runs apiece.

South Africa's 4-1 series win over England in 1905-6, along with their 1907 tour of England, marks the summit of googly history when they showed that they were still a force on pitches less lively than South African matting. R. E. Foster has left us an account of the bowling of the famous quartet, Schwarz, A. E. E. Vogler (1876–1946), G. A. Faulkner (1881–1950) and G. C. White (1882–1918), in which he describes them as coming off the pitch at an extraordinarily fast pace in spite of seeming to be comparatively slow through the air and not very deceptive in flight. They were all in fact closer to medium or slow-medium pace than to slow. Although Foster was one of the three or four really great batsmen of the early 1900s he had to learn to cope with a quickish off-break of a new type, one that carried heavy top-spin. Later batsmen familiar with the left-hand chinaman would be less surprised by this delivery. It appeared to be slow because it needed to be thrown a little higher to allow for the downward push from the top-spin component. The loose balls that came along were hard to hit because of the speed with which they came off the bouncy pitches; six men frequently placed on the leg side made the big hit risky.

Vogler was the finest of the four, concealing his grip well during the run-up and possessing very deceptive variations of pace. He often started with fast-medium off-spin with out-swerve or outswing; then, with the shine off the ball, he bowled slow-medium leg-breaks, with the googly introduced perhaps once every two overs. His leg-break turned from 2 or 3 inches up to 18 inches (46 cm); the googly spun rarely more than 3 or 4 inches, often coming straight through as a top-spinner. A dangerous ball of his was a slow yorker which seemed 'more to quiver than swing in the air'. Who knows what witches' brew of varying swerve and swing, each possibly changing in dominance during flight, this ball represented? C. S. Marriott also records that the leg-break:

... sometimes performs an amazing kink about three-quarters of the way along its flight; I have generally heard this called 'corkscrew', which is near enough, but not strictly true because there is no circular motion. What actually happens is that the ball suddenly swings very sharply and swiftly in the air three or four inches to right and left, and then goes straight on. I have often done it, but never knew when it would happen nor what caused it. The bowler can usually see it himself, although I have noticed that it shows up more plainly in a certain light. One of the finest examples I can remember was when A. E. Relf was coaching. Although then getting on in years, he was still bowling that beautiful leg-break at medium pace; quite often his leg-break performed this astonishing kink in its flight from side to side. Once or twice I even saw a bit of real evidence for calling it the corkscrew, when it occurred so late that the ball had already begun to dip: the first short swing was to leg, which meant that it began by moving in a semicircle, and although the quick return-swing was horizontal, the illusion of a genuine corkscrew movement was apparent enough. I asked him about it afterwards: he said he had always done it, but could offer no explanation beyond the blend of leg- and top-spin on the ball.'

The famous Mailey full tosses that dismissed Jack Hobbs twice in Test matches, at Melbourne in 1925 and the Oval in 1926, came out of the same aerodynamic box of tricks. Later Mailey said of one of them that it was not a full toss but a high one that dipped suddenly.

Faulkner bowled the leg-break and googly at slow-medium pace with great control and fierce spin, concealing the googly well. White was similar but spun the ball less. Schwarz was the odd one because he had the googly but not the leg-break. Foster thought that he should have been scored off more than he was. Batsmen didn't need to worry about possible spin in the other direction; he was purely a top-spinning off-break bowler with a googly action. Too many batsmen tried to hit him. Foster's advice was to play him off the pitch for twos and threes, rather than going for the big hit. Many tried the latter and made his figures compare well with the others.

The averages in 1907 were: Schwarz 137

wickets at 11.79; White 56 at 14.73; Vogler 119 at 15.62; Faulkner 64 at 15.82. Schwarz required 31 balls for each wicket, the others 30. In the 1909-10 series, played in South Africa, Vogler took 36 wickets and Faulkner 29 in beating England, while Schwarz and White were not selected. Vogler, Schwarz and Faulkner toured Australia with the South Africans in 1910-11, but met with little success. Vogler had taken to the bottle, and batsmen were learning about googlies. For the 1912 Triangular Tournament in England Vogler did not go, Faulkner had partly lost the knack, and Schwarz had lost it completely. The great quartet had finished.

The origin of the name googly is about as clear as the googly itself was to its early victims. 'Googler' is a word known to have been used in 1898-9 to describe some unspecified type of bowling in England, before Bosanquet. The Australians called it the 'bosey', and to the South Africans it was the 'wrong 'un'.

'Googly' and 'wrong 'un' gave way to 'bosey' after the First World War. No English googly bowler was a world force after that time, in spite of the excellent home records of Freeman, Wright, Hollies and others.

H. V Hordern (1884–1938) led the way for the Australians in the pre-war period, giving the South Africans a taste of their own medicine in a 4-1 series win in 1910-11. He took a long run and bowled accurate googlies and leg-breaks with a high action at medium pace. In the following season, also in Australia, he took 32 wickets for 24.37 against England. Returning to full-time dentistry, Hordern retired from top cricket after two seasons, never having toured England with an Australian team. Brilliant bowler though he was, relatively brief exposure at the top level must preclude any claim of greatness for him.

Coming after Hordern were two, and I think it is correct to say the only two, right-hand googly bowlers who pass the test of being successful with the googly and who maintained success at a reasonable level throughout the whole cricket world over a number of years. These were Mailey

and O'Reilly. The Indian leg-break and googly bowler S. P. Gupte (1929–), with his 149 Test wickets at 29.55 in 36 Tests, pushes for a place alongside Grimmett and O'Reilly. Grimmett's 216 wickets at 24.21 in 87 Tests is undoubtedly better and, unlike Gupte, he was a force in England. Comparisons such as these are difficult however, because by the time Gupte appeared on the scene, conditions in England had already become less favourable for spin. However, at the same time, the cricket world had expanded to include the West Indies, India and Pakistan, in all of which Gupte was very successful.

Grimmett tells us that he virtually abandoned the googly during his career, since it didn't fit in with his bowling plan. Herb Collins told him during the 1926 tour of England not to bowl any more googlies on the tour, although he could bowl them quite accurately. Grimmett thought Collins feared that he would lose the leg-break. The subsequent development of Grimmett's bowling, and the way in which he was able to maintain a low trajectory and off-break without the googly, has been discussed earlier. Although he says he used the googly very rarely — and then mainly against left-handers — anyone who knows the difficulty of pulling out a delivery like that for rare occasions only would be surprised to find Grimmett, with his exacting standards of accuracy, taking such a risk, especially when he already possessed an effective top-spinner and possibly the flipper.

Ring and McCool bowled googlies, but through no fault of their own were denied the chance to walk the larger stage. Dooland, who also had limited exposure in international cricket, could bowl the googly, but it was the flipper that took him to the heights. Benaud, during long hours practising leg-breaks and googlies, eventually damaged his shoulder, and, more than once in a less than brilliant early bowling career, was on the point of giving up before adopting the flipper.

Arthur Mailey moulded the leg-break, top-spinner and googly, all at a higher altitude than that of his famous googly predecessors, into a match-winning combination. He dominated the world of spin in the 1920s and with the possible exception of S. P. Gupte, no bowler of the slow googly has matched him since that time. Ian Peebles admired a fellow leg-spinner with the following description:

The enormous spin was the product of an ideal leg-break bowler's action. Mailey ran a few springy paces at an angle to the wicket, curled his wrist up in the region of his hip-pocket, and flipped the ball out with nicely co-ordinated movement of arm, wrist and fingers. He was a dangerous bowler in the air as well as off the pitch, for the fast-revolving ball dropped steeply at the end of its flight. The batsman who made any misjudgment of length was in poor case to combat the sharp break in either direction. Mailey played twenty-one times for Australia and took 99 wickets. That they cost 33 runs apiece is neither here nor there. In 1920-21 he took 36 wickets in the series, an Australian record. [10]

Mailey's brand of all-or-nothing cricket, his humour and wonderfully refreshing approach reached the public not only through his deeds on the field, but also through his pen as a cartoonist and writer. Anyone interested in an expert's account of the hey-day of spin, and in a warm and human attitude to the game of cricket, should read his book *10 for 66 And All That,* [11] the title being his figures for one innings against Gloucestershire in 1921. Such was his faith in his methods, that, as his career developed to Test-match level, he gave the ball more air than he had done earlier.

O'Reilly bowled with aggression, pace, spin and accuracy of length and direction during twenty years for New South Wales and twenty-seven Tests. Others before him had spun the leg-break further and bowled it faster; others had bowled the googly at speed. When he came on the scene the googly had long since lost its novelty value against top batsmen, but in O'Reilly's hands the combination was indeed formidable. Only on

pitches made dead and gripless was he defeated, as at the Oval in 1938. Coaches presuming a right to change a bowler's action should note O'Reilly's ungainly run-up and delivery, 'all flailing arms and suggestion of a stoop', and ponder its effectiveness.

As for a bowler's attitude to his craft, O'Reilly recommends a version of the martial arts mentality, in an article he wrote for his club report:

You can never become a good attacking bowler if you do not develop a bowling 'temperament'. A happy-go-lucky, good-natured and carefree outlook is of no use whatever to an ambitious and competent bowler. He must be prepared to boil up inwardly on the slightest provocation, and opportunities are so common that there is no need to cite even one.

Conceal that desirable temperament from the public, but reveal it in all its force and fury to your opponent, the batsman. [12]

Adding to the batsman's discomfort, he was better at concealing his googly than his temperament. In another account written in his old age, he revealed details of his technique and strategy:

With my bowling, my cardinal rule was that I always had my eyes glued on the spot where I was going to pitch the ball. I wasn't a slow leg-spinner, I bowled medium pace. The leg-spinner was my stock ball, but I bowled the wrong 'un more frequently than any other leg spinner I've seen. It was nothing for me to bowl it three times in an eight ball over: I had complete confidence in my ability to bowl a wrong 'un to length and direction, and I could really get it to bounce, so I used it as a variation of flight and bounce as well as spin.

When I started I used to bowl the orthodox off-break, but I gave that up because it interfered with my rhythm, but my straight faster ball got me a lot of wickets — I even had a bouncer of sorts. [13]

The question of how to 'pick' it, or whether in fact it can be 'picked' at all, is virtually the province of the googly and nothing else in the entire art of spin bowling. When were cricketers last drawn into an intense speculation on whether it was possible to pick an arm-ball or a top-spinner from an off-break?

A. A. Thomson tells of the attitude of a seasoned veteran Arthur Shrewsbury, whom W. G. Grace considered the next best batsman in England to himself:

'If this kind of bowler,' said Shrewsbury, 'pitches a ball outside my off stump, I expect it to break in from the off and I'm ready to play it that way. If it breaks the other way I leave it alone. But if it pitches on my legs or between my legs and the wicket, I expect it to break in from leg; if it does, I play it, if it doesn't, I leave it alone. And what's more,' added Arthur shrewdly, 'I bide my time, because I never saw one of those chaps who didn't bowl one or two bad balls in an over, and I'd get a four off those ... "[14]

Bosanquet, always inclined to be wayward in length, gave up county cricket in 1905, and his career as an effective bowler ceased at that time. He had good days, but his length was described as generally 'irregular' and his claim to fame must be more as pioneer than polished practitioner. Defending the googly against the accusations of the type made by R. E. Foster, he wrote in 1925: 'But, after all, what is the googly? It is merely a ball with an ordinary break produced by an extraordinary method. It is not difficult to detect, and, once detected, there is no reason why it should not be treated as an ordinary break-back!'

Bowlers wishing to try this 'extraordinary method' may find the following description useful. The hand must hinge in at the wrist at delivery earlier than for the leg-break. The back of the hand faces the batsman and there is a feeling that the ball is being flipped out over the top of the little finger. As the bowling arm comes up the wrist should not stiffen, while the hand rolls over to bring the palm facing upwards. Dipping the left shoulder earlier than for the leg-break, and perhaps turning more to face the batsman, make this difficult delivery a little more feasible.

Unless the whole action is completed at a height close to that of the leg-break, the difference is likely to become obvious to many batsmen. A variation of the googly action, which may make it more difficult to detect, is to point the hand more to the rear than down to the side as it comes over high. This may well be the secret of its more successful exponents.

Whereas the final stage of the leg-break action involves the fingers flicking over the ball in a direction somewhere between the slips and extra-cover, the googly action involves the fingers flicking over towards the leg side.

All else failing, most batsmen go on the back foot and try to read the ball off the pitch, or make sure they get out to it and smother the spin.

The caution required of the batsman in sensing and combating the added danger gives the bowler an advantage, especially when there is no guarantee that the ball will actually grip and turn as expected. This danger applies every time a batsman 'reads' a bowler, fast or slow. The really successful googly bowlers possessed the flexibility to carry out these actions quickly and easily and with a minimum of strain.

Every possible give-away sign has been spotted by batsmen at some time or other: the run-up, the grip, a little finger sticking out, the lower hand, the higher flight, the way the ball spins in the air. Their conspicuousness may depend on the rapidity of the finger action, the clarity of the light and the type of background.

Abdul Qadir, a bowler of great interest to the cricketing world, spun his googly with a quick enough action to make it difficult to detect from his hand; but his impressive attacking qualities were too often unaccompanied by the necessary consistency and patience.

The Somerset batsman Harold Gimblett, who was having trouble playing leg-breaks and googlies, asked Walter Hammond for advice. The reply he received follows.

Hammond gave me a long stare. 'Forget 'em Harold. Ignore 'em'. 'That's all very well for you,' I said. 'You can play them with your eyes shut. It's something I haven't learned to do.'

'First of all, clear your mind of this nonsense about them turning one way or the other. Just play every ball on its merit, where it pitches.'

Hammond was not an easy man to talk to. But he was very helpful to me. He explained that if the ball was a half-volley I should aim for somewhere between mid-on and mid-off, that arc. If it was a leg-spinner, the shot would go past mid-on.

'There's one golden rule,' he said. 'Normally to play back, you're supposed to get into a position where you are absolutely right behind the ball. But not with these boys. They can catch you with a top-spinner or one that hurries off the wicket. You've got to give yourself a bit of room. Go forward and backwards on the leg stump. If it's slightly short, you can play back and, outside the off stump, you have all the arc in the world, square to cover-point and beyond, to hit it where you like as hard as you like. If it comes into you (the googly) you've still got plenty of time and room to play wide of mid-on for 2, 3 or 4.'

I couldn't wait for leg-spinners after that.[15]

Writing of googly bowling in 1907, W G Grace said:

Now the genuine googly requires even more effort of a peculiar kind than does the leg-break. In my opinion, a bowler cannot last who has any trouble over his delivery. The longest-lived bowlers are those whose action is the reverse of troublesome.'

Grace was right; a significant number of googly bowlers have suffered serious problems of one sort or another. R. O. Schwarz lost the ability to bowl the leg-break. Ian Peebles (1908–1980), the great hope of English spin in the 1930s, severely damaged his shoulder bowling leg-breaks and googlies; after only four Test series he was forced to withdraw and ended his career bowling off-breaks. Likewise, J. H. Cameron, a West Indian, found the strain of bowling leg-breaks and googlies too much during the 1939 tour of England and settled for off-breaks. Garfield Sobers' spinning career ended in 1966 when his shoulder went as a result of bowling the googly; an injury that never completely healed. Richie Benaud developed chronic fibrositis during his Test career. Benaud, like Peebles, had been prepared to devote the great amount of time to practice that is demanded of a bowler attempting to tame the googly. R. S. Whitington described the pain:

Benaud had withdrawn from the Lord's Test owing to his very painful, fibrositic bowling shoulder. Watching Richie don and remove his sweater during that cold summer was as excruciating as two hours with a dentist. I watched the expression on his face through binoculars once, and once was enough. Few noticed how Richie always faced away from those on the field when he donned and removed that sweater.

He could hardly have suffered a less favourable preparation for the ordeal he knew he must undergo on that last day at Manchester. He had to eliminate the googly from his scheme of things as his shoulder could not allow him to deliver it.[16]

Problems like these have afflicted googly bowlers at all levels of cricket. Apart from causing injury and loss of the leg-break, the googly among all the possible deliveries in cricket is the one most likely to be punished. It may not necessarily be the most inaccurate, although the awkwardness of the 'pull' rather than the 'push' nature of its release, makes it likely to be so. It is the combination of this basic inaccuracy, with a generally slower speed, and inward turn, that makes it more vulnerable than most other bowling.

Bob Holland, a successful Australian Test leg-spinner in recent years, said in a television interview that he didn't bowl his googly in international cricket because it wasn't one of his good balls and he hadn't full control of it. The reply from the interviewer encapsulated perfectly the widespread ignorance of the googly and displayed a lack of appreciation of the honest, considered, and successful strategy that had just been revealed to him, by saying: 'I think you should bowl a few wrong 'uns just to make the batsman think', adding the advice that Holland should work on that ball at the nets!

History tells us that Mailey and O'Reilly were unique in their own different ways. If better bowlers of their type should ever appear, such an event will be just as freakish as they were themselves. Because the googly is such a poor ally, it is harmful to the re-emergence of spin bowling to regard either of them as practical models for young bowlers to imitate.

It is easy to knock the record of the googly for six, as did Alan Fairfax, an Australian Test batsman of the 1930s:

This type of delivery attracts more attention than it deserves because it is a freak which few can bowl. Anyway, it is used much less frequently than newspaper writers would have us believe. It is my firm belief that the overrated googly is the ruination of many potential leg-break bowlers. [17]

Nevertheless, when spin regains a significant place in the game, new generations of bowlers will rise to the challenge of the googly and cricket will be all the richer for it. If they do, then a little gentle cynicism is called for, along with R. C. Robertson-Glasgow, who penetrates the world of at least one googly bowler and perhaps of nearly all of them:

They are always going to do the trick. They feed on hope, die by murder, and are born again. Reasons, evasions, and open lies live around these googlies. It is the wrong end, the wrong slope, or too cold. Some day all will be warm and right. But I don't think so. Never the time and the place and the googly all together. [18]

Even if we could rid the googly of all the doubtful baggage that it has accumulated, it can't escape from the sameness of its flight compared with the leg-break. One could claim that this is an advantage; same flight, different turn, but turn is not nearly enough against a good batsman. In earlier chapters we looked at the ways that bowlers seek to escape from this dilemma.

The story of the googly is one of the most fascinating in cricket. Those who use the term in a careless way, such as in describing a ball that merely fails to turn, among an over of those that do turn, should consider the possibility that, by their irresponsibility, they will devalue its true meaning.

22

LEFT-HAND BOWLING

Right-hand cricketers, both batsmen and bowlers, outnumber their left-handed counterparts by about four to one. Untangling the reasons for the handedness of the human race has kept a great number of people busy for many years. Somewhere in the background of it all we must accommodate the fact that the right side of the brain carries out some functions not carried out by the left, and vice versa; but I doubt that this explains why we are so lopsided in our attitude to left-hand bowling.

If ever a bowler was the victim of stereotyped thinking along the most unimaginative lines possible it is the left-arm spinner. For some reason we have come to regard a left-hand bowler who wheels up a gently spinning ball, which will drift a little in the air if the wind is in the right direction, and may very occasionally turn on landing, as indispensable to the attack (if that is the appropriate word) of every cricket team. A simpering off-break action that would be eminently un-remarkable from a right-hander is elevated to a sublime level.

Colin Blythe and Tony Lock were left-hand spinners in the very best sense. They spun the ball with an action which if transferred to the mirror hand would rank with that of the most notable off-spinners. Unfortunately they were not the models for the droves of left-arm, so-called spinners whose principal function it seems is to bowl inexpensively enough to impress a certain type of captain, take up so much time that victory is out of the question, regard wicket-taking as something for others, and ultimately play batsmen into form. The sight of one such delivery actually turning is a noteworthy event at any level.

If any logic does exist within this gentle occupation, it is most likely to be found in the emphasis which is placed on flight. Fortunately, right-arm leg-spinners operating from the same side of the wicket and actually succeeding in their appointed task of turning the ball away from the bat, are not allowed to base their career on such a narrow foundation. The delicate finger pressure required would at least guarantee a minimum of lost skin.

Everything discussed earlier in connection with the right-hand off-break and its accompanying variations can be applied to the left-hander. The implication in this set of deliveries is that the stock ball is the leg-break, the ball which will cause the right-hand batsman the most embarrassment.

Wilfred Rhodes (1877–1973) was a spinner of high class, a slow left-hander who, as well as scoring nearly 40 000 runs in 37 seasons, took 4187 wickets. He was one of the most successful bowlers ever, a master craftsman of curving flight, subtle variations and spin. Some details of his methods, as passed on by Hedley Verity and C. B. Fry, are included in the biography by A. A. Thomson. First Verity:

... the left foot behind the bowling crease, the right foot out on the off side. Then, just before the left arm comes out to deliver the ball, the batsman catches a glimpse of the bowler's right shoulder-blade.

The ball is spun on a line from mid-on to third man. On delivery, the wrist turns and the knuckles go up and out from the hand, the ball being spun from the first finger.

The momentum of run-up, through arm, shoulder, body, and turn of wrist, goes into the action, the bowler following through automatically, up and over his front foot.

In such an action there is both ease and power, and the curving flight, with the ball travelling upwards from his fingers, takes the spin better than any straight flight.[1]

and Fry:

How does the batsman see Wilfred Rhodes? Hostile meaning behind a boyish face, ruddy and frank; a few such easy steps and a lovely swing of the left arm, and the ball is doing odd things at the other end: it is pitching where you do not like it, you have played forward when you do not want to — you have let fly when you know you ought not; the ball has nipped away from you so quickly; it has come straight when you expected a break; there is discomfort.[2]

Verity's observation that the ball was 'spun' on a line from mid-on to third-man refers to the direction of the hand twisting across behind it.

Tony Lock based his career on the conviction that left-hand spinners should be attacking bowlers, able to turn the ball on most pitches. Even Rhodes and Verity were frequently stock bowlers rather than wicket-takers. But Lock bowled at a brisk slow-medium pace, seldom using the chinaman and almost never the googly. His leg-break and associated variations brought the rewards he sought, and in his time he was the most dangerous attacking left-arm spinner in the game. In 49 Tests he took 174 wickets at 25.58 each.

Derek Underwood's spinning action was discussed earlier. What more damning commentary could be made on modern cricket than that of his team-mate Chris Cowdrey[3] when he expressed the widely held view that Underwood was: '... a freak talent ... no other modern cricketer has successfully bowled medium-pace spinners'? The line of great slow-medium spinners of earlier years was virtually down to one survivor. On his retirement Underwood complained bitterly about the bounceless pitches on which he was forced to bowl. Earlier he pointed out the drastic reduction

in the use of spin in one-day games.

At the beginning of his county career Underwood grappled with the problem facing all left-handers, that of bowling around or over the wicket. Over the wicket he found it necessary to pitch just outside the leg stump in order to hit the wickets, allowing for the angle of delivery. To the slow left-hander this may sound far-fetched; but it must be remembered that a good length for a faster bowler like Underwood is somewhat shorter, and that the shorter it pitches the wider is the straight path missing the off stump. The problem is even more acute for medium and fast left-handers. Underwood's ball that swerved and possibly swung from off to leg also caused him problems, it tending to carry on down the leg side and remove any chance of an lbw decision. He also found it difficult to avoid running on to the pitch; running across in front of the umpire standing back would have required a drastic change in his entire bowling action because of the completely new angles involved. Wisely making his own decision in the face of advice to the contrary from some highly-regarded cricketers, he settled for bowling at his normal pace, around the wicket with the umpire standing up. He pitched between wicket and wicket or just outside off and the in-swerver was always likely to get an lbw.

Underwood revealed the basis of a memorable career in these words:

I rely on subtle variations of pace for my wicket-taking ability, allied to bowling a tight line and length, just as any other spinner would do on a good wicket, the difference being that my stock ball is faster than their's. If the conditions help the ball turn more sharply, then I consider that a bonus. Again just as any spinner would do.

Length and line coupled with the ability to disguise a slower delivery have always been my main assets ever since my school days... More often than not this was sufficient to take wickets at schoolboy level and even at village green level. Moving up a class to play club cricket for Beckenham made me realise I had to do a little extra.

That was the time I added a great variety to my bowling. It was at this stage that Kent began playing a part in my development and Claude Lewis, a left-arm spinner himself, influenced these variations when he told me, 'For every wicket on which you play there is a pace to bowl.'

My stock delivery then was fairly flat and from that I developed a quicker ball, a slower ball, another one slightly slower still, giving it more air, and so on. My bowling remains basically the same today. The one great difference being that I have now become better at adapting my style to different wickets and at exploiting wickets which really give me encouragement.[4]

We have been discussing the left-hander's leg-break, delivered with the same action as a right-hander's off-break. When we move on to its opposite number, the left-hand action mirroring the right-hander's leg-break, we come to something of a cul-de-sac in the development of left-hand bowling.

Used by the left-hander, the right-hander's range of techniques for the leg-break will deliver a range of off-breaks. But we seem to have gone out of our way to make left-handers feel odd when they wish to bring the ball back in from the off. We adopted a curious name, the 'chinaman', and to add to the confusion, sometimes wrongly apply it to the left-hander's googly, which of course is a leg-break to a right-hand batsman. The name is thought to have been coined by an English batsman during the 1950 MCC tour of the West Indies. After being bowled by an off-break from Ellis Achong, a Trinidadian of Chinese extraction, he uttered the remark, 'Fancy being bowled by a Chinaman'.

Perhaps it is the relatively small number of such bowlers which attracts this sort of treatment. Unless we encourage such left-hand bowling, a significant proportion of cricketers will not be testing their potential skills to the fullest extent. Research indicating that about one-quarter of all young children have no preference for a particular hand raises the possibility that the game could be enriched by more young cricketers being encouraged into left-handedness. Even mature cricketers are known to have changed over, and there are some who could bowl with both hands.

Fast, medium, and slow, left-handers have always been valued members of many bowling attacks. For their stock ball they all bring the hand down to the left of the ball during release and, depending on the axis of spin, obtain varying degrees of inswing, in-swerve and leg-break. A few can also swing the ball away from the right-hander by drawing the hand down on the right side of the ball and using an action which mirrors that of a right-hand inswing bowler.

Fry's analysis[5] treats only a few left-handers but there is one, S. Hargreave (1876–1929) of Warwickshire, a slow-medium bowler whose methods point to a deficiency in our modern approach. Hargreave was noted for his accuracy, his ability to vary pace and length, and his effectiveness on all types of wicket, fast and slow. After describing Hargreave's ability to bowl a leg-break at full pace using 'finger-spin', Fry describes his slower ball, which 'drops shorter than expected and nips along quickly'. The ball 'is a very good one which is liable to beat the batsmen not only off the pitch, but in its flight'. The accompanying photo shows the first-and-third-finger grip, the mirror image of the one found to be most effective for right-hand leg-break bowlers. Fry's caption under the photo reads: 'The ball is held apparently for the off-break. But this bowler does not break from the off in using this grip unless he turns his hand at the moment of delivery so as to put on intentional finger-spin'. Hargreave's ball was therefore a chinaman of slow-medium pace, which, because such a ball always carries some top-spin, would behave as Fry described.

An interesting feature of the above account is the apparent acceptance that the first-and-third-finger grip is normal for the left-hander's off-break. This is exactly what we would expect as a natural technique if left-handers reflected the method of right-handers. In other words, medium-pace left-handers of a century ago were rotating their forearms, turning their hands and working their fingers as right-hand leg-break bowlers have been ever since. Whether they hinged their wrists is immaterial because, as we saw earlier, finger movement and hand rotation at speed give ample spin.

But why the slow-medium pace off-break, carrying (like its leg-break mirror image) a good deal of top-spin, the very ball that modern right-hand off-break bowlers strive for as an invaluable variation, should be adopted so rarely is difficult to understand.

Cricketers clever enough to see the great worth of such a ball can do no better than study the highly effective methods of Ernest Toshack, who played for Australia just after the Second World War. The war and the fact that he lived in the Bush combined to make his debut late and his Test career short, but in twelve Tests he took 47 wickets at 21.04 runs each. His pace was medium to slow-medium and he bowled his stock delivery from over the wicket, spinning the ball from off to leg. He could curve the ball either way in the air and occasionally spun one from leg to off. His faster ball was exceptionally good and he had remarkable accuracy. Toshack was therefore in a direct line of descent from Hargreave half a century earlier. It is said that he practised every morning at five o'clock in the nets across the road from his home in Sydney, bowling to a single stump to improve his accuracy.

Certain left-hand spinners, slower than Hargreave and Toshack, form a truly amazing group. Not content with the uncommon, though not exceptionally difficult, skill of being able to bowl the left-hander's off-break, they also adopted the googly. The South African C. B. Llewellyn (1876–1964) has been credited with being 'The Bosanquet of the Left'. After him the better-known exponents were the Australians Fleetwood-Smith (1910–1971), Jack Walsh (1912–1980), George Tribe, Johnny Martin and David Sincock; Johnny Wardle (1923–1985) and Dennis Compton (1918–97) being the only Englishmen.

Following our critical analysis of the right-hander's googly, with all its problems, it would be surprising if the mirror images appeared any different. Fleetwood-Smith was a right-hander who changed to left near the end of his school days, following a broken arm. His stock ball, at a pace above slow, was the off-break which spun at an exceptional rate; the leg-break was the googly. For Victoria he took 295 wickets at 24.40 runs each, with some exceptional performances. Sometimes he was unplayable, but in Tests his erratic form meant that he was not a match winner in the Mailey mould. He played ten Tests, taking 42 wickets at 37.58 runs each.

Walsh went to England in 1936 at the age of 23 and remained there for the rest of his cricket career as a prodigious spinner and a batsman. His 1127 first class wickets cost 24.25 each. Tribe had three Tests for Australia against England in 1946-7, beating the bat often enough but not having the success needed to remain in the side. Like Walsh he enjoyed a long and successful career after moving to England.

Martin is remembered more as an enthusiastic cricketer and an aggressive batsman than as a bowler. Although he took 3 wickets in 4 balls in his Test debut against the West Indies in 1960-1, he never repeated that success and in 8 Tests took only 17 wickets at the high cost of 48.94 runs each. Sincock, once described as Australia's most exciting wicket-taker, whilst bowling some unplayable deliveries, was also erratic and failed to hold his place after three Tests in which his 8 wickets cost 51.25 runs each. Wardle's bowling career reflects the problems facing anyone who sets out to master every type of spin known at that time to a left-hander. J. M. Kilburn said of Wardle: 'Spin sometimes took precedence over the need for basic accuracies and on occasions he neglected opportunities presented by the circumstances'.[6] In 28 Tests he took 102 wickets at 20.39, not a great number per Test, but economical enough.

This tiny band of pioneers attracted plenty of interest, including that of selectors willing to give them a role. They enriched the game and deserve the gratitude of cricket lovers everywhere. But like most of the disciples of Bosanquet, the China men had feet of clay; none reached the height of a Mailey or an O'Reilly, and on the evidence available to us they would have been well advised to seek something other than the left-hand googly as a ball to accompany their left-hand off-break.

If there is to be a future for the left-hand off-break bowler we must find a way out of the impasse described by A. G. Moyes:

A left-handed 'bosey' bowler runs counter to nature, in that his normal delivery is an off-break, and the leg-break, which should be his normal turn, is the surprise. He suffers because the greater proportion of batsmen play right-hand, and thus his usual delivery is an off-break to them. The result is that he must use over-many 'bosies' if he wants big results. The right-hand 'bosey' bowler is rarely at his best against the left-hand batsman, and the same applies to the left-hand bowler and right-hand opponent. That is why it never surprises me if they fail against the men who are tops in the batting art. Fleetwood-Smith was often a demon against ordinary first-class batsmen, but when he met the Hammonds, Huttons, and Comptons he mostly seemed to have left his trident in the dressing-room... He had some good days, but not proportionate to his natural ability. Taking it on the average, I don't think that the left-hand 'bosey' bowler can ever be a consistent menace in the highest circles, simply because nature is against him.[7]

First we will ignore the googly (a leg-break) and, concentrating on the off-break, consider whether the left-hander's off-break is the same as, or better, or worse than, the right-hander's off-break. If both types of bowler were operating from behind a screen, would 'Johnny' Moyes be able to distinguish one from the other? The answer would depend largely on whether they were bowling against an appreciable wind or not, whether or not they used a low trajectory, and how fast they were bowling. Into a wind of even moderate force, the top-spinning off-break from the left-hander would need to be thrown up higher because it would dip more quickly. It would also lose more forward momentum on a slow bounceless pitch than would the right-hander's off-break. Such a delivery dropping even slightly short is easily forced away on the leg side. Bowling *with* the wind there is no problem.

Delivered at a pace at least a little faster than slow, and possibly extending right through into medium pace or faster, the left-hand off-break will, because of the substantial amount of spin it is likely to carry, be an attacking delivery of the highest order. The finger action will probably be based on a first-and-third-finger grip (the reflection of the right-hand leg-spinner's grip), along with any amount of hand- and arm-rotation and wrist-hinging which is possible within the limited action time.

The opportunity for left-handers to become top-class off-spin bowlers, in the manner set out here, is nothing fanciful, but merely a reminder of the methods of successful bowlers of the past. We can now address the assertion that because most batsmen are right-handers, this form of bowling, in which the stock ball is an off-break, will be less effective than a leg-break. Moyes' basic idea is true, but in the context of a well-developed set of bowling skills, it is quite misleading. Why, as Moyes claims, should he use 'over-many bosies'? Does this mean that Moyes, to be consistent, wants all right-hand off-spin bowlers to use many leg-breaks? First it implies that an off-spin bowler, right- or left-hand, has not added danger to his attack by developing the ball that swerves in the air away from the bat. This ball will be delivered from over the wicket in both cases. Over the wicket is an excellent angle for the left-hander because his sharply turning off-breaks will not deviate so markedly to the leg side as they would from around the wicket. Just as the natural swerve of the right-hand leg-break bowler is from off to leg, so the left-hand off-break will swerve *away* before biting back off the pitch. Needless to add, the top-spinner from the left-hander bowling over the wicket will also be useful.

Returning to Moyes' claim that it is too much to ask the left-hand bowler to base an attack on bowling a great number of googlies and because this is so, the whole strategy is doomed to failure, we know enough about googlies now to be able to support that statement. But it is based on the erroneous assumption that the googly is the only worthwhile variation that is available. If Moyes implies that no other variation but the googly can be disguised, then the history of bowling says otherwise. Plenty of googly bowlers have not disguised their intentions very well and plenty of non-googly bowlers have done so effectively.

What can the left-hand bowler who is good at turning the ball in to a right-hand batsman do about variations? The practical possibilities for a left-hander wishing to turn the ball from leg to off have been well tried, and tried successfully. We looked at the parallel situation in an earlier chapter: the leg-break bowler adopting the off-break or the thumb-generated back-spun balls or the nothing ball. These escape routes from the sameness of an attack dominated by top-spin dipping flight, as discussed in Chapter 17, are just as open for the left-hand spinner as they are for the right-hander. The only difference required for this strategy, as compared to the classical left-hand attack, would be that it should mostly be delivered from over the wicket. But even here there is scope for variation around the wicket, especially if the leg-break (off-break action) is really turning back, away from the batsman.

Everything we have discussed about the machinations of spin, spin-swerve, wind, and grip on the pitch, applies to left-hand bowling; good hauls of wickets are there for the taking.

If I seem to have ignored left-hand bowlers of the fast variety in this discussion, it does not mean that they are not catered for, since I believe that the earlier chapters on swing and swerve allow for an easy conversion of those principles for use by the other hand.

23

THE BATSMAN'S POINT OF VIEW

This chapter is not really about batting technique, but about entering the mind of the batsman. Apart from any intentions the batsman may have, what do we know about his basic capabilities? A few years ago scientists published a paper entitled 'Do baseball and cricket players keep their eyes on the ball?'[1] Human performance was being studied by means of a sophisticated electronic arrangement which revealed exactly where the subject was looking as a ball approached. They concluded that baseball and cricket players do not keep their eye on the ball because it is physiologically impossible.

Using subjects who included amateur baseball players and one professional, tracking balls travelling at speeds between 80 to 150 km/h (50 and 93 mph), they found that it was possible to keep up with the ball only for the first 90 percent of its flight. Some were able to track the ball over the first portion of its trajectory, draw on their years of training to guess its future position, make a quick, position-correcting, eyeball-rolling movement to this predicted location, and then resume tracking. The top subject, a member of the Pittsburgh Pirates, also used a little head movement during this process, prompting the authors of the paper to suggest that the old batting axiom 'Don't move your head' should be amended to 'Don't let your body move your head, but it's fine to move your head to track the ball'. He was also able to repeat his head position and stance most consistently as well as having smoother eye movement and the ability to track the ball for a longer time.

The inability to track the ball the whole distance arises from the fact that, as the ball gets closer, it is passing *across* the view at an increasing rate. A fast ball passing at a distance from the body equal to that between the eyes and the sweet spot on the cricket bat, will cross at about 500-1000° per second. Untrained people are unable to cope with this, and cannot normally track targets moving faster than 70°/sec. The professional baseball player however had a smooth tracking speed of up to 120°/sec with his eyes and, coupled with a 30°/sec speed for his head, reached 150°/sec overall. Such is the value of a special natural ability coupled with years of training under conditions almost identical to those in which the scientific test was conducted. Top-class batsmen would also be expected to display this exceptional ability.

Since little was said in the report about cricket I have carried out some calculations to show what their work means for the game. The baseball player uses a cylindrically-shaped bat, demanding great accuracy in controlling the point of contact with the ball on a curved face. But he does not face the problem of coping with a ball bouncing off the ground. Although the cricketer has this problem, the greater chance of a controlled hit using a flat-faced bat more or less compensates. A baseball travels about the same distance as a cricket ball on delivery, and in both sports the point of impact with the ball is about the same distance from the eyes.

In what sense do both players line the ball up? Depending on whether the deliveries from both pitcher and bowler are left- or right-hand, to a left- or right-hand bat, and whether (in cricket) they are from round or over the wicket, and whether they are swerving or not, the ball in both sports is seen early in flight to be moving across the field of vision to some extent. The closer the ball is to the batsman or batter the faster it moves across the vision.

Baseball players are required to contact the ball within a fairly limited space alongside them, whereas for cricketers it extends on both sides from well above eye level to the level of the meanest grubber. A fast ball at 129 km/h (80 mph) travelling 15.5 m (17 yd) from the bowler's hand to pitch on a full length (2 yd in front of the batsman) will travel towards the batsman and downwards for 2.5 yd, in 0.44 sec. If we divide its trajectory into four periods we can find some of the problems faced by the batsman as the ball approaches. For the first quarter it crosses the vision at 17 °/sec, the second 36°/sec, the third 61°/sec and the last, before it pitches, 183°/sec. Thus with 70°/sec as the normal limit, tracking is outside the capabilities of the untrained only in the last quarter. However, it is obvious that closer to the batsman a good deal of the rapid and unpredictable movement, which at this speed will be confined mainly to bounce, lies outside the limits of visibility. An 129 km/h (80 mph) yorker, pitching at the batsman's feet, presents an impossible tracking task of over 1000°/sec movement. However, because it does not bounce, the yorker with its straight path allows a trained batsman to make the anticipatory eye movements detected by the researchers. In other words, training allows the eye to move ahead of the ball to where it is expected to be. Tracking takes place by a series of such movements. The *swinging* yorker is a different matter! For a bowler of half the speed, assuming a straight line trajectory and pitching on the same spot, the above figures are halved.

If tracking was everything, then slow bowlers might never get the wicket of a trained batsman. Fortunately for the bowler, seeing does not necessarily mean doing. The sight of a batsman, bat raised, watching the ball hit his stumps is a common enough demonstration of the need to react in time. Reaction time varies tremendously. The good news for batsmen and a stern warning for bowlers is that it can be greatly reduced by training. The bowler who, after bowling four inexpensive overs to a batsman, thinks that he is

on top must not forget that, whatever happens next, he has been training that batsman. A painful shock may be in store. At worst, every ball was the same stock ball making the batsman so comfortable that the subsequent run-getting surprises nobody except the bowler. Just because runs were not being scored, there is no reason for the bowler to think he is on top to the extent that he can forget variety. But, in the hands of a good bowler, such training may be brilliantly designed to lead the victim into the one trap necessary for his demise, whether it is through being lulled, or frustrated and unsettled.

The scientific work we have been discussing has interesting things to tell us about this all-important learning process. The human eye, trying to track unpredictable targets, has a time delay of about 159 milliseconds before it gets into action at a new position. Such a delay in following a cricket ball could leave the eye several feet away from the ball, depending on whether the bowling was slow or fast. *Predictable* moving targets were a different story as the subjects quickly learned a high level of accuracy with no time delay. They did this by means of quick anticipatory eye and head movements. During a two hour period the best results were obtained when each subject was given 18 seconds of training every five minutes. Since a batsman cannot react rationally without first seeing the ball, the work discussed here demonstrated the vital part played by training, both within a game and before it. Reducing the amount of predictability and devising ways of manipulating all this training to the benefit of the bowler is the very summit of his art.

A century before the scientists moved in the Demon Bowler had worked out a few things for himself:

'What is the first duty of a bowler, Mr Spofforth?'

'To lead astray the batsman, to lead him astray by never allowing him to guess what is coming. So far as I am concerned I may send a very quick ball (I have never yet put

all my strength into it), the next may be corresponding slow. Therein, I consider, lies any power I may have as a bowler — this ability to vary the pace from the very quick to the very slow. Then I try to deceive him by break and variety of pitch. If you know your batsman from previous meetings, a good bowler knows his weak points. I am speaking of the best known men in the world of cricket. When I am bowling against a batsman whose peculiarities I am not acquainted with, I generally gauge him by his style, and have his stock in three or four overs. I dare say a batsman would tell you the same thing about a bowler. We try to lead each other astray, but the batsman is generally the first to betray himself. Having penetrated the armour, then I go for him, tickling him and tempting him. He fancies he has got my gauge by one style of break. Then I try another and suddenly revert to the first; or one puts, by the manner of holding the ball, a spin on that will not cause it to turn out of its course. The batsman may think by the action of the delivery that the ball will turn out of its course when it possibly finds its way to the wicket. But it is a difficult matter to explain. As I find a batsman is inclined to hit, to play back, or to play forward, so I tempt him, sometimes trying to 'beat the bat' — that is, going straight for his wicket, at others alluring him to hit so as to place the ball in the hands of one of the field'.[2]

William Lillywhite, the star of the round-arm era, puts bowling firmly on an intellectual pedestal: 'I suppose if I was to think every ball, they would never get a run.'

Although the response of the batsman to each delivery may tell the bowler something useful, there are times when the bowler must be guided by principles rather than reacting to what happens at the other end. If things are not going in the bowler's favour and he has tried all his tricks —

change of pace, variation of spin, flight and angle — to no avail, the temptation is strong to assume that there is no point in maintaining this variety. Such a retreat is based on a false interpretation of what the batsman has done. Even if he looks comfortable, he has been forced to solve one problem after another. The scientists we discussed earlier found that fatigue in problem-solving reduced the success rate in the tracking experiments. Every new problem posed is a potential wicket-taker: persistence is necessary if the batsman is to be the one who capitulates, rather than the bowler himself.

Another type of misinterpretation of the batsman's situation by bowlers arises from timidity in a tense situation. Instead of bowling normally and employing his full complement of variations, the bowler 'freezes up' and becomes predictable at the very time when variety would put more pressure on the batsman. Since the variations are not usually quite as reliable as the bowler's stock ball, the decision to forsake tidy but sterile controllability, for the possibly riskier option, is something that must be faced by all good bowlers.

The bowler who refuses to try variations in case they don't work may not only be accused of lack of courage but of selfishness. Although he may argue that the threat alone of these tricks is sufficient for the purpose, the real reason is more likely to be his own inability to face the risk of failure. In other words, he puts his own feelings ahead of his duty to his side. Only a captain with a thorough understanding of bowling and the powers and make-up of a particular bowler will provide the encouragement and reassurance required by a bowler in this situation.

Cricket has many situations of the swings-and-roundabouts type. The tall batsman looks *downwards* on the approaching ball more than does the short batsman. This means that the tall man suffers earlier from the problem of tracking, since the ball is moving across his vision to a greater extent. Tony Greig had much more difficulty with Jeff Thomson's yorker in Australia in 1974-5 than did John Edrich who was much shorter. On the other hand, the tall batsman is better able to deal with the bouncing ball. Where there is little bounce the shorter player is better off. We are dealing here with faster bowling.

Now consider slower bowling, where better tracking is possible. The average movement across the field of view over the last quarter of the flight of a slowish 64 km/h (40 mph) delivery is only about 90°/sec. Both batsmen can now see it nearly all the way, except for the last few feet which they deal with either by moving forwards and destroying that part of the flight, or else going back for a longer look at it. But because he looks down on it to a greater extent, the tall man is in a better position to judge how far away it is. It is always easier to judge the speed of something from the side or top than by looking along its line of flight. Clarrie Grimmett's dictum, stating that the longer the ball remains at eye level or slightly above it the better, is based on this principle and describes perfectly the mean trajectory for which he was famous. Tony Greig looked down towards Thomson's yorker but his eyes were unable to cope.

Role reversal, lion one day, mouse the next, is hard for a bowler to take. The batsman, now scoring freely at the other end, was all at sea the last time they met. Give him credit, he may have done some hard thinking in the meantime, but more likely every batsman looks better against this bowler today. From all the possible reasons and excuses, we can extract one which holds useful lessons. *Failure to adjust to the conditions prevailing on the day* sums it up; a failure made all the more likely, almost inevitable, by the bowler failing to come down from that shaky pinnacle — success in the previous game.

That game was played on a fast pitch where the bowler did well by bowling short; today it is slow and he is being punished off the back foot. The atmosphere helped his swing and swerve; not so today. The light and the background are better today. The pitch took spin so that he did well by aiming his leg-break at the leg stump for it to take the off stump or the edge of the bat; today it skids straight through and he is constantly being hit through the on side. The list could be longer. Just as a batsman, having made a big score, must start afresh to build another innings, so too must the bowler avoid any prior fixation on particular tactics, and be prepared to adapt to those required on the day.

A certain mysticism surrounds the subject of flight; language is inclined to soar into regions of scant practical interest to the bowler. What exactly is flight? The cynic might suggest that flight is the last resort of the bowler who can't do anything else with the ball, either in the air or on landing. One must agree that there is not much else to some bowlers.

For a newcomer unfamiliar with the game, it might be hard to accept that there could be anything subtle in tossing a ball to a certain area of ground about 16 m (17 yards) away. Unless the bowler is clear in his own mind to be able to deal with this question, he has little chance of divining what the batsman might find difficult about it.

There have been a few ultra-slow bowlers in the game and some of them have been quite effective. Jack White (1891–1961) who played for Somerset and England was one such bowler. He bowled left-hand at a pace described by Jack Fingleton as 'slow to stationary' and turned the ball only a little each way; yet he played in 15 Tests and took 49 wickets at 32.26 runs each. The steeply dropping ball, bowled by the expert, may on occasion pose problems even for the best batsmen. Only the quick-footed will be able to cope with it. A batsman interested in developing another string to his bow could find this type of bowling a rewarding sideline. In yet another attack on slow bowling, designers of the all too common low-roofed artificial practice nets have ensured that such deliveries will never reach the batsman.

If there is to be deception, it will only take place in relation to another delivery or series of deliveries. A 'well-flighted group' may be a preferable phrase; 'training the batsman into oblivion' the bowler's aim. Most of this book is designed to help the bowler achieve that aim.

Extending our description further, we now include spin bowling of a pace and length which makes it difficult for the groping batsman to be sure of smothering the spin. Beating the bat may in that case have nothing whatsoever to do with flight; the batsman may have followed it well in the air only to be beaten off the pitch. Since that happy situation is not as common as the bowler would like, he must work for a little advantage from *both* directions; the turning ball may be enough to cap off just a small mistake in picking up the flight. Again we have a situation where it would be wrong for the bowler to give up using one or more of his variations simply because the batsman seems to be coping. Although any one of these variations on its own may not worry the batsman, the *sum total* of small misjudgments of length, pace, angle, and spin, may be sufficient to bring about his downfall.

Underwood, O'Reilly, Grimmett and Mailey all used flight superbly, but within a range appropriate to their methods. Nevertheless explosive changes of pace can wreak their havoc before the batsman has time to react. The suggestion that bowlers of any type should harness flight merely by bowling slower reveals a lack of understanding. One of Underwood's variations of flight was a ball slightly *faster* than normal.

The term 'loop' carries a strong suggestion of slowing down. Bill O'Reilly regarded it as fatal:

My advice to the talented tyro is to shun these words as if they were germ-laden. So often one hears them bandied about that one tries hard to assess the woeful damage they have caused in the bowling department. To me they are anathema. The young bowler who thinks that he must toss the ball high in the air to satisfy his claims for recognition as a promising spinner is a fool. Tossing the ball high should be regarded as an unfailing sign that the bowler is wasting everybody's time, and would be much better off if he turned his attention to batting, or feeding the chooks.

I have seen looping bowlers never given the chance to hit the pitch when bowling to a quick-footed batsman free from the embarrassment of not knowing whether to go forward or back. A quick-footed batsman will always crucify a looping slow bowler.[3]

One bowler whom O'Reilly may have had in mind was Walter Robins (1906–1968), who Ian Peebles described as the best English leg-spinner he ever saw. He bowled at around medium pace, but after accepting advice to slow down, he was never as good again.

24

AIR RESISTANCE AND WIND

A long throw from the boundary of 64 m (70 yards), projected at 45° to the ground, would go about another 27 m (30 yards) if there was no air. The large turbulent wake that cricket balls make as they push the air aside means that drag is slowing the ball. As we saw earlier, both swing and spin-swerve take place when this wake is diverted to one side or the other. Although drag slows a ball slightly in its flight towards the batsman, this slowing is of little consequence for cricket. But sideways deflection resulting from the combination of wind and drag can be significant.

It used to be thought that fast bowlers could break through some imaginary barrier into a region where both drag and swing suddenly decrease, but this is not so.

Bowlers know that wind resistance causes the ball to be blown off track occasionally. Maurice Tate's only wide in his whole career was when a sudden gust of wind caught the ball at a seaside ground. Wind at ground level is usually far from steady; trees, buildings and other obstacles cause all sorts of changes in strength and direction. Used cleverly, wind is a valuable ally. But it can also ruin a well-directed delivery. The difference between a good ball and a bad one, when bowled to a good batsman, may be no more than a matter of inches. The slower the delivery the more it is blown off course; yet another reason why spin bowlers, not wishing to make life unnecessarily difficult for themselves, should in the main seek to push the ball through.

We saw earlier how air speed generally increases both the swerve and the swing force, and the use to which an up-wind bowler can put this extra air speed. Unfortunately, an opposing factor operates for bowlers applying top-spin in any form, because, as we noted earlier, of the fatal effect of loss of forward speed when the ball against the wind dips into a slow pitch. On fast pitches however, this down-dipping, high-bouncing delivery is an excellent combination.

Into the wind, the swing bowler has a good opportunity of exploiting the extra air speed. Without the wind against him the swing bowler can only obtain higher air speed by bowling faster. Although the swing force increases with speed the flight time is shortened at the same time. There is also a probable delay at the beginning of the flight while the wake deviation develops. Against the wind the ball moves through more air in order to get to the batsman and therefore will swing more. The down-wind delivery passes through less air, making it more reliant on pace and/or turn, since both swing and swerve will be reduced.

Another important effect of wind is the way it slows or quickens the bowler's run-up and delivery. The human body, as every cyclist knows, has a considerable wind resistance. Strength and stamina, always important, particularly for faster bowlers, are vital if long up-wind spells are to be sustained. Problems of balance and timing during delivery can arise for both fast and slow bowlers under these conditions. A slow bowler being pushed over a little by a strong wind from behind can find himself bowling short at a time when he expects the wind to make him over-pitch.

Since swing requires a smooth flow of air around one side of the ball, we must regard all wind as potentially destructive of swing; wind near ground level is usually turbulent. Turbulence will vary however, and may not always be destructive. The sideways push of the wind may also be in the same direction as the intended swing and will enhance it. If the wind blows against the intended swing, we have an unpredictable situation which depends on which force wins the contest. Good bowlers seem to be capable of swinging against moderate side winds.

Swing bowlers should be conscious of the way in which a cross wind can effectively alter the seam angle they have chosen to use. An alert bowler will be experimenting with different seam angles and perhaps bowling from different ends in order to try and take advantage of the situations we discussed in the chapters on swing.

25

PITCH AND BAT MAKE THE BALL SPIN

The surface of even the most heavily-spun ball is moving around the ball many times slower than the ball is moving through the air. When it lands the bottom of the ball catches on the ground to some extent and is slowed down, while the rest of the ball moves on above it (Fig. 60a).

The friction during this all-important contact depends both on the ball and on the pitch. We discussed earlier how, as the ball wears, it begins to come off the pitch slower, and that the slowing can result only from changes in the *surface* of the ball, and need have nothing to do with changes in the pitch or changes in the bounce of the ball.

The universal effect as discussed earlier, no matter whether the ball initially had back-, top- or side-spin, is that the tendency towards top-spin is increased. This does not necessarily mean that the ball will actually acquire top-spin; depending on the friction of the contact, it may merely experience a decrease in back-spin. This situation would arise from a fast or medium-pace delivery which is given a fair amount of back-spin and lands on a 'skidding' pitch. This same delivery on a 'gripping' pitch may be turned over to come off with heavy top-spin. If the bowler has applied top-spin in the first place, then such a pitch will impart even more.

Depending on the amount of off- or leg-spin applied by both fast and slow bowlers, the ball coming off the pitch may also carry a certain amount of rotation towards one side or the other. Fry mentions leg-spin from one bowler coming off the pitch with 'a curious upwards curl', probably a mixture of dip and inswerve on the rising ball. Nevertheless the predominant spin a ball acquires on landing will be top-spin.

Ground-induced spin has all manner of interesting consequences, not only for bowler and batsman, but also for the wicket-keeper, the fieldsman and the umpire. The fieldsman at point, reaching down for the ball only to find it spinning away to his left, or his team mate at square-leg, equally embarrassed on the right hand, are classic victims of ground-induced spin. Because the batsman has turned the ball square, the top-spin becomes spin on an axis pointing in the same direction as it is travelling. The ball rolls to one side as it travels along the ground, or worse, will kick sideways as it bounces.

The wicket-keeper, always under pressure, is more than ever deserving of our sympathy now that television has revealed what can happen between the pitch and his gloves. Movement after pitching is mentioned several times in cricket literature. This can include the most vicious antics where a ball can climb, dip or swing violently and unexpectedly. Ground-induced spin lies behind this behaviour, but its nastiness will be manifest in a witch's brew involving spin-swerve and possibly swing; in fact it may be confused with late swing.

The simplest of these gyrations is the downward dip, resulting from ground-induced spin and causing pronounced top-spin, especially marked on a gripping pitch. The rising ball seems to be drawn downwards by some invisible force. The wicket-keeper, standing back, seems to be in some trouble; perhaps the ball is dropping in front of him, or he is always having to bend to take it. The casual observer would simply say that he is standing too far back. Others may wrongly interpret what they see as indicating a pitch with poor bounce. The same problems worry slip fieldsmen and the hooking batsman who can't

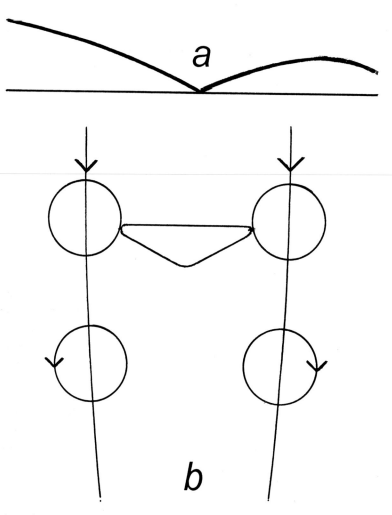

Fig. 60 The pitch and the bat making the ball spin. By gripping the ground during contact (*a*) the ball acquires top-spin which makes it dip in flight after bouncing. By gripping the bat on either side (*b*) the passing ball acquires side-spin which makes it curve in behind the bat.

understand why he was caught behind off a bottom edge.

This accentuated top-spin and dipping flight resulting from the contact of the ball with the ground has two possible effects of interest to the fast bowler firing the ball in short. The delivery that fails to rise much and strikes the batsman's pad may be experiencing a dip or at least a flattening of trajectory. This would increase the chance that a ball striking the pad fairly high could still be heading for the stumps; in other words, a justifiable lbw decision. The other consequence relates to the danger in attempting to dodge a rising ball which, because of the effect we are discussing, rises less than expected.

Less frequently a ball appears to climb as it approaches the wicket-keeper. All other things, such as the speed of the delivery and the spot where it landed, being equal, it could rise more, and, incidentally come off significantly faster, because it has landed on the smooth leather, gripped less, acquired less top-spin, and therefore dipped less than a previous delivery, as well as losing less forward speed.

Landing changes spin, including the axis of spin. It may even twist the ball around a little. All sorts of changes in flight may result.

These problems facing the wicket-keeper will come and go depending on the amount of grip the ball obtains on the pitch. Both the ball and the pitch will affect this grip. If the pitch is at all gripping it will be at least somewhat abrasive; in this case the ball will most likely be changing more rapidly than the pitch. The wicket keeper must be aware of the cycle of behaviour that starts every time a new ball is unwrapped. If the seam is new, or if it is kept clean, and if it is not too flattened, it will grip better. If the bowler is getting a good deal of movement off the pitch, these effects are more likely to be seen, but I doubt whether wicket-keepers would complain; if they themselves are in trouble, then the batsman is being called upon to exercise real skill.

We can extend our discussion to what happens when a ball comes off the edge of the bat. This must have at least some effect, both on the path and the rotation of the ball. The ball coming off an outside edge will experience side-spin (bat-spin!). The direction of the induced spin as the right-hand batsman looks down on it, on the offside, must be clockwise; therefore, with spin swerve, it will curve from off to leg as it approaches the wicket-keeper and the slips. I wonder how many slip catches are dropped because of a combination of ground-induced spin and bat-spin, dip and swerve? Leg-side snicks, including inside edges thick enough to influence the rotation of the ball, will make it swerve from leg to off. In both cases the snick curves back inwards, justifying the old rule which says that if there is any doubt about who should go for the catch, it must be left to the wicket-keeper. It is up to wicket-keepers and slip fieldsmen to make themselves aware, as early as possible, of anything that might be happening in the air after pitching.

Umpires cannot take much comfort from all this because the ball off the edge of the bat swerves in the opposite direction to the deflection. Many of the classic umpiring controversies, where batsmen have apparently been wrongly judged not out, may have been caused by this side swerve. Whilst the thick edge will not cause any trouble because the deflection is greater than any opposing swerve, the fine edge, especially the one where the ball grips the bat as it goes past, places the umpire in an impossible position. Not only does he fail to see any deflection, he may well see the opposite, an inward curve past the bat. In this case we must sympathise with him when he assumes that the curve was the work of the bowler alone. Cricketers must accept that umpires will always be obliged to say 'not out' under these circumstances. Will we now see devious batsmen applying a strip of gripping material along the outside edges of their bats?

It is worth noting that this same grip of ball on bat will allow the top-spinner that originates from ground-induced spin to grip and climb up off the face of the bat, making it generally more difficult to keep shots down: another bonus for the bowler on a gripping pitch.

Spinning balls from edges, or even balls carrying ground-induced spin, also add to the problems of out-fielders, especially catchers. All these problems arise from spin, but how often do we see fielding practice based on fielding the spinning ball? Bowling machines set to fire with side-spin should prove useful in this area, but bouncing the ball off a gripping surface added to a bat would be a substitute.

26
PRACTICE

Good quality cricket practice is not easy to come by. Quantity is rarely a problem, but cricketers too often settle for nothing more. Three bowlers queuing up to bowl to one batsman is a laughable rehearsal for actual play, and it is obvious that cricketers have opted for nothing more than some sort of physical work-out.

Gary Sobers says he practised very little, and this should remind us of the greatly differing needs of cricketers. Players like Sobers, playing several days a week, may merely be wasting energy practising. If they need to brush up on technique, or even experiment a little, they are good enough to do at least some of it in the games they play. Most cricketers are developing at one level or another and usually require training of as high a quality as possible.

Since the bowler in the queue has no chance of developing his ability to deliver a series of six carefully related deliveries intended to lead the batsman astray in subtle stages, the basic design of such practice is incapable of educating bowlers beyond the cricket equivalent of the kindergarten. In earlier chapters we looked at spin-induced flight variations and the way good practice time for this can be wasted, both for the batsman and the bowler, when more than one bowler is operating at a time. Nor does standing in a queue help develop stamina, as would a series of full overs.

We will assume that a great deal of prior development has taken place when the bowler practised alone, as it did with many famous bowlers. Likewise, batsmen may have been using throw-downs or bowling machines. When they come together for practice worthy of the name, one batsman one bowler is the only rational way to improve both. After six deliveries from one bowler another takes over for his six and they continue to alternate. Time can be saved by having several balls available which the resting member of the pair helps to return.

Quality practice also demands that the bowler should not be treated as a sort of human bowling machine. Batsmen may benefit from bowling delivered in tired drudgery, as in the days when the wealthy class employed strong lads to bowl to them in the nets, but for bowlers it is nothing more than that, and a source of all manner of bad habits both physical and mental. Repetitive work is certainly necessary, but it should be strictly on the bowler's own terms. The risk of suffering from any number of repetitive stress-related injuries, including crippling tendonitis of the shoulder, is too great to justify a bowler being a batsman's hack.

Today's coaches could learn something from Jack Massie, writing more than sixty years ago about practice for boys aged 12 to 18 years:

No boy should be allowed to bowl continuously for longer than ten minutes at a time at practice, and twenty minutes in all on one day.

Every boy should be taught to bowl at practice with some definite plan in view the whole time. He should practise some particular ball or some particular plan of attack, and should be able to say what he is practising at any time when asked. A boy, or any bowler for that matter, should bowl at practice exactly as if he were bowling in a match; that is to say, he should have a definite bowling crease of the correct width, and should pace out his run in the same way as he would do in a match, and he should be called for a no-ball should he go over the crease.

On no account should a bowler be allowed to bowl haphazard just for the sake of giving a batsman a strike.[1]

Massie's warning about over-bowling young bowlers at the nets can only be acted on if two bowlers bowl alternative overs, thus allowing accurate timing.

Synthetic surfaces, with their boring predictability, are basically at odds with the essence of the game; they can never replace turf. In some situations they allow play to take place where none would have been possible otherwise, and, for that reason, will have been gratefully accepted by many keen players. But cricket evolved for more than two hundred years on turf, and, as is painfully obvious on too many occasions on artificial surfaces, the fine balance between bat and ball, which has also evolved, and which is codified in the Laws, is easily upset. Used outdoors, artificial surfaces soak up water in wet weather and may not dry out until long after the surrounding grass has dried. The ball will not grip under these conditions. In spite of claims that these surfaces when dry behave like turf pitches, they are disappointing. Laid over crushed limestone they inevitably trap moisture underneath, no matter where they are laid, and they generally lack bounce. Laid over concrete they generally bounce too much, as well as greatly increasing the risk of stress injuries (see Chapter 9).

Modern practice nets are in most respects a backward step compared to those used thirty or more years ago. I refer to the damage inflicted by metal and concrete on balls, bats and on the frames of faster bowlers jarring down on the hard surfaces. Ian Peebles wrote vividly of the shock he experienced early in his career when he moved, in the reverse direction, full of enthusiasm from months of highly promising indoor practice, to playing outdoors on turf. Everything felt so different, and his bowling suffered as a result.

Bowlers who have practised intensively indoors wearing boots without sprigs should expect to experience problems with rhythm until they get used to wearing spikes on turf, and they should not sustain the problem by going back indoors during the summer. However, indoors during winter is both an enjoyable pastime in its own right as well as being a time for working on new skills. If the area is well planned to avoid ball-damaging surfaces the ball will swing and swerve well in the non-turbulent air. But faster bowlers must remember that the human frame was not designed to withstand the repeated impact of coming down on hard or even partially softened artificial surfaces. Even dry turf has a certain degree of 'give' in it. Indoors therefore they must cut their pace substantially.

Good bowling is a matter of inches; only a bowler can appreciate the way bowling in boots fitted with metal spikes feels different from bowling in spikeless boots. Not only does it *feel* different during that crucial time in the delivery action when feet and ground are in contact to move the body into a precise position, it *is* different. The absolute requirement for a bowler, fast or slow, is to experience a firm and reproducible grip on the ground. Outdoors, the run-up to synthetic practice wickets should be turf, kept in good repair, and on which metal spikes should be worn. Limestone or other stony types of run-up are hard on the feet, are often dangerously unstable on the surface, accelerate ball wear, and are unacceptable substitutes for earth or clay. I hope that no bowler, particularly of fast or medium pace, is forced into the dangerous situation of having to bowl using boots without metal spikes and running on to a damp synthetic mat.

Bowlers wishing to practise spin-swerve and accompanying break off the wicket, might wish to try the method used by the great M. A. Noble, as told to S. F. Barnes, who did not distinguish between swing and swerve, and who used the latter with memorable results:

I asked Noble if he would care to tell me how he managed to bring the ball back against the swerve. He said it was possible to put two poles down the wicket, one ten or eleven yards from the bowling crease and another one five or six yards from the batsman and to bowl a ball outside the first pole and make it swing to the offside of the other pole and then nip back and hit the wickets. That's how I learned to spin a ball to make it swing. It is also possible to bowl in between these two poles, pitch the ball outside the leg stump and hit the wicket. I spent hours trying all this out in the nets.[2]

27

CAPTAINS

A captain can make or break a bowler. He either provides an acceptable framework within which a bowler feels free to operate at his best or, as sometimes happens, exerts a corrosive influence on all concerned and allows the game to seep away in forgettable time wasting.

Bad captaincy manifests itself in various forms: taking bowlers off for no apparent reason; regarding any questioning of decisions as contrary to team discipline, selfishness on the part of the bowler and destructive of team spirit; acting alone in the absence of any mechanism for hearing complaints; and reacting to criticism by making life unpleasant for that individual, including removing the bowler from the crease for periods longer than normal.

A bowler quickly learns that, under some captains, if he wants to bowl, it doesn't pay to speak out. Perhaps it is wise to regard the effect of power, or the dumb response of incompetence, as a potential problem with all captains, unless there is good evidence that, for once, a bowler has found someone with whom he can engage in constructive dialogue.

The work of the Test captain, or at least the visible results of this work, is for all to see, analysed and discussed down to the last wave of the finger. At levels below this the opportunities for captains to harm the game, and in particular the morale and development of bowlers, are legion. Clubs failing to take seriously the appointment of captains do harm to themselves and to cricket.

Many club captains don't understand the simple concept of bowlers maintaining pressure on batsmen from both ends; of working in tandem. A bowler may sink down onto the dressing-room seat at the end of the day without a wicket to his name, yet through his consistency and the understanding of his captain he may have pressured batsmen into rash shots against the other bowlers and into attempting suicidal runs.

Cricket would benefit from a sort of Captains Anonymous which puts to them the question 'Do you really want to win?' If the question is too frank it can be rephrased as 'I know that you would like to win, but are you doing all you can to bring this about?' The answers, if honest, would reveal no surprises to experienced cricketers: 'I wanted to give everybody a bowl'; 'An old friend of mine is captaining the opposing side and I regard this game principally as a social affair'; 'We haven't won all season and it's no use trying now'; 'Look at this team, a bunch of no-hopers'; 'The committee just want me to keep everybody happy'; 'I played cricket at a high standard earlier in my career, and I've got no real interest in this grade'; 'Winning doesn't mean much to me, sport is far too competitive'; 'I used to be keen to win when I was younger'.

A bowler engaged in the long and absorbing task of developing mastery of his craft has the right to receive recognition and respect for his efforts. If he is powerless to change these attitudes and circumstances by himself, his own cause — and the cause of good cricket — are best served by a rapid and quiet move to another team or club which offers better prospects.

One aspect of that disconcerting and subversive attitude to the competitive element in sport was nicely put by a writer in *The Times Literary Supplement*:

> *The ability to tap the boyhood sources of energy and illusion is essential in most*

highly competitive activities, and one would hesitate to back a fully adult person (should one exist) in any serious contest. There is nothing like a sudden upsurge of maturity to impair the will to win.[1]

Happy is the bowler whose captain continually brings out the best in him; no tension, no frustrations. Cricket is a complex game. For many field changes there is an equally strong case for the opposite course; do you close the gap, or feed the batsman's strength hoping for him to make a mistake? Out in the middle is not the time for extended discussion. If a captain has not taken the time to work out these tactics with the bowler before the game starts, then, in the event of a disagreement on the field, he must accede to the bowler's wishes. To do otherwise is to presume to know more about the bowler's craft than does the bowler himself, without giving the latter the chance of putting his case.

But in order to bring some balance to this discussion we need to consider what happens when the bowler's halo slips a little. Where better can a good captain display his qualities than in handling a chronically ineffective bowler or a bowler with no guts? We will assume that the problem lies deeper than a day off form, or difficulty in coping with an unusually good batsman or two. Good captains might have a check-list which includes the following, both long term and short term measures: suggest particular remedial work in the nets; suggest work on variations ; bring on bowler against less competent batsmen; suggest to the bowler that he examine his own motivation. If these measures fail, then more is being expected from the bowler than he is capable of giving. In other words, he is in the wrong team.

This conclusion raises an important issue of greater significance to cricket than the fate of one inadequate bowler. I refer to the conflict between a bowler's continuing development and the expectations placed on him. Consider a young medium-pace bowler, included at an early age in a squad from which will be selected a team to play a series of games for an elite group. Because he is young, let us assume about twenty, he has a range of ability limited to little more than the ability to bowl straight with reasonable control at a brisk pace. At what stage does he embark on learning the skills which will take him above the hordes of straight-up-and-down medium-pacers? These new skills are not the skills which brought him selection in the first place, and their demanding, and perhaps lengthy, period of development, the outcome of which is uncertain, could require his removal, for a considerable period, from the ladder of advancement. In other words, the system discourages the very development that it purports to foster in the most promising material available.

Common observation seems to indicate that more young bowlers should be showing some sign that they are grappling with the challenge of technical development. Instead of lavishing time and money on bowlers in the type of system described, we should seek ways of informing young bowlers about the full range of options available to them and then ensure that conditions exist in which they can develop. The large number of exceptional bowlers who have taken relatively lengthy periods to develop tells us that such expertise is not acquired overnight, and raises fears that their early inclusion in a performance-based selection system might even stifle such development.

Returning to our inadequate bowler, let us hope that he is placed at a level where he can experiment a little, overcome his problems and develop without embarrassment. Is it too revolutionary an idea to suggest that certain cricket teams should be selected, not with winning but with the development of every member of the side as their principal objective? I am not referring to the fine thoughts normally expressed by captains and coaches, but to the genuine requirement of every player, batsmen as well as bowlers, that they must reach out and try new techniques if they are to remain in the side. There need not be an age limit and the composition of the team could change quite rapidly depending on the needs of its members. In such a team bowlers would be charged with the exciting and demanding task of breaking away from the need to rely on uninspiring uniformity.

Our hypothetical captain, not only of the type of team suggested above but of all teams, should be just as concerned with promoting attacking and penetrative bowling as with helping the expensive bowler. If he does not, then he and his team may merely drift into mediocrity.

No book on bowling appears complete without diagrams and notes on field placing. In my young days I copied them into notebooks and added more from important games I attended. Looked at now they remind me of nothing so much as the products of a group of racing tipsters making their picks for the big race, and between them seeing nearly every horse as a potential winner. The possible range of variations in bowling skills, pace and spin, pitch conditions, wind and batsmen, from day to day or even minute to minute, make a mockery of any attempt to lift predetermined plans from a book. If the precise positions used by famous bowlers are of interest, and it is precise positioning that good bowlers do require, the published diagrams, casually scaled down to the size of a printed page, are unreliable.

Trial and error, a flexible approach and a careful noting of the results obtained with different placings, is the way towards fields which will suit a particular bowler under particular conditions.

Jack Massie said it in 1926:

The bowler decides where he wants his field placed and the captain places the men in these positions. Each bowler should be taught right from the jump to study this matter of placing his own field to the best advantage for his own bowling, and it is a matter which each individual bowler must study very closely.

The most important thing to be borne in mind is that fieldsmen must not be wasted by placing them at random in order to stop the result of bad balls, but they must be placed where they will be most useful for good bowling and the bowler must see to it that he cuts the 'loose stuff' down to a minimum. Further, because it is desirable to have a man in a certain position for one batsman, it does not follow that he should be in the same position for every batsman and a boy should be taught to study the batsman accordingly in order that he may make the best use of his field.

It will not pay as a general rule to plug away at a batsman's weakness the whole time as this will have the effect very often of giving him practice in this particular point with anything but the desired result. It may be found far more effective to go through strength to weakness.[2]

Captains, flushed with the success of a bowler and perhaps living out some boyhood fantasy, are at times prone to go overboard in bringing fieldsmen in around the bat. Whilst all concerned may imagine themselves as re-enacting Jim Laker's 19 wickets at Old Trafford, a little cool thinking should be directed towards the gaps in the out-field which, particularly for a spinner, will do his cause no good at all when desperate shots put balls in the air.

Cricket is more a game played by eleven individuals on a team list than by a team. The bowler with ball in hand and the batsman at the other end are on there own. Captains who fail to recognise this individuality do so at their peril.

'I'm absolutely ashamed to be associated with you crowd, the way you played, pitiful!'

In every cricket team there are players with a range of skills in various different stages of development; players with different motivation and different natures. Blanket condemnations fired out sergeant major-like are certain to be inappropriate for the majority of the recipients. They will merely antagonise and alienate. If a captain does not wish to go to the trouble to analyse a player as an individual, and talk privately to him in an attempt to understand him and his cricket, then he is not doing his job.

The Bowler's Art

When the purely physical problems of hitting or bowling a ball have been mastered there remains the biggest problem of all; the mental problem. Mental toughness is needed to go on batting and bowling well for long periods, particularly under difficulties. It is not surprising that many of the greatest cricketers have been gritty individualists; they needed to be able to get on with their teammates, but they also needed to be something independent, different, even awkward and difficult in some respects. Such is the quality that brings them success when the rest of the team might be crumbling around them. What is the use of hugging and huddling on the field when the same deeply inculcated group ethos may engender an overwhelming feeling that if the others are doing badly in a particular game then the whole group will inevitably fail?

DICTIONARY OF SOME IMPORTANT BOWLING TERMS

ABRASION : The wearing process that roughens the leather and cuts down the exterior stitching. Abrasion results from the friction between the ball and the pitch. If there is no abrasion it is a sign that the pitch is not gripping and therefore not giving the spinners, i.e. the twisters and the cutters, a fair return from their efforts.

ARM BALL : Arm ball is the term usually applied to a delivery which does not turn but which goes straight through, or swings or swerves in a direction opposite to the usual turn. Examples are the off-spin bowler making the ball beat the *outside* of the bat, or the lefthand leg-break bowler beating the *inside* of the bat, both balls behaving in an opposite manner to what the batsman might have been expecting. There are two ways of delivering each of these balls; two of them are swung and two are spin-swerved.

ASSISTED SWING : Swing where the influence of the seam is assisted by minor to moderate roughness, either accidentally or deliberately inflicted on one side of a new or only slightly worn ball, and which causes the ball to swing towards that side. (See REVERSE SWING for the swing *away from* the rougher side.) The damage acts like the seam in making the boundary layer of air cling longer to the ball on that side. With assisted swing the ball will swing even if the seam is pointing straight down the pitch.

BACK-SPIN : As the fingers usually come more or less straight down the back of the ball during release, back-spin is the natural spin of most fast and medium pace bowlers. While back-spin is not essential for swing it has the effect of ensuring that the sides of the ball stay on the side during flight. Back-spin is also a common variation of many slower spinners as well as being the main component of cut (see CUT). Some slower bowling actions use the thumb to obtain back-spin and thereby flatten the flight, introduce an unexpedcted increase in length, and reduce the angle at which the ball lands (see FLIPPER).

BOSIE : An Australian word for the googly (see GOOGLY).

BOUNDARY LAYER SEPARATION : The layer of air moving around close to the surface of the ball is the boundary layer. At cricket speeds this air layer will not cling to the ball all the way but flies off the surface to leave it about half way around. All swing and swerve depends on this air layer leaving the ball a little earlier or later on one side than on the other. From a shiny surface it leaves early; from a slightly rough surface it leaves late; and from a very rough surface it leaves somewhere in between the two. Pointing the seam to one side is the equivalent of changing the roughness of that side. (See SWERVE for the effect of spin on boundary layer separation.)

BREAK : The change of direction on pitching; caused by the bowler's twist or cut.

CHINAMAN : The ball bowled by a lefthand spinner (twister) that turns in from the off. Like the righthander's leg-break it will normally carry a certain amount of top-spin.

CUTTER : A ball that is spun by dragging the fingers down off the back of the ball and somewhat to one side or the other. The rotation comes from pushing against the natural inertia of the ball. Whereas in twist the spin is applied to *both* sides of the ball from a *two-point* contact, e.g. the first and third fingers for the leg-break, in cut the action is applied from *one side only* (see TWIST). Depending on which side of the back of the ball the fingers come down across, the result will be either a leg-cutter (fingers a little to the left), or an off-cutter (fingers a little to the right). The bottom of the ball is moving mainly forwards in both cases but slightly to one side or the other, hence the turn.

FINGER SPIN : Finger spin is the basic twisting action involving fingers on opposite sides of the ball applying pressure against each other while moving in opposite directions. But finger movement is only part of a more widespread set of movements involving twisting of the hand, and movement of the bones of the fore-arm. The wrist, not being capable of significant twisting, acts as a forward hinge to give the ball speed through the air. *This hinging action is not spinning* but it varies among different bowlers; nevertheless, in the light of a close examination of the mechanics of bowling actions, there does not appear to be any substantial basis for separating bowlers into finger spinners and wrist spinners. All spinners use the wrist hinge to some extent.

FLIPPER : See THUMB-GENERATED BACK-SPIN.

FRICTION : The pitch and the ball grip each other through friction. The friction will depend on the nature of both surfaces in contact. Friction allows the ball to turn in response to spin. Friction also slows the pace of the ball coming off the pitch and makes it more likely to 'kick' up into a slightly higher bounce. Friction of the ball against the bowler's fingers is also essential if he is to retain control while applying the twisting action.

GOOGLY : An off-break delivered with what has some of the appearance of a leg-break action. Googlies usually carry a certain amount of top-spin.

GO WITH THE ARM : See ARM-BALL.

GRIP : An adequate grip of the fingers for the ball and the ball for the pitch is essential if the full range of bowling skills is to play a part in cricket.

IN-SWINGER : A delivery that curves in the air towards the leg side and which derives this curve from the different roughness of the two opposite sides of the ball; roughness which causes the boundary layer to separate at different positions on the two sides. This different separation leads to different air pressures on the two sides : hence the sideways swing force (see BOUNDARY LAYER SEPARATION).

LEG-BREAK : A delivery that, on landing, turns from leg to off.

MICRO-TURBULENCE : Small scale turbulence in the air. It is of vital importance in two cricket situations. One is in causing swing (see SWING). Swing involves induced micro-turbulence from the seam or other roughness, more on one side of the ball than on the other. The other is in the atmosphere over a cricket ground where microturbulence can upset the early boundary layer separation of air on the smooth side of the ball and therefore prevent new ball swing and assisted swing.

MOVEMENT : Movement is a word commonly used in connection with fast and medium pace bowling to indicate sideways deviation in the air, or turn (cut) from the pitch. Careful watching and listening frequently reveal that those who speak of 'movement' have little idea whether it is swing or cut or both that they are talking about.

NOTHING BALL: A useful and uncomplicated delivery carrying moderate back-spin as would be applied by any young meduium pace bowler. Bowled among deliveries dominated by top spin it challenges the batsman to detect the flatter flight and the fuller length.

OUTSWINGER : A delivery that swings towards the off side (see SWING).

OVER-SPIN : Another name for top-spin. The top of the ball is rotating forward and the bottom backward.

OVERHEAD CONDITIONS : Hearing the term 'overhead conditions' we know that the user appreciates that the behaviour of a ball after it leaves the bowler's hand is influenced, to some extent, by its surroundings. While cricketers are acutely aware of these influences, the way in which they take place has, most often, been left unclear and obscured by the incorrect attachment to humidity. *Moisture, either in the air or in the pitch, has no effect on swing.* The true critical factor for new ball swing, or for assisted swing, is whether the air is microturbulent or not. The various conditions either favouring, or getting rid of, microturbulence are described in detail in the main text of the book. Another area influenced by overhead conditions is the rate of drying of damp pitches. A damp pitch will respond more to cut because the surface may allow the ball to make a little indentation and therefore better contact. Also, if the surface is covered with grass, the friction on greenish grass is better than on dry grass: the ball from cutters will then grip and turn a little better.

REVERSE SWING : Reverse swing is sideways deviation of the ball in the air, resulting from minor roughness on one side and major roughness on the other. Major roughness usually involves the presence of at least some furriness in the leather on that side. Since this overall state of difference cannot be arrived at as a result of normal play it must be the result of human interference with the ball. *Because the direction of reverse swing is away from the rougher side instead of towards it as in normal new ball and assisted swing, it is called reverse swing.* Reverse swing is much less affected by microturbulence than is normal or assisted swing.

SEAM : In terms of the dictionary meaning 'seam' is where the four leather pieces of the ball are joined together by almost invisible stitches. These are what hold the ball together. The visible stitching, in four prominent rows that go right around the ball, does not hold it together, but merely goes in and out through the leather. These rows are what cricketers call the 'seam' and they are there solely to provide a grip for the ball in the bowler's fingers and a grip for the ball on the pitch.

SEAMING : Seaming is a term that has been misused so often that it has lost its value. As used by many, it applies both to swing, and to turn from cut, frequently as a result of careless observation which incorrectly reports the swinging ball as having cut off the pitch. The best that can be said for the term is that it reminds us that fast and medium pace bowlers do use the seam both for swing (to influence air flow) and cut (to apply the cutting spin, and for the grip of the cut ball on the pitch). However there are two ways in which 'seaming' has been devalued. The first is through the incorrect claim that a bowler can make a ball turn off a pitch merely by delivering it 'seam up' to land on the seam. The second is the use of 'seaming' in a way that avoids any distinction in describing whether a particular delivery has swung, or swung and turned (from cut), or simply turned (from cut) without swinging. These are important distinctions which 'seaming' obscures.

SPIN : Rotation of the ball. Spin makes the ball *swerve* in the air and, if friction on the pitch is adequate, it will, with most spin types, lead to *turn*.

SPIN-SWERVE : Curving of the ball in the air through applied spin and not through different roughness on the two sides (see SWERVE).

SWERVE : Whereas for swing the different roughness makes the air layer separate differently on the two opposite sides of the ball, in swerve it is the different *speeds* of the two sides of the ball that makes the air separation different. For example a top-spinner has the top surface of the ball moving faster *against* the on-coming air than the bottom which is moving *with* the air. With most roughnesses and most air speeds and most spin rates, this leads to the top of the ball behaving like a smooth face of a swinging shiny new ball and giving early boundary layer separation compared to the bottom of the ball. The air stream is deflected upwards and therefore the ball is deflected downwards. That is why the top-spun ball dips.

SWING : Swing is the curving of the ball in the air without the need for any applied spin on the ball. The ball *will* be spinning backwards in the air simply because it is virtually impossible to release it and propel it to the other end of the pitch at speed without applying back-spin to it. But the back-spin is unnecessary for swing and the amount of back-spin has little or no effect on the swing. The roughness arising either from the seam placed on one side, or from the accidental or deliberate uneven damage to the ball, makes the air layer near the surface, the boundary layer, leave the ball later on that side than on the other less rough or non-seam side. Where the air is a little more turbulent it clings longer, such as on a slightly worn side. The area under the clinging and flowing layer is a low pressure area, lower than on the other side, say, of a shiny ball where the air leaves early. The result is a sideways push from the shiny side towards the rough side. Unless a bowler grasps the true picture of swing he will never understand all the other features of swing, including assisted swing and reverse swing.

THUMB-GENERATED BACK-SPIN : Gripped with the thumb under the ball and released with a mixture of back-spin and a little off-spin as the thumb flicks out forward, both generated from a predominantly clockwise rotation of the hand and arm, the back-spinning off-spinner is a worthy variation in anybody's bowling. Once thought to have originated with Clarrie Grimmett, it has now been shown to have been well known to at least two successful bowlers of the late nineteenth century, Walter Mead and W. G. Grace. The Australians named their discovery, or rather their rediscovery, the flipper. The essence of the flipper and its English precursor is the opportunity it offers for an escape from the dipping flight that is so dominant among all deliveries carrying top-spin; i.e. the leg-break, the googly, and the top-spinning off-spinner. The flight is flatter, making it land closer to the batsman than he expects. Because it lands at a flatter angle it will also come off the pitch at a lower angle; both of which can embarrass a batsman. (See NOTHING BALL for another way of introducing a variation which shows an escape from top-spin dominated flight.)

TURN : Change of direction from the pitch; achieved by cut or twist, and friction on the pitch. All turn, whether from cut or from twist, depends on at least some sideways movement of the bottom of the ball contacting the pitch.

TWIST : The act of spinning a ball by applying counter movement to the *two opposite sides*. The term 'twist' is used in some of the earliest writings on cricket and is an essential term for distinguishing the two main ways of spinning a ball, the other being cut, which involves a drag on *one side* of the ball only (see CUT).

UNDER-SPIN : See BACK-SPIN.

WICKET : It is less confusing to the uninitiated to confine 'wicket' to the three stumps and two bails at each end of the pitch. Calling the pitch the wicket is perhaps the least harmful among the examples of language that sometimes obscures the truth about the game.

WRONG 'UN : Originally the South African term for the googly (see GOOGLY). Nowadays wrong'un, as used by some as a 'jack-of all-trades' term, describing any unusual delivery whatsoever including balls that don't turn at all, is losing its value as a descriptor of a particularly intriguing and historic delivery. This is irresponsible and regrettable.

REFERENCES

CHAPTER 1

1 John Nyren, *The Young Cricketer's Tutor* (David-Poynter, 1974), p.31.

2 C. V. Grimmett, *Grimmett on Cricket* (Thomas Nelson and Son, 1948), p.42.

3 R. Bowen, *Cricket, A History of its Growth and Development Throughout the World* (Eyre and Spottiswoode, 1970), p.77.

4 John Nyren, *The Young Cricketer's Tutor*, p.62.

5 F. Gale, *Cricket* 1893.

6 ibid., p.62.

7 ibid., p. 80.

8 E. Parker, *The History of Cricket*, The Lonsdale Library of Sports and Games, Vol. 30 (Lonsdale, 1950), p.231.

9 ibid., p.234.

10 John Nyren, *The Young Cricketer's Tutor*, p.32.

CHAPTER 2

1 H. M. Barkla and L. J. Auchterlonie, J. Fluid Mech. 47 Part 3 (1971), p.437-47.

2 J. W. Macoll, J. Roy. Aeron. Soc. 32 (1928), p.777-98

CHAPTER 3

1 B. Hollowood, *Cricket on the Brain* (Eyre and Spottiswoode, 1970), p.62.

2 C. Wieselsberger, 'Der Luftwiderstand Von Kugeln' Zeitschr. f. Flugtchn. u. Motorluftschiffahrt, 5 (1914) p.142-4.

3 J. C. Cooke, Math. Gazz. 39 (1955), p.196-9.

4 R. A. Lyttleton, *Discovery* 18 (1957), p.186-91.

5 D. Bradman, *The Art of Cricket* (Hodder and Stoughton, 1958), p.139.

6 N. G. Barton, Proc. Roy. Soc. London A 379 (1982), p.109-31.

7 L. J. Briggs, Am. J. Phys. 27 (1959), p.589-96.

8 K. Bentley, P. Varty, M. Proudlove and R. D. Mehta, Imperial College Aero Tech. Note (1982), p.82-196, Nature, 303, June 30 1983, p.787-8 and R. D. Mehta, 'Aerodynamics of sports balls' (Ann. Rev. Fluid Mech 17, 1985), p.151-181.

9 K. Sherwin and J. L. Sproston, Inst. J. Mech, Eng. Educ. 10 (1982), p.71-95.

10 Central Institute of Technology, Heretaunga, New Zealand.

11 Kookaburra brand balls manufactured by A. G. Thompson Ltd. Victoria, Australia.

12 E. Achenbach, J. Fluid Mech 62 Pt 2 (1974), p.209-21.

13 S. Taneda, J. Fluid Mech 85 Pt 1 (1971), p.187-92.

14 A. G. Moyes, *Australian Bowlers* (Angus and Robertson, 1953), p. 187-92.

15 A. Imbrosciano, 'The swing of a cricket ball', Project Report, Newcastle College of Advanced Education, Australia, 1981, p.54.

CHAPTER 5

1 P. Smithers, *Melbourne Age*, 17 November 1990, p.32.

2 D. Oslear and J. Bannister, *Tampering with Cricket* (Collins Willow, 1996).

3 E. Achenbach J. Fluid Mech. 65 Pt.1 (1974) p.113-125.

CHAPTER 7

1 C. B. Daish, *The Physics of the Ball Games* (English Universities Press, 1972), p.72.

2 K. Bentley, P. Varty, M. Proudlove and R. D. Mehta, Imperial College Aero. Tech. Note (1982), p.82-196.

3 K. Sherwin and J. L. Sproston. Inst. J. Mech. Eng. Educ. 10 (1982), p.71-9.

4 N. G. Barton, Proc. Roy. Soc. London A 379 (1982), p.109-31.

5 K. Sherwin and J. L. Sproston, Inst. J. Mech. Eng. Educ 10 (1982).

6 A. Ibbetson, *Weather* 33 (1978), p.369-82.

CHAPTER 9

1 B. Elliott, D. Foster and B. Blanksby *Send the Stumps Flying* (University of Western Australia Press, 1989).

2 D. N. Kulund, *The Injured Athlete* (Philadelphia, Lippincott 1988).

3 P. N. Sperryn, *Sport and Medicine* (London, Boston, Butterworth 1985).

4 B. J. Wilkins, Synthetic surfaces are not cricket (Leisure Management, New Zealand, Winter 1994), pp 5-6.

CHAPTER 10

1 A. A. Thomson, *Hirst and Rhodes* (The Epworth Press, 1950), p.57

2 C. S. Marriot, *The Complete Leg-Break Bowler* (Eyre and Spottiswoode 1968).

CHAPTER 11

1 A. Bedser, *Twin Ambitions* (Stanley Paul, 1986), p.43.

2 F. Trueman, *Freddie Trueman's Book of Cricket* (Pelham Books, 1967).

CHAPTER 12

1 R. Bowen, *Cricket, A History of its Growth and Development Throughout the World* (Eyre and Spottiswoode, 1970), p.104.

2 H. S. Altham, *A History of Cricket,* Vol. I (Allen and Unwin, 1962), p.102.

3 ibid., p.173.

4 ibid., p.173.

5 ibid., p.146.

CHAPTER 13

1 D. Allen (ed), *Cricket on the Air* (BBC, 1985), p. 81.

2 G. W. Beldam and C. B. Fry, *Great Bowlers and Fielders* (Macmillan, 1906).

3 D. Underwood, *Beating the Bat* (Stanley Paul, 1975), p.29.

4 Chris Cowdrey, *The Cricketer* (October 1988), p.11.

5 S. Cameron-Lee and K. W. McAuliffe, 'Principles of Pitch Preparation', New Zealand Turf Management Journal, February 1989, p. 18.

CHAPTER 14

1 J. A. Lester (ed), *A Century of Philadelphia Cricket* (University of Pennsylvania Press, 1951).

2 D. R. Allen (ed), *Cricket on the Air* (BBC, 1985), p. 81.

3 E. W. Swanton (ed), *Barclays World of Cricket,* (Collins Willow 1986), p.218.

4 R. Benaud, *Willow Patterns,* (Hodder and Stoughton, 1969) p.173.

5 M. Atherton *Test of Cricket* (Hodder and Stoughton, 1995).

6 C. S. Marriott, *The Complete Leg-Break Bowler,* (Eyre and Spottiswoode, 1968) p.46.

7 G. W. Beldam and C. B. Fry, *Great Bowlers and Fielders* (Macmillan, 1906).

8 D. Underwood, *Beating the Bat* (Stanley Paul, 1975).

9 M. Brearley, *The Art of Captaincy* (Hodder and Stoughton, 1985), p. 192.

CHAPTER 15

1 C. J. Kortright, Interview in *Wisden Anthology* 1940-63, p.987.

2 P. Walker, *Cricket Conversations* (Pelham Books, 1978), p.69.

3 R. S. Whitington, *Bradman, Benaud and Goddard's Cinderellas* (Bailey Bros and Swinfen, 1964), p.145.

4 K. Gregory, *In Celebration of Cricket* (Hart-Davis, Magibbon, 1978), p.155.

5 J. A. Lester (ed), *A Century of Philadelphia Cricket* (University of Pennsylvania Press, 1951), p.167.

6 W. J. O'Reilly, *Tiger: 60 Years of Cricket* (Collins, 1985), p.45.

7 A. Mailey, *10 for 66 And All That* (Phoenix Sports Books, 1958), p.113.

8 R. Illingworth, *Spinner's Wicket* (Stanley Paul, 1969), p.62.

9 I. Peebles, *Bowler's Turn* (Souvenir Press, 1960), p.142.

10 M. Williams, *Double Century*, from an article by John Woodcock (Collins Willow, 1985), p.525.

11 W. Shakespeare, *The Tempest*, Act 3.

12 G. Broadribb, *Next Man In* (Putnam, 1952), p.74.

13 R. Letham, 'Cricket — More Than Ever a Batsman's Game', The Cricketer, December 1985, p.31.

14 A. Mailey, *10 for 66 And All That*, p.113.

15 I. Peebles, *Bowler's Turn*, p. 142.

16 L. Watts, *The Fine Art of Baseball* (Prentice-Hall, 1975), p.58.

CHAPTER 16

1 G. W. Beldam and C. B. Fry, *Great Bowlers and Fielders*, p.195.

2 L. Duckworth, *S F Barnes — Master Bowler* (The Cricketer-Hutchinson, 1979) p 21.

3 ibid. p 21.

4 Coaching notes written by Barnes in 1948, edited by L. Duckworth and published in The Cricketer, March 1978, p.25.

5 L. Duckworth, *S. F Barnes — Master Bowler* p. 21.

6 Coaching notes.

7 C. S. Marriott, *The Complete Leg-Break Bowler*, p 25.

8 A. Ross (ed), *The Cricketer's Companion* (Hutchinson, 1979), p 256.

CHAPTER 17

1 D. Underwood, *Beating the Bat*, p. 29.

2 C. S. Marriott, *The Complete Leg-Break Bowler*, p. 73

CHAPTER 18

1 Earl of Lonsdale and E. Parker (eds), *The Game of Cricket* (The Lonsdale Library, 1930), p.79.

2 P. Murphy, *The Spinner's Turn*, p. 166.

3 C. S. Marriott, *The Complete Leg-Break Bowler*, p.73.

4 T. Graveney, *Cricket Over Forty*, p. 155.

CHAPTER 19

1 R. Benaud, *Willow Patterns*, p.174.

2 C. S. Marriott, *The Complete Leg-Break Bowler*, p. 132.

3 P. Philpott, *Cricket Fundamentals* (Batsford, 1982), p. 88.

4 G. W. Beldam and C. B. Fry, *Great Bowlers and Fielders*, p. 326.

5 C. G. Macartney, *My Cricketing Days*, p. 134.

6 F. Keating, *High, Wide and Handsome — Ian Botham* (Collins Willow, 1986), p. 120.

7 G. Broadribb, *Next Man In*, p. 82.

CHAPTER 20

1 N. O'Neill, *Ins and Outs* (Pelham Books, 1964), p.214.

2 P. May, *A Game Enjoyed* (Stanley Paul, 1985), p.160.

3 C. V. Grimmett, *Grimmett on Cricket*, p.42.

4 C. V. Grimmett, *Tricking the Batsman* (R. M. Osborne, 1932), p.59.

5 C. V. Grimmett, *Grimmett on Cricket*, p.40-3.

6 G. W. Beldam and C. B. Fry, *Great Bowlers and Fielders*, p.234.

7 C. Martin-Jenkins, *The Complete Who's Who of Test Cricketers* (Orbis Publishing, 1983), p.104.

8 H. S. Altham and E. W. Swanton, *A History of Cricket*, p.214.

9 G. W. Beldam and C. B. Fry, *Great Bowlers and Fielders*, p.338.

10 ibid., p.338.

11 C. V. Grimmett, *Grimmett on Cricket*, p.42.

12 R. C. Robertson-Glasgow (Alan Ross, ed), *Crusoe on Cricket* (The Pavilion Library, 1966), p.171. Dan Leno (1860-1904) was the greatest comedian in the history of music hall. He was able to convulse his audience with a look.

13 R. Benaud, letter, 1982.

14 J. Pollard (ed), *Cricket — The Australian Way* (Landsdowne Press, 1961), p.110.

15 C. S. Marriott, *The Complete Leg-Break Bowler*, p.62.

16 J. Fingleton, *Fingleton on Cricket* (Collins, 1972), p.167.

17 R. Robinson, *On Top Down Under* (Cassell, 1975), p.218.

18 M. Rundell, *A Dictionary of Cricket* (George Allen and Unwin, (1985), p.89.

19 P. Murphy, *The Spinner's Turn*, p.59.

20 T. Graveney, *Cricket Over Forty* (Pelham Books, 1970), p.147.

21 E. W Swanton (ed), *Barclays World of Cricket*, p.478.

22 N. O'Neill, *Ins and Outs*, p. 216.

23 D. B. Close, *Close on Cricket* (Stanley Paul, 1986), p.56.

24 R. Benaud, *Richie Benaud's Way of Cricket* (Hodder and Stoughton, 1969).

25 R. Benaud, *Willow Patterns*, p.182-3.

26 W. J. O'Reilly, *Wisden Anthology 1963-82*, p.924.

27 G. W. Beldam and C. B. Fry, *Great Bowlers and Fielders*, p.232.

28 A. Border, *Ashes Glory* (Swan Publishing, 1989), p.101.

29 W. J. O'Reilly, *Wisden Anthology 1963-1982*, p.924.

30 B. Scovell, *Ken Barrington — A Tribute* (Harrop, 1982), p.79.

31 ibid., p.79.

CHAPTER 21

1 *The Wisden Book of Obituaries 1892-1985* (Queen Anne Press, 1986), p.93.

2 C. H. B. Pridham, *The Charm of Cricket — Past and Present* (Herbert Jenkins Ltd.) 1949, p.130.

3 ibid., p. 131.

4 *The Wisden Book of Obituaries 1892-1985*, p.93.

5 Letter to *The Times* by Bosanquet's brother Nicholas, October 14, 1936.

6 E. Parker, *A History of Cricket*, The Lonsdale Library, Vol. 30, p.119.

7 ibid., p.119.

8 Letter to *The Times*.

9 C. S. Marriott, *The Complete Leg-Break Bowler*, p. 146.

10 E. W. Stanton (ed), *Barclays World of Cricket*, p.209.

11 A. Mailey, *10 for 66 And All That* (Phoenix Sports Books, 1958).

12 J. Pollard (ed), *Cricket — The Australian Way*, p.151.

13 W. J. O'Reilly, *The Bradman Era* (Collins Willow, 1984), p.102.

14 A. Ross (ed), *The Cricketer's Companion*, p.275.

15 D. Foot, *Harold Gimblett, Tormented Genius of Cricket* (Heinemann, 1982), p.85.

16 R. S. Whitington, *Bradman, Benaud and Goddard's Cinderellas*, (1964) p.20.

17 A. Fairfax, *The Science of Cricket* (1953).

18 R. C. Robertson-Glasgow, *More Cricket Prints* (Werner Laurie, 1948), p. 137.

CHAPTER 22

1 A. A. Thomson, *Hirst and Rhodes* (The Epworth Press, 1959), p. 183.

2 ibid., p. 183.

3 Chris Cowdrey, *The Cricketer* November 1987, p. 12.

4 D. Underwood, *Beating the Bat*, p. 29.

5 G. W. Beldham and C. B. Fry, *Great Bowlers and Fielders*, p.288.

6 E. W. Swanton (ed), *Barclays World of Cricket*, p.246.

7 A. G. Moyes, *Australian Bowlers* (Angus and Robertson, 1953) p.141.

CHAPTER 23

1 A. T. Bahill and T. La Ritz, 'Do baseball and cricket players keep their eyes on the ball?' Proceedings of the 1983 International Conference on Systems, Man and Cybernetics (India), p.79-88. See also A. T. Bahill and T. La Ritz, 'Why can't batters keep their eyes on the ball?', American Scientist, 72, May-June 1984, p. 249-53 and A. T. Bahill and D. E. McHugh, 'Learning to track predictable targets', Investigative Ophthalamology and Visual Science, 26 July 1985, p.932-7

2 Interview in *The Pall Mall Budget*, 1886.

3 W. J. O'Reilly, *Tiger: 60 years of Cricket*, p. 211.

CHAPTER 26

1 R. J. A. Massie, *Bowling*, p.14.

2 G. W. Beldam and C. B. Fry, *Great Bowlers and Fielders*, p.232.

CHAPTER 27

1 *The Times Literary Supplement*, June 26 1981.

2 R. J. A. Massie, *Bowling*, p. 13.

INDEX